Acclaim for
The Second Greatest Story Ever Told

God's mercy is the gift that's so great it makes us wonder: Can it really be true? There must be a catch. Father Gaitley tells the story of Divine Mercy and Marian consecration in this popular history of the great devotional currents of the century just past.

This is not an academic exercise. This is a page-turner — and a life-turner — because so much turns on the question of God's love for us, and the ways we love him in return. This book about Divine Mercy and Marian consecration in our time needs to become the backstory of my devotional life and yours.

— SCOTT HAHN, PH.D.
St. Paul Center for Biblical Theology

The Second Greatest Story Ever Told

Now Is the Time of Mercy

Fr. Michael E. Gaitley, MIC

MARIAN PRESS
STOCKBRIDGE   MA 01263

2015

Available from:
Marian Helpers Center
Stockbridge, MA 01263
1-800-462-7426
TheDivineMercy.org

ISBN: 978-1-59614-316-6
First edition: 2015

Cover Design: Mark Fanders
Cover Art: "John Paul II" © Marian Fathers of the Immaculate Conception
Page Design: Kathy Szpak
Editing: David Came, Sarah Chichester, and Chris Sparks

Imprimi Potest:
Very Rev. Kazimierz Chwalek, MIC, Provincial Superior
The Blessed Virgin Mary, Mother of Mercy Province
Congregation of Marian Fathers of the Immaculate Conception
February 2, 2015

Excerpts from *The Kolbe Reader*. Edited by Anselm W. Romb, OFM Conv.
© 1987 Franciscan Marytown Press, Libertyville, IL.

Diary of St. Maria Faustina Kowalska: Divine Mercy in My Soul
© 1987 Marian Fathers of the Immaculate Conception

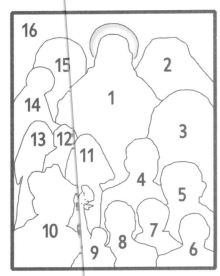

1. Jesus, The Divine Mercy
2. St. Thérèse of Lisieux
3. St. Faustina Kowalska
4. Bl. Michael Sopocko
5. St. Maximilian Kolbe
6. Fr. Seraphim Michalenko, MIC
7. Bl. Jerzy Popiełuszko
8. Fr. Joseph Jarzebowski, MIC
9. Lech Wałęsa
10. Karol Cardinal Wojtyła
11. Bl. Jacinta Marto
12. Bl. Francisco Marto
13. Lucia Santos
14. Our Lady of Fatima
15. St. Margaret Mary Alacoque
16. Blessed Martyrs of World War II

Printed in the United States of America

To St. John Paul II

In our time, humanity needs
a strong proclamation and witness
of God's mercy.

John Paul II, a great apostle of Divine Mercy,
prophetically intuited this urgent pastoral need.

— *Pope Benedict XVI*

Listen to the voice of the Spirit
that speaks to the whole Church in this our time,
which is, in fact, the time of mercy. ...

Pope John Paul II had the "intuition"
that this was the time of mercy.

— *Pope Francis*

Contents

Acknowledgments

"Boom! Boom! Boom!" Last night, as I was concluding the last chapter of this book, I was interrupted by several explosions. "What was that?" I looked down at my watch. "Oh, yeah, midnight. It's a new year."

Fireworks were fitting for the New Year's Eve conclusion of this book. I say that because I research as I write, and while I had the general plan for this work when I started, I was surprised by so many new and exciting discoveries. It really did go, "Boom! Boom! Boom!" all the way through. I hope you'll enjoy it as much as I have. Just know that like a real fireworks show, the blasts build, so make sure you stick with it for the grand finale.

When the fireworks started going off last night, I also got some texts from friends, wishing me a happy new year. That was fitting, too, because as I look back on the year, so many of them helped make this book possible.

First of all, I'd like to thank Sarah Chichester and David Came whose comments, suggestions, and edits were particularly helpful. Fr. Seraphim Michalenko, MIC, and Christopher Sparks also contributed useful comments and edits. Finally, Mark Fanders worked long hours on the cover, patiently putting up with my many tweaks and changes.

I'd also like to thank Mark Middendorf, president of Lighthouse Catholic Media, who organized a retreat last summer for me and a group of men called the Marian Missionaries of Divine Mercy. It was during that retreat that I had the time to begin this book. And I certainly can't forget the generosity of Fr. Joseph Fessio, SJ, and John Galton, who hosted and led the retreat for the men, which freed me up to write. Even more unforgettable was Mary Galton's delicious cooking, which ensured that at least natural consolation filled everyone's retreat.

Many friends prayed particularly hard for this work, not the least of whom were the men of the Marian Missionaries themselves: Eric Mahl, Lewis Brooks, Brian Kelly, Br. David Guza, OMV, Marcus and Adam Fluty, Ruben Mendoza, Mark

Wakely, Nicholas Sully, and Joseph Gohring. Also, I'd like to acknowledge my other prayer warriors: the Oblate Sisters of the Most Holy Eucharist, the Norbertine Sisters of St. Joseph, the Visitation Sisters of Tyringham, Fr. David Lord, MIC, Erin Flynn, and Brian Gail.

Finally, I'd like to thank the Lord for giving us the second greatest story ever told in our own day. May its amazing testimony help us to realize and respond to the good news it points to, namely, that *now is the time of mercy*.

Fr. Michael E. Gaitley, MIC, STL
National Shrine of The Divine Mercy
Stockbridge, Massachusetts
January 1, 2015
Solemnity of the Mother of God

Introduction

In 2012, I gave a talk at a parish, a brief history lesson, that was later produced on a CD by Lighthouse Catholic Media. By the end of the year, it became Lighthouse's bestselling CD. Apparently, more people liked history than I realized! Or, more likely, I think it was the title, "The Second Greatest Story Ever Told," that grabbed their attention.

The second greatest story ever told? Really? Maybe people were expecting a comedy CD — but it wasn't a joke. The story I told that evening, I believe, really is the second greatest story in the history of humanity. (Not because of the teller, obviously, but because the story really is *that good*.) Yet few people are telling it! And there wasn't a book that gave the whole, remarkable story. The purpose of this present work is to offer the full story, which includes material I couldn't fit into a 60-minute talk.

The main protagonist, the central figure of this amazing story, is St. John Paul II. Now, you may be saying, "But I already know his story. I've read this book or that book about him." If you already know his story, that's great. But I bet you still haven't heard what's *most important* about him. Or, if you have heard it, you've probably only gotten bits and pieces and not the full, glorious picture. That's because, for whatever reason, this "most important thing" is hardly mentioned by most of John Paul's biographers — and even if it does get mentioned, it's often lost in a thousand other details. Yet this overlooked part of the story is precisely what makes it "the second greatest story"!

Alright, so what's this often-overlooked-part of John Paul II's story? What's this thing that makes his life the second greatest story ever? It's *Divine Mercy*. It's what John Paul himself described as a "special task" assigned to him by God for our time,[1] something that "formed the image" of his pontificate.[2] It's the mystery that, according to Pope Benedict XVI, "was at the center" of John Paul's papacy[3] and is a kind of "synthesis of his magisterium."[4] It's what Pope Francis recognizes as a "great intuition" of John Paul II for our time.[5]

At this point, you may be saying, "Oh, is that all? I've already heard that John Paul II loved Divine Mercy. I know that Pope Francis keeps speaking about it. I've seen the Divine Mercy pictures and all that. I've heard this story before." Again, you may have heard bits and pieces, but here you'll get the *whole* story. Here you'll discover amazing, unheard of connections involving Our Lady of Fatima, Saints John Paul II, Faustina Kowalska, Maximilian Kolbe, and others. Here you'll learn that *right now* is a time of great grace and mercy for the whole Church and the entire world. Here you'll find out how the second greatest story in the history of humanity can also become *your* story.

Before we begin, I first need to give some background. I'll cover that background in the first three chapters, which will help us to fully appreciate this amazing story.

CHAPTER ONE
Regarding the First Greatest Story

*Man, tempted by the devil, let his trust in his
Creator die in his heart and, abusing his
freedom, disobeyed God's command.*

~ Catechism of the Catholic Church

The "second greatest story" implies that there's a *first* greatest story. What's the first greatest story? Of course, it's that of Jesus, Mary, Joseph, and the Apostles, the story of Biblical salvation history, the story that begins with Genesis and ends with the Revelation of John. But because this book isn't called *The First Greatest Story Ever Told*, I'm not going to spend too much time on *that* story here — yet I should say something about it. That's because a central part of the first greatest story is essential for understanding the second greatest story. I call it "God's School of Trust."

*G*OD'S SCHOOL OF TRUST. At the beginning of the Book of Genesis, we read about God's glorious act of creation and man's inglorious sin. Of course, the story is familiar to us all: The serpent tempts, and Adam and Eve give in. And then what happens? Let's read from the Biblical account itself:

> And they heard the sound of the Lord God walking in the garden in the cool of the day, and the man and his wife hid themselves from the presence of the Lord God among the trees of the garden. But the Lord God called to the man, and said to him, "Where are you?" And he said, "I heard the sound of you in the garden, and I was afraid, because I was naked, and I hid myself" (Gen 3:8).

Now, notice a few things here. When Adam and Eve hear God walking in the garden, rather than run to him, *they run away*. Rather than acknowledge their sin, confess it, and jump into the embrace of God's merciful love, *they hide*. Rather than trust in our infinitely good and merciful God, *they're afraid of him*. The *Catechism of the Catholic Church* explains what's going on here:

> Man, tempted by the devil, *let his trust in his Creator die in his heart* and, abusing his freedom, disobeyed God's command. This is what man's first sin consisted of. All subsequent sin would be disobedience toward God and *lack of trust in his goodness*.[6]

The key word here is TRUST.[7] Truly, sin begins with a lack of trust: "Man let his *trust* in his creator die in his heart." Sure, pride was in there, too. But the starting point, the origin of sin, is *lack of trust in God*. And this applies not only to the first sin but to "all subsequent sin." Indeed, every one of our sins involves "lack of trust" in God's goodness.

As if to underscore this point, the *Catechism* goes on to describe "the tragic consequences" of Adam and Eve's first sin. It says that "they become *afraid* of the God of whom they have conceived a *distorted image* — that of a God jealous of his prerogatives."[8] In other words, as a result of original sin, not just Adam and Eve but *every one of us* tends to fear God and lacks trust in him. This is because, like Adam and Eve and as a result of original sin, we hold a "distorted image" of God in our hearts. We now tend to see him as one who just wants to ruin our fun, one who is always ready and eager to give us the divine smack-down, one who's just "jealous" of his power. Yet this image of God couldn't be further from the reality! So what is the reality? Here it is: *God is our infinitely merciful Father who burns with love for us, longs to make us happy, and deserves all of our trust*.

Now, I suggest to you that the "trust issue" gets to the heart of salvation history. I suggest that *the whole of the Bible can be summarized as one long "school of trust,"* where our good and merciful God is simply trying to get us skittish, fearful creatures to give up our fear of him and trust in his love and goodness.

I suggest that this long school of trust is God's effort to heal us of the distorted image of him that too often has embedded itself in our hearts.

I said that the school of trust is long, and I do mean *long*. It started after the fall of Adam and Eve, and it still goes on. To this day, God continues to try to heal the false image we have of him in our hearts, so we will trust in him. But why so much effort? Why does it take so long? Why doesn't God just snap his fingers, heal our hearts, and make us trust in him?

It's because God *can't* do it. God can't do things that make no sense. For instance, he can't make a square circle. That's nonsense. Similarly, the idea that you can force someone to trust you or love you is nonsense. Trust and love require freedom, and if they're forced, then they're not trust and love.

So, God has a problem. He wants us to trust in him, but he can't force it. And to make matters worse, because of original sin, we already have a distorted image of him that makes us afraid of him. The deck is stacked against him! So what's a poor God to do? Well, he could have destroyed us as we deserved and started all over. Thank God that's not what he did. Instead, with mercy, he began the long, difficult process of healing our hearts and winning our trust. Thank God that's what he did, and we get to see exactly how he did it in the Bible, which we'll continue to look at now.

A KEY TO THE BIBLE: *"COVENANT."* One of my favorite professors in college, Dr. Scott Hahn, taught us something that blew me away. He said there's a key that opens up the treasures of the Bible and summarizes its teaching: a concept called "covenant." He said that if you look at the Bible through the lens of covenant, then the whole thing suddenly makes sense — and I believe he's right. Let's begin by looking at what a covenant is.

According to Dr. Hahn, the best way to understand what a covenant is, is to contrast it with what it's not. A covenant is *not* a contract, which is an exchange of goods or services. Rather, a covenant is an exchange of *persons*. To put it bluntly, it's the difference between prostitution and marriage: the former is an exchange of services; the latter is an exchange of persons. Well, it's that exchange of persons, that mutual giving in love, that explains what God is up to in the Bible.

Basically, God wants to woo us and make us his bride. (Guys, this is the imagery God uses in Sacred Scripture, so don't freak out. It's just an image.) For his part, he's more than willing to give himself to us, but we're not so ready to give ourselves to him. Again, we're not ready because of that distorted image of him that's stuck in our hearts, and so we're afraid and lack trust. It's like we're the luckiest woman in the world who is being pursued by the most handsome, powerful, kind, and loving man in the universe, but for some reason, we see him as a mean, ugly, and frightening ogre. The good news is that he doesn't stop pursuing us as he leads us through his school of trust, which, in the Old Testament, he teaches through Israel's experience of the covenant.

*T*HE OLD COVENANT. Later in this book, we're going to focus on the hero of our story, St. John Paul II. But for now, we're just going to draw from a particularly brilliant section of his encyclical letter *Dives in Misericordia* (*Rich in Mercy*) where he explains how, in the Old Testament, God led his people Israel through his school of trust.

John Paul begins by pointing out that Israel had drawn "a special experience of the mercy of God" from their age-long history, a history of the covenant:

> Israel was, in fact, the people of the covenant with God, a covenant that it broke many times. Whenever it became aware of its infidelity — and in the history of Israel there was no lack of prophets and others who awakened this awareness — it appealed to mercy. In this regard, the books of the Old Testament give us very many examples.[9]

And what did God do after Israel continually broke the covenant and then appealed for mercy? He gave mercy. He forgave. He healed. He brought back. For Israel, therefore, the process of breaking the covenant and then experiencing mercy from God *taught them about who God is.* God is not someone to hide from out of fear. Rather, he's someone to whom we can run with contrite hearts, ask for mercy, and from whom we can expect to receive it.

Perhaps nothing illustrates this point more clearly than during the time of the Exodus, when Israel rejects God and sets up the Golden Calf. This is a direct slap in the face to the Lord. The people he had just miraculously saved from 400 years of slavery in Egypt, the people to whom he had given himself in covenant, dramatically depart from their Creator, Lord, and Redeemer by setting up a statue of an animal that has eyes but cannot see and ears but cannot hear. For this insult, Israel deserves to be destroyed! But what happens? John Paul explains:

> The Lord Himself triumphed over this act of breaking the covenant when He solemnly declared to Moses that He was a "God merciful and gracious, slow to anger, and abounding in steadfast love and faithfulness" (Ex 34:6). It is in this central revelation that the chosen people, and each of its members, will find, every time that they have sinned, the strength and the motive for turning to the Lord to remind Him of what He had exactly revealed about Himself[10] and to beseech His forgiveness.[11]

Thus, John Paul points to the central lesson of God's school of trust: In the time of man's greatest infidelity and sin, God remains "merciful and gracious, slow to anger, and abounding in steadfast love and faithfulness." If only Adam and Eve would have understood this after the fall! Instead, it took centuries for this lesson to begin to hit home. And as it did, John Paul observes, "It is easy to understand why the psalmists, when they desire to sing the highest praises of the Lord, break forth into hymns to the God of love, tenderness, mercy, and fidelity."

Let's conclude this section by meditating on some of these songs of praise to the One who, Israel delights to discover, is really the God of mercy and love:

> Bless the Lord, O my soul; and all that is within me, bless his holy name! Bless the Lord, O my soul, and forget not all his forgivings,[12] who forgives all your iniquity ... who crowns you with mercy and compassion ... . He made known his ways to Moses, his acts to the people of Israel. The Lord is merciful and gracious, slow to anger and abounding in mercy. He will not always chide, nor will he keep his anger forever. He does not deal with us according to our sins, nor repay us according to our iniquities. For as the heavens are high above the earth, so great is his mercy toward those who fear him; as far as the east is from the west, so far does he remove our transgressions from us (Ps 103:1-4, 7-12).

> O give thanks to the Lord, for he is good,
>   for his mercy endures forever.
> O give thanks to the God of gods,
>   for his mercy endures forever.
> O give thanks to the Lord of lords,
>   for his mercy endures forever;
> to him who alone does great wonders,
>   for his mercy endures forever;
> to him who by understanding made the heavens,
>   for his mercy endures forever;
> to him who spread out the earth upon the waters,
>   for his mercy endures forever;
> to him who made the great lights,
>   for his mercy endures forever;
> the sun to rule over the day,
>   for his mercy endures forever;
> the moon and stars to rule over the night,
>   for his mercy endures forever (Ps 136:1-9).

*T*HE *NEW COVENANT.* God's revelation of his love and mercy through the long history of Israel is an important lesson in God's school of trust — but it's not the final word. God's final word comes when his words of love and mercy given in the Old Testament become flesh in Jesus Christ. And this is a lesson that, when accepted, has the power to completely obliterate the false image of God that comes from original sin. It has the power to bring us from fear to trust. In a certain sense, it's the conclusion of God's school of trust.

Again, our focus here isn't on the first greatest story ever told, a story that culminates in Jesus Christ. So let's just look at the key points of how the incarnation of God's love and mercy help heal the fear of God we inherited from our first parents.

Who's Afraid of a Little Baby? When the Word became flesh, God did not come to us as a striking, noble figure dressed in purple robes and surrounded by a retinue of fearsome soldiers or glorious angels. Rather, amazingly, he came into the world as a newborn baby. But who's afraid of a little baby? Especially a newborn baby with no teeth (he can't even bite us) and who's wrapped in swaddling clothes (he can't even smack us with his little hands — after all, swaddling clothes are like a mini straitjacket). And he is born not in a majestic castle but in a little cave to poor, humble parents.

What's God's lesson here? I think it's loud and clear: "Don't be afraid to approach me!" And we get this. Every Christmas season, we happily sing, "O come, let us adore him!" Yes, there's no reason to be afraid to approach our humble God who comes to us in such a lowly state.

Who's Afraid of Such a Good Man? Even when Jesus grows up and begins his public ministry, everything about him draws us to him. First of all, he makes it a point to hang out with sinners and the most rejected by society. And the message is clear: "Whoever you are, I do not hesitate to come to you. In fact, the more weak, broken, and sinful you are, the more I seek you out. So do not be afraid."

Second, as we read in the Gospels, Jesus spends much of his time teaching, healing, forgiving, and feeding people. It explicitly says that his heart is moved with pity for the people. So what is there to be afraid of? Certainly, the people in Jesus' day were not afraid to approach him. They came to him by the thousands, drawn by his goodness, and in their eagerness to be close to him and touch him, they nearly crushed him (see Mark 3:9; Luke 8:42). It seems that he's the one who should be afraid of us! — not the other way around.

Who's Afraid of the Greatest Love? Part of God's final lesson for us in his school of trust is his Son's suffering and death on the Cross. As Jesus himself taught, "Greater love has no man than this, that a man lay down his life for his friends. You are my friends … " (Jn 15:13-14). And he manifested this love when he gave up his life for us, his friends. Yet, even though he calls us friends, we were actually his enemies because of our sins. This fact shows his love even more, as St. Paul explains: "But God shows his love for us in that while we were yet sinners Christ died for us. … [W]hile we were enemies we were reconciled to God by the death of his Son" (Rom 5:6-8). The message is clear: "If you do not believe my words, at least believe my wounds. See my pierced hands and feet. I really, truly love you." With his arms stretched wide on the Cross, it's as if God were saying to us, "I love you *this* much!"

Who's Afraid of the Image of Divine Mercy? Three days after Jesus' death, the apostles were all gathered in the upper room where they had locked the doors out of fear. They were probably thinking, "Might the same people who crucified Jesus come for us next?" They were also probably feeling ashamed and guilty because, with the exception of John, they had all abandoned their friend in his time of greatest need. In the midst of this darkness, fear, and shame, and despite the locked doors, Jesus appeared among them (see Jn 20:19).

Like Adam and Eve in the garden after the fall, the first inclination of the Apostles may have been to run and hide. They may have been thinking, "Oh, no! The ghost of the

Master has come to punish us!" But Jesus puts them at ease as he immediately greets them with the comforting words, "Peace be with you." Then, he shows them his pierced hands and side, and the disciples rejoice. He also breathes on them, saying, "Receive the Holy Spirit. If you forgive the sins of any, they are forgiven" (Jn 20:23).

What's God's lesson here in the school of trust? He's saying, "Even after you've abandoned me and have locked the doors of your heart because of fear, I come to you, not to punish you, but to give you my peace, forgiveness, and joy." In summary, at his Resurrection, Jesus gives us what would later be called the Image of Divine Mercy, the image of his appearance to his disciples in the upper room. What's there to be afraid of? "Jesus, I trust in you."

Jesus, I Trust in You

Who's Afraid of a Piece of Bread? So we will never forget who he is and what he has done for us, so we will never forget God's school of trust, Jesus leaves us a memorial of everything he has done for us: the Eucharist.

The Eucharist is the coming of the Lord in a humble form, even more humble than a little baby! Obedient to the words of the priest, he comes to us under the appearance of bread and wine. Who's afraid of a piece of bread or a chalice of wine? And that bread and wine, which truly become his Body and Blood, make present his death on the Cross, where his Body and Blood were separated for us.

And then he allows us to eat his flesh and drink his blood so as to enter into the deepest intimacy with us, so as to renew his covenant with us, a covenant of mutual, self-giving love. And as if this were not enough, he remains in our churches, in our tabernacles, where he waits for us in the Sacrament of Love. Why does he wait? So we will not be lonely, so we will always have "manna in the desert" in this life. He waits so we will always have him near, so we will always have an in-the-flesh friend, even if everyone else has abandoned us. The Eucharist is the perfect lesson in God's school of trust! How can we fear such a good and gracious God? How can we not trust in him?

Yet, despite all these proofs of God's love, goodness, and mercy, we still struggle with fear. We still have a hard time giving God our trust. And so, God's school of trust continues in the history of the Church as the Holy Spirit tries to convince us of the truth about God that has been fully revealed in the *first* greatest story ever told.

CHAPTER 2

God's School of Trust in Church History

Behold, this Heart, that so deeply loves mankind,
that it spared no means of proof —
wearing itself out until it was utterly spent!

~ Jesus to St. Margaret Mary Alacoque

While this book is not called the *first* greatest story ever told, it's also not called *The History of the Catholic Church*. So, here again, I'm only going to summarize and trace some key points from God's school of trust, this time during the history of the Church. The "second greatest story," I will eventually argue, is the *first greatest story* in the history of the Church.[13] By tracing the points below, we'll better appreciate the greatness of this story when we get to it in Chapter 4.

*J*ANSENISM AND THE SACRED HEART. Regarding God's school of trust presented in Sacred Scripture, the faithful almost always more or less "got it." In other words, to varying degrees, for at least the first millennium of Christianity, they basically understood the message of God's love and mercy. Thus, by God's grace, to varying degrees, they were able to overcome the wound of original sin, the false image of God that made them afraid to draw near to God and to trust in his love and goodness. But there's one period in Church history when God's school of trust, all his efforts to convince us of his love and goodness, did not seem to be working — people were *not* getting it.

This terrible period in the Church's history, which reached its high point in the 17th century, is that of the *Jansenist heresy*.

Jansenism has been called "Catholic puritanism" and "the heresy that breaks the Lord's heart more than any other," because it teaches a joyless moral rigorism that keeps people running away from the Lord. It makes the spiritual life into a kind of puritanical olympics of painful penances and deprivations such that only the elite, self-denying, gold-medal winners get to receive God's love. As for the rest of us losers, all that's left is bitter despair as we nervously await the fiery wrath of a vengeful God. And there's no consolation in the Sacraments of Confession or the Eucharist either, because these, too, are the precious rewards reserved only for the few, pure, perfect people who get admitted to them by the merciless gate-keepers, the pitiless priests and bishops who have bought into the Jansenist lie.

Let's picture the period of Jansenism. Imagine a church where the self-righteous hypocrites, the Scribes and Pharisees, rule the day and sinners have no hope of God's mercy. Imagine a church where the key words are justice, wrath, and punishment. Imagine a church where Adam and Eve were *right* to run and hide from God. If you can imagine that, then you can imagine Jansenism. And you can also probably imagine what all this must have been doing to Jesus Christ, who had come not for the self-righteous but for sinners, who had borne the sins of the world and given his life to prove God's love for us. Truly, the whole sad scenario of Jansenism was breaking his heart and led to one of the most dramatic events in the whole mystical tradition of the Catholic Church. Here's what happened.

On December 27, 1673, from the tabernacle, Jesus cast his gaze out on all of Europe, searching for a true friend on whom he could unburden some of his heartache and through whom he might finally convince people to believe in his tender love and mercy. Eventually, he found such a friend: a little nun in a convent in France named Sr. Margaret Mary. To this blessed soul, Jesus released an ocean of anguish as he disclosed his divine Heart. Appearing on the Cross, he said to her in a voice full of sadness and grief:

> Behold, this Heart, that so deeply loves mankind, that it spared no means of proof — wearing itself out until it was utterly spent! This meets with scant appreciation from most of them; all I get back is ingratitude — witness their irreverence, their sacrileges, their coldness and contempt for me in this Sacrament of Love.[14]

On another occasion, the Lord appeared in front of the
exposed Blessed Sacrament with a similar message. Margaret
Mary describes the experience:

> Jesus Christ, my kind Master, appeared to me. He
> was a blaze of glory — his five wounds shining like
> five suns, flames issuing from all parts of his human
> form, especially from his divine breast which was
> like a furnace, and which he opened to disclose his
> utterly affectionate and loveable Heart, the living
> source of all those flames. It was at this moment
> that he revealed to me the indescribable wonders
> of his pure love for mankind: the extravagance to
> which he'd been led for those who had nothing for
> him but ingratitude and indifference. "This hurts
> me more," he told me, "than everything I suffered
> in my passion. Even a little love from them in return
> — and I should regard all that I have done for them
> as next to nothing, and look for a way of doing still
> more. But no; all my eager efforts for their welfare

meet with nothing but coldness and dislike. Do me the kindness, then — you, at least — of making up for all their ingratitude, as far as you can.[15]

This revelation of the Sacred Heart of Jesus to St. Margaret Mary began a powerful process in the Catholic Church of overcoming the scourge of Jansenism. While it came in the form of a private revelation, it certainly wasn't a "new" revelation. Rather, it simply brought people back to God's school of trust that's revealed in the Bible. It got people to see God as he truly is. It got them to stop running away from the Lord. And moved by his tenderness and mercy, it got people to draw closer to Jesus and to his Heart. In other words, people were beginning to "get it." They started to know and believe in the lesson of God's school of trust.

But the Jansenists weren't going to give up without a fight.

JANSENIST COUNTERATTACK. While the revelation of the Sacred Heart of Jesus struck a stunning blow to Jansenism, this horrible heresy was far from over. Before I explain how Jansenism launched a powerful counterattack, let me first make two points about the "Jansenist context" to give us a better idea of why it wasn't going anywhere anytime soon and why it was well positioned to reassert itself.

(1) French Pride and Power. In the 17th century, Jansenism's home base was France. There, the Jansenist lies had found a rich and welcome soil. That's because, at least at the time, French culture tended to a kind of elitism that overflowed into popular French spirituality. So, pious French people of the time tended to be overawed and amazed by any spiritual elites who could boast of extraordinary penitential achievements and mystical gifts. Indeed, many of them sought to be part of a "holier than thou" crowd that enjoyed looking down on everyone else.

Now, because Catholic France was the world super-power at the time, it could and did spread this spiritual elitism throughout the Catholic world. Think of the United States of

America today, which has spread its corrupt Hollywood culture of sex, violence, and greed to the ends of the earth. In a similar way, French Catholic culture spread the web of Jansenism to the far-off corners of the Catholic world.

(2) The Protestant Reformation. The Protestant Reformation, which began in the 16th century and continued to flourish into the 17th, also contributed to Jansenism's power. We can find the reason in the father of the Reformation, Martin Luther.

Luther had been a German Catholic priest who fell prey to a Jansenist-like spirituality. He was extremely fearful of God, felt he had to earn God's love, and was terrified of being sent to hell for the slightest infraction against God's rules. Luther found freedom from this torturous spirituality when he read St. Paul's Epistle to the Romans and received a deep insight into the power of God's saving grace that comes through faith in Jesus Christ.

That's great for Luther. The only problem was that he took his freeing insight too far. Going beyond Romans, he said that we are saved by faith *alone*. This addition contradicted the Epistle of St. James, which explicitly says that we are saved *not* by faith alone but by faith and *works*. After dismissing the Book of James as "an epistle of straw," Luther took himself and his heretical teaching right out of the Catholic Church.

When the Catholic Church launched its Counter-Reformation against Martin Luther and the Protestants at the Council of Trent, it rightfully emphasized the Biblical teaching that we are saved by both faith *and* works. And so you had the two camps set: On the Protestant side, the battle cry was "Faith alone!" On the Catholic side, the motto was "Faith and works!" And when the theological battles of these two camps spilled into the extremely violent military battles of the 17th century, such as the infamous Thirty Years War that absolutely devastated Europe, the positions of the two camps were confirmed in blood.

Now, while it's true that we are saved by faith *and* works, because of the animosity between the two sides, it's not surprising that a rigorous "works" spirituality such as Jansenism, the idea that you have to earn God's love and grace, found a ready welcome on the Catholic side. You might say that in their fervor to oppose the Protestants, and while being egged on by the Jansenists, many Catholics were chanting "WORKS! WORKS! WORKS!" And maybe they were forgetting the importance of faith (trust) in the mercy of God.

Of course, the Church's doctrine was never wrong, but many a Catholic ethos or attitude surely fell into a "works" mentality, such that works were seen as a way of earning God's love (rather than as a response to it). And this only helped to confirm the suspicions of Protestants that Catholics believed they could earn their salvation apart from having a living faith based on a personal relationship with Jesus Christ. With the spirit of Jansenism running rampant within the Church, reinforcing a false image of God, how could one develop a personal relationship with someone who just seemed like a mean ogre?

And so, the Jansenist heresy, French pride and power, and the Protestant Reformation created a perfect storm against God's school of trust, a storm that continued to blow through the Church, despite the Church's strong wall of defense: the Sacred Heart revelation. More specifically, the counterattacking winds of Jansenism were able to breech that wall by twisting devotion to the Heart of Jesus to Jansenism's own ends.

Jansenism Twists the Sacred Heart of Jesus. Shortly after my conversion back to my Catholic Faith in high school, I made an effort to become more pious. For instance, I started going to daily Mass, regularly prayed the Rosary, and picked up some devotional books on the Sacred Heart.

According to those books, if I really wanted to be a friend to the Sacred Heart of Jesus, it seemed I'd have to spend much of my time giving up food (fasting) and sleep (vigils). Well, as a growing young man, giving up food and rest were not so easy, but I did my best. The books also suggested that I choose sacrifices as much as possible to make reparation for sins committed against the Sacred Heart of Jesus. I tried to do that, too. But soon, my spiritual life became a joyless marathon of penances and self-denial that made me begin to resent my "relationship" with Jesus. Who was this guy who just wanted me to suffer all the time? I became particularly sad because, as I showed up less and less for all-night adoration, as I began to eat a dessert here and there, I saw myself as a failure in my friendship with Jesus. After all, he was relying on my fasts and vigils to cheer him up for all the rejection of his love, and I was letting him down. Right?

What's wrong with this picture? The Sacred Heart devotion, as I was following it, sure looks a lot like Jansenism. There's the emphasis on personal effort, earning God's love, and a spiritual life dominated by penance and self-denial. Of course, penance and self-denial are part of the Christian life, but they're not the most important things. Yet, that's the way much of the Sacred Heart devotion appeared to me (and, I found out later, to many other people).

So, I began to avoid thinking of or drawing close to the Heart of Jesus, because for me, it represented not a call to love but to pain and suffering without the relationship of love. Jansenism had won after all! Jesus had revealed his Heart, hoping to remind us of God's school of trust, that he is love and mercy itself, but for many people it just scared them off. Thus, one might say that Jansenism hijacked the Sacred Heart devotion and foiled God's effort to bring many of us back to his school of trust.

But like the Jansenists, God also wasn't going to give up without a fight.

*G*OD'S *MULTI-PRONGED OFFENSIVE AGAINST JANSENISM.* In what follows, I'm going to highlight two spiritual soldiers whom God raised up to fight against Jansenism and bring people back to God's school of trust. There are actually several more after them, but they're part of the "second greatest story," which begins in Chapter 4. I'll tell their stories then.

A Redeemer (Redemptorist) from Jansenism. In 1696, just 22 years after the Sacred Heart revelation, a woman in a village near Naples, Italy, who suffered from scruples and a highly penitential piety, gave birth to a son who would free many people like her from the grip of Jansenist rigorism. He would eventually be known as St. Alphonsus de Liguori, founder of the Redemptorists, Doctor of the Church, and hammer of the Jansenist heretics.

Saint Alphonsus contributed to God's cause against Jansenism above all through his moral theology. By the 18th century, most priests in Europe received their training in moral theology from Jansenist-influenced professors. The terrible influence of their teaching was felt not only in frightening fire-and-brimstone sermons that left the faithful absolutely terrified of God, but it was also felt in the confessional. More specifically, this meant that going to confession often entailed that one would meet not the mercy of God but a strict and exacting priest who would withhold absolution.

Imagine being truly sorry for your sins, confessing them to a priest, and having him tell you, "No, you're not sorry enough. I'm not giving you absolution." That often happened! But St. Alphonsus de Liguori put a stop to it. He developed a merciful moral theology that became wildly popular as it spread through seminaries and parish rectories like a fire. Alphonsus's teachings also encouraged laypeople to receive Jesus in the Eucharist more frequently. (Many people, scared away by Jansenist teaching, only received Communion once a year.) In recognition of his inestimable gift to the Church, Blessed Pope Pius IX made St. Alphonsus a Doctor of the Church in 1871.

A "Little" Warrior for God. Even with St. Alphonsus's moral theology routing the Jansenists, Catholic spirituality still had deep Jansenistic overtones. By the end of the 18th century, many Catholics remained fearful of God, focused on his justice, and confused by his love. This was a problem even in the convents, which became bastions of Jansenistic spirituality, especially in France. Yet it was in one of those very convents, amidst all the thorns and thistles, that a flower blossomed and bloomed, giving off a captivating fragrance that would open the hearts and minds of millions of people to the God of merciful love.

Of course, I'm talking about St. Thérèse of Lisieux, the Little Flower, the little warrior for God against Jansenism. However, it may come as a surprise that before Thérèse valiantly fought against Jansenism, she first had to suffer greatly as one of its victims. As her sister Pauline (Mother Agnes) reported, Jansenism poisoned her early religious life through excessive fear.[16] Also, it led Thérèse to focus too much on sacrifices and penances. For instance, in preparation for her first Holy Communion, she made more than 1,000 sacrifices. That's not bad in itself, but against the backdrop of Jansenism, it points to a problem in Thérèse's early spirituality.[17]

Eventually, the Lord led Thérèse from the turmoil of Jansenism and into the "Little Way," the spiritual path that set her "full sail along the waves of confidence and love."[18] It was this Little Way that brought Catholics back to the primacy of faith (over works) in the spiritual life. It was this Little Way that led Cardinal Christoph Shönborn, editor of the *Catechism of the Catholic Church*, to say, "St. Thérèse of Lisieux is the Catholic response to the Protestant Reformation."[19] It was this Little Way that led Pope Pius XII to declare that she "rediscovers the Gospel."[20] It was her living of this Little Way that made St. Pope Pius X state that she is "the greatest saint of modern times." It was her Little Way that led St. John Paul II to declare her a Doctor of the Church. It was because of her Little Way that St. Thérèse, a young woman who died at 24 years old, became one of the most popular saints in the Catholic Church today.

At its heart, the Little Way teaches us something well before it's time, namely, that the "universal call to holiness" of Vatican II is real. Thérèse convinced "little souls," as she called them, that they truly can become saints, not by relying on their own merits and works but by repenting of sin, showing mercy to others, and trusting in the infinite mercy of God who can do all things, even make us modern sinners into great saints

I'd love to say more here about St. Thérèse and her revolutionary Little Way, but that's for another book. Suffice it to say that, after the period of Jansenism, Thérèse almost single-handedly reintroduced the Church into the way of confidence and love, God's school of trust. But the story does not end there. God was still leading the Church through his school of trust, and the Church's most important lesson would soon begin in the relatively small, often-overlooked country of Poland. That amazing lesson would become the second greatest story ever told.

CHAPTER 3

Amazing Moments in Polish History

Here comes our Slavic Pope to the rescue,
Brother of mankind.

~ Juliusz Słowacki, Polish poet, 1848

In my opinion, Poland has the most amazing history of any country in the world. (I'm not Polish, so I think I can say that without bias.) But this book is not titled *Polish History*, so in what follows, I'll only cover those points that provide background for the second greatest story ever told, which begins in the next chapter. By the way, if you're not much of a history buff, don't worry. This chapter provides lessons that *everybody* can get into, so stick with it!

WHY GOD CHOSE POLAND. To me, the most amazing part of Polish history is how God used Poland several times *to save the world* — well, at least Europe. Really. Before I share the ways he did so, let me first give some of the reasons why I believe God would use Poland for such a mission.

(1) The Most Jewish. The Jews continue to be God's chosen people. As St. Paul writes, "The gifts and call of God are irrevocable" (Rom 11:29). And the highest concentration of Jews in the world from the time of the Middle Ages until World War II was in Poland, which was known as "the paradise of the Jews." It had that reputation because the laws in Poland from the time of the Statute of Jewish Liberties at Kalisz (1264) had given its Jewish citizens more rights than anywhere else in Europe, and the Jews flourished. Of course, most Jews lived separately from the ethnic Poles, but there were also many assimilated Jews who blended in with the rest of the population. It's not surprising, then, that God would use for his saving work a country with so many people called to be "a light to the nations" (Is 49:6) and with whom "God keeps his covenant and merciful love to a thousand generations" (Dt 7:9).

(2) The Most Catholic. Not only was Poland filled with God's chosen people of the Old Covenant (Jews), but it was also made up of some of the most fervent of God's people of the New Covenant (Catholics). Indeed, for centuries, Poland has had the reputation of being one of the most Catholic countries in the world — if not *the* most Catholic. And rightfully so. The reason goes back to the very beginnings of its fascinating history.

The official adoption of Roman Catholic Christianity with the Baptism of King Mieszko in 966 represents the single most momentous event in Polish history. Prior to that Baptism, pagan Poland had been in danger of being conquered and absorbed by its powerful Catholic neighbor to the west, the Holy Roman (Saxon-German) Empire. After the Baptism, however, the Holy Roman Emperor no longer had a religious excuse to conquer Poland. Yet freshly baptized Mieszko, with the Germans off his back, suddenly had a religious excuse to proceed to conquer and absorb into his kingdom his own pagan neighbors.

Poland further solidified its independence from Germany (and confirmed its new territorial conquests) when in 968, Pope John XIII appointed a non-German priest to be the first bishop of Poland with his seat at the Polish city of Poznan. This upset the German bishops, especially because there was already a German archdiocese of Magdeburg close by.

But it wasn't just the German bishops who were upset. Many Germans of the Holy Roman Empire resented that little Poland was now both politically and ecclesiastically independent from them and acting on its own. It's not surprising, then, that in 972, Margrave Hodo, a military commander who ruled the March of Lustania (a border province of the German Empire) attacked Poland. What is surprising is not only that he was defeated and lost German land to Poland but also that the German Emperor at the time, Otto I, upheld the victory and confirmed Polish independence later that year.

Otto required only one thing in return for his official recognition of Polish independence: King Mieszko's 7-year-old son, Boleslaw. In other words, to make sure Mieszko

would behave and that future Polish kings would be loyal
to the German Empire and the Catholic faith, Otto wanted
Boleslaw to remain at the imperial court to be given proper
Catholic training that couldn't be had in newly Christian
Poland. Despite the pain that separation from his young son
would cost him, Mieszko agreed. However, he sent a lock of
his son's hair to the Pope as a way of entrusting him to the
special care of the Holy See.[21] This began more than a thousand
years of close relations between Poland and the Pope. In fact,
almost exactly a thousand years later, in 1978, this relationship
took on a very special significance when Poland gave not just a
lock of hair from one of her precious sons, but one of her most
precious sons himself — as Pope.

(3) The Most Suffering. The Book of Isaiah, chapter 53,
speaks of the "suffering servant" who is Christ, the one who
"bore the sin of many, and made intercession for the trans-
gressors," the one who was "wounded for our transgressions
… bruised for our iniquities," the one "upon whom was the
chastisement that made us whole," and the one "by whose
stripes we are healed." But we are also "suffering servants,"
because we are the Body of Christ. And whenever the Body of
Christ lovingly suffers with Christ the Head of the Body, it has
a saving, healing effect. We see this, for example, in the early
Christian martyrs, about whom it was famously said, "The blood
of the martyrs is the seed of the Church."[22] It is also true of the
blood of the martyrs, the suffering servants, of later centuries.

I believe God chose Poland to save Europe and the
Western world so many times because Poland is an extraordinary suffering servant. So many times in its history, it has
suffered unlike any other country.

What other modern country suffered a deluge of attacks
and destruction by no less than *six* neighboring peoples who
mercilessly wielded weapons of fire, sword, and rape while the
dying victim lay prostrate and barely conscious? This happened
to Poland during the terrible decades of the 1640s-1660s.

What other modern European country was partitioned
and then completely wiped off the map of Europe by conspiring

European countries? This happened to Poland at the end of the 18th century at the hands of Germany, Austria, and Russia. (Miraculously, Poland then rose again from the ashes of World War I.)

What other country suffered an 18-percent casualty rate during the bloodiest war in human history? During World War II, Poland suffered this, as we shall soon see.

The point is this: Poland is a remarkable suffering servant. Moreover, its role as such was recognized by some of the country's greatest poets during the time of the partitions (the time when the country was divided up and then wiped off the face of Europe, making it illegal to even use the name "Poland"). For instance, here is a poem by the greatest Polish poet, Adam Mickiewicz, in which, after summarizing modern world history, he speaks defiantly in the third paragraph to the partitioning powers of Germany (ruled by Frederick), Russia (ruled by Catherine), and Austria (ruled by Maria Theresa). Then, in view of later events, he goes on to speak prophetically of Poland's redemptive role:

In the beginning there was belief in one God, and there was Freedom in the world. And there were no laws, only the will of God, and there were no lords and slaves, only patriarchs and their children. But later the people turned aside from the Lord their God, and made themselves graven images, and bowed down ... . Thus God sent upon them the greatest punishment which is Slavery ... .

Then the Kings, renouncing Christ, made new idols which they set up in the sight of the people, and bade them bow down. ... So the kings made an idol for the French and called it HONOR; and this was the same that was called ... the Golden Calf. And for the Spaniards, their king made an idol called POLITICAL POWER; and this was the same that the Assyrians worshipped as Baal ... and for the English, their king made an idol called SEA

POWER AND COMMERCE, which was the same as Mammon ... . And for the Germans, an idol was made called ... PROSPERITY which was the same as Moloch ... . And the nations forgot they had sprung from one Father ... .

Finally, in idolatrous Europe there rose three rulers ... a Satanic Trinity, Frederick, whose name signifieth "Friend of Peace"... Catherine, which in Greek signifeth "pure"... and Maria Theresa, who bore the name of the immaculate Mother of the Savior ... . Their names were thus three blasphemies, their lives three crimes, their memory three curses ... . And this Trinity fashioned a new idol, which was unknown to the ancients, and they called it INTEREST... .

But the Polish nation did not bow down ... . And finally Poland said: "Whosoever will come to me shall be free and equal, for I am FREEDOM." But the Kings when they heard were frightened in their hearts, and said ... "Come, let us slay this nation." And they conspired together ... . And they crucified the Polish Nation, and laid it in its grave, and cried out, "We have slain and buried Freedom." But they cried out foolishly ... .

For the Polish Nation did not die. Its body lieth in the grave; but its spirit has descended into the abyss, that is into the private lives of people who suffer slavery in their country ... . But on the third day the soul shall return again to the body, and the Nation shall arise, and free all the peoples of Europe from slavery.[23]

The next poem, by Juliusz Słowacki, reads even more prophetically than Mickiewicz's. It's called "Into the Midst of Riotous Squabblers," and from the dreary darkness of 18th century Poland, it looks forward to the bright day of a coming Slavic pope, which would have seemed completely absurd at the time:

Into the midst of riotous squabblers
   God sounds his gong;
Here is the Slavic Pope, your new ruler;
   Make way, applaud.
This one will not, like Italians before him,
   Flee sworded throngs;
Our world-disdainer will fight like a tiger,
   Fearless like God.
Sunshine resplendent shall be his countenance,
   Light shining true,
That we may follow him into the radiance
   Where God resides.
Multitudes growing obey all his orders,
   His prayers too:
He tells the sun to stand still in the heavens,
   And it abides.
Now he approaches, the one who distributes
   Global new might,
He who can make blood circulate backwards
   Inside our veins.
Now in our hearts the pulsation starts flowing,
   Heavenly light;
Power is a spirit, turns thought into action
   Inside his brain.
And we need power in order to carry
   This world of ours;
Here comes our Slavic Pope to the rescue,
   Brother of mankind.
Angel battalions dust off his throne with
   Whisks made of flowers,
While he pours lotion onto our bosom,
   Pontiff benign.
He will distribute love like a warlord
   Passes out arms;
His strength sacramental will gather the cosmos
   Into his palms.
Then will he send glad tidings to flutter

Like Noah's dove ... .
His voice will transform the nations to brethren. ...
He will redeem the world and bring to it
  Both health and love. ...
And then reveal the Lord our Creator
  Shining above.[24]

As unlikely as it sounds, God eventually did choose a Slavic pope, a "fearless" pope, who did not "flee" mortal danger and who "fought like a tiger," a pope who truly had a "resplendent countenance" and whose "prayers" did indeed work miracles, a pope who "distributed Global new might," who set "blood pulsating" through our veins by his stirring witness, who "came to our rescue" in the face of Communism and a culture of death, who was a true "brother of mankind," a pope who "distributed love [whose second name is mercy] like a warlord passes out arms" by tirelessly promoting the message of Divine Mercy, and above all, a pope who taught us not to be afraid as his message "cleansed our wounds" and pointed us to the "redeemer of the world" from whom merciful rays "shine above." It's this pope, whom Słowacki foresaw, who would become the central figure of the second greatest story ever told.[25]

*H*OW POLAND SAVED THE WORLD. Having looked at *why* God chose Poland, now we can look at *how* God used this unique country to save the Western world.

The Siege of Vienna, 1683. In the United States, September 11th is a day of infamy. You don't even need to mention the year. Just say, "September 11th" or "9/11," and everyone gets it. For extremists in the Muslim world, September 12th was also such a day. You didn't even need to mention the year. They all knew that "9/12" was the high-water mark of Islam's grand push into Europe.[26]

That push was stopped dead in its tracks by a Polish king at the famous Battle of Vienna. Were it not for King Jan Sobieski of Poland, we may all be speaking Arabic now and bowing east five times a day. The Muslim terrorists who flew commercial airliners into buildings full of people knew this, knew they'd suffered a humiliating defeat centuries before, and that's why they attacked on September 11th. They wanted to erase their own day of infamy, September 12th, through a smashing victory of their own — one day previous. They knew their story well. It's good that we know it, too. Here it is, beginning with some background.

For some 300 years, an epic struggle raged between the Ottoman (Muslim) Empire and the Holy Roman (Catholic) Empire. The Battle of Vienna marked the turning point in this struggle as it stopped the Muslim advance into Europe and led to the eventual dismemberment of the Ottoman Empire in Europe. Leading up to the battle, this empire had conducted a siege of Vienna with a massive, 200,000-man army. The siege began on July 14th after the Ottoman commander demanded that the city surrender. The leader of the city's defenders (only 15,000 troops) refused to give up, especially after hearing that a few days earlier, the people of a nearby town had surrendered to the same Muslim army and were summarily slaughtered.

The siege was not easy on the courageous defenders of Vienna. Food and water would soon run out, and who would come to save them? The other princes and kings of Europe were bickering among themselves, and nobody wanted to come running to face a vicious 200,000-man army. Would anyone come? This was the burning question in the hearts of Vienna's defenders, who were barely holding out hope.

Thankfully, the Ottomans' 130 field guns were no match for the 370 cannons on the city walls, which held the Muslims at bay — for a time. To counter their artillery disadvantage, the Muslim army dug massive tunnels under the city walls and began to blow them up from below. This process was effective but time-consuming and bought enough time for tens of thousands of Polish relief forces to arrive at the city and join the Austrian soldiers, who were not strong enough to fight the Muslims alone.

Yes, the Poles came. To the rest of Europe's shame, *only* the Poles came to engage the battle. But before they arrived, on September 8, the situation had become desperate. The Ottoman army had succeeded in blowing a 13-yard hole through the city walls. The city's defenders, who were starving and severely weakened by the siege, prepared for a fight within the city walls, which could come any day. The Muslims laid one last round of explosives with 10 mines that would have finally torn the walls of the city wide open, letting in the Muslim legions of destruction. But it didn't come to that.

On the night of September 11, as the Poles were celebrating Mass, the Ottomans noticed the fires of the Polish camp and knew that reinforcements had arrived. At 4:00 a.m. on September 12, the Muslims launched a preemptive attack on the Austrian forces gathered to the west of the city. At the same time, they assaulted the city itself, thinking they could take it before the Poles would have time to engage. They were wrong. There was no time to detonate the final 10 mines, because the Polish infantry launched a massive counterattack on the Ottoman flank. The battle raged for hours, and as it did, the Muslim commander, showing his merciless savagery, personally ordered the execution of 30,000 hostages, mostly women and children.

These innocents would be avenged as the hour of victory finally arrived. At 5:00 p.m., King Jan Sobieski himself led the largest cavalry charge in the history of the world. He and his "Winged Hussars," Polish cavalry with giant feathered contraptions that make a terrifying hissing noise in the wind, screamed straight for the huge white tent of the Muslim commander. They rode through that tent like a terrible storm, as their slashing and slicing spread panic and confusion throughout the commander's closest ranks. As the other Ottoman soldiers looked on from afar and saw their leader's tent in the hands of the enemy and their battle standards falling, terror gripped their hearts, and they fled the battlefield in disarray. The rout of the Muslims was complete.

The next night, from the very same tent where he'd aimed his victorious charge, King Jan Sobieski wrote to his beloved wife Maryanska about the victory and the heartless and decadent Ottomans:

They left behind them a mass of innocent local Austrian people, particularly women; but they butchered as many as they could. Bodies of dead women lie in great numbers; but there are also many wounded, and those who might yet live. Yesterday I saw a three-year-old child, a most pretty little boy, whose face and head had been savagely slashed by an infidel.

The Vizir had captured a marvelously beautiful ostrich from one of the Emperor's palaces here; but this too he had killed so that it would not fall into our hands. What luxuries he had surrounding his tents it is impossible to imagine. He had baths; he had a garden and fountains; rabbits; cats; and a parrot which kept on flying about so that we could not catch it.[27]

Sobieski went on to describe his reception by the defender of the city: "He hugged and kissed me and called me his savior."[28] And then, the Polish king wrote another letter. This one he addressed to the Vicar of Christ on earth, the Pope. It was much briefer, echoing Caesar's famous words of victory in Latin: "VENI, VIDI, VINCI" (I came, I saw, I conquered) — but with a twist: "VENI, VIDI, DEUS VINCIT" (I came, I saw, *God* conquered).

The elated Pope eventually commemorated the momentous battle, which Sobieski had entrusted to the Blessed Mother beforehand, by extending the feast of the Holy Name of Mary to the entire Church and setting its new date for September 12th, a new day of glory for Christendom, a new day of infamy for Muslim extremists. God had used Poland, Mary had used Poland, to save Europe. Let's not forget it.

The Miracle on the Vistula, 1920. Earlier, we learned that the Polish state had been wiped off the face of the map by three other countries, the "Satanic Trinity," as Adam Mickewicz called them: Germany, Austria, and Russia. Now, while it surely had been common practice to strip a defeated enemy of territorial possessions, never before had one of Europe's historic states been deliberately annihilated by a neighbor. This unprecedented injustice transpired in three dastardly acts, called the "partitions of Poland," during the years 1772, 1773, and 1775. See for yourself the incredible shrinking map of Poland below:

After one of the partitions, the instigator of it all, Fredrick the so-called "Great" of Germany, a Protestant, joked that he had "just partaken of the Eucharistic body of Poland."[29] Then, he and the other partitioning powers proceeded to persecute the Poles in their newly stolen lands — even Catholic Austria, the same Austria that Poland had helped earlier by saving its capital, Vienna.

On a positive note, the political martyrdom of Poland and persecution of the Church led to a dramatic growth in Polish national consciousness, the heart of which was the Poles' Roman Catholicism. In fact, in the minds of the Poles, the country and the faith were intimately united, with cultural resistance a matter of religious duty — and resist they did. For more than a century, without a country of their own, the Poles kept alive their language, history, culture, and faith while producing some of their finest cultural works, works that kept hope alive that the Polish state would rise again.

President Woodrow Wilson stoked the flames of hope in Polish hearts when on January 8, 1918, in his famous Fourteen Points speech, he included the following point, number 13:

> An independent Polish state should be erected which should include the territories inhabited by indisputably Polish populations, which should be assured a free and secure access to the sea, and whose political and economic independence and territorial integrity should be guaranteed by inter-national covenant.

Such an independent Polish state was indeed erected immediately following the surrender of the German Army on November 11, 1918, which ended the fighting of World War I.

But who erected the new Polish state? It was neither the United States nor any other Allied power. Poland herself, by the grace of God and the determination of a Polish military leader, Marshal Josef Piłsudski, rose again from the ashes of the Great War 123 years after being annihilated by her Christian neighbors. More accurately, Piłsudski simply walked into the vacuum created by the retreating German forces and then reestablished Poland while Austria and Russia tended to their war wounds.

As the British historian Norman Davies put it, "To at least one skeptical commentator, the creation of an independent Poland in 1918 was the result of 'a fluke.' To people of a religious turn of mind, it looked like a miracle."[30] Miracle or not, Poland was back, and the Poles were ecstatic — but there wasn't time to celebrate. The new Polish state had to immediately fight for its life and also, without knowing it, that of

Western civilization. One might say that if Poland were miraculously resurrected in 1918, it was so it could work another type of miracle for Europe, which we'll learn about now.

As German soldiers retreated west to their smoldering homeland following World War I, they left a power vacuum not just in Poland but in the entirety of the "Ober-Ost." The Ober-Ost had been Germany's Eastern front, consisting of the lands of present-day Lithuania, Latvia, Estonia, Belarus, Russia, and Poland. At first, there were just small skirmishes among the multitude of ethnic groups of the region, which led Winston Churchill to observe, "The war of the giants has ended, [and] the wars of the pygmies have begun."[31] But then, from these skirmishes, to everyone's surprise, a new giant emerged from the fray, a giant that had both the will and the power to conquer all of Europe and make it into a godless, anti-Christian society.

The giant was the Soviet Red Army, consisting of more than a million men drawn from the endless sea of Russian peasants. The ideal that fired them was Vladimir Lenin's Marxist, atheistic ideology. The path to conquering post-war Europe — which lay flat on its back, totally spent, but for that very reason, ripe for the Red Revolution — crossed resurrected Poland. Now, what could this fragile and fledgling country do in the face of such a massive army? As the Red Army's atheistic soldiers would soon find out, Polish faith could work miracles.

In March 1920, the Soviet High Command ordered a massive western offensive, the goal being to spread the Soviet revolution to Western Europe. At first, Marshal Piłsudski and his Poles held off the offensive through several sharp, preemptive maneuvers. But things changed in the summer when the Red Army broke through Polish lines. On July 2, the Red Army's commands from Moscow exclaimed, "To the West! Over the corpse of White Poland lies the road to worldwide conflagration."[32] The Red Army marched west, straight for Poland's capital city, Warsaw.

By the beginning of August, five armies of the Soviets were closing in on Warsaw. Meanwhile, Piłsudski was at work, implementing a plan for a daring, complex counterattack from the south that required Warsaw's fragile defenses to hold firm. Amazingly, outnumbered four to one, Warsaw withstood a direct Russian assault, giving Piłsudski time to cut through the Red Army's rear, flanking, encircling, and routing it. A hundred thousand Russians were taken prisoner while hundreds of thousands more fled eastward in panic and disarray. The General of the Red Army, Mikhail Tukhachevski, went from euphoric confidence to mind-numbing shock and despair. The Poles had pulled off a David-and-Goliath styled miracle, the "Miracle of the Vistula," as it's been called, because it all happened on the banks of the Vistula River.

In the weeks that followed, Piłsudski pressed his advantage and forced Lenin, who feared a Polish march on Moscow, to seek peace. By mid-October, the Polish-Soviet War was finished, along with the Soviets' immediate plans for world domination.

The significance of Poland's victory against the massive Red Army was not lost on contemporaries. For instance, the British Ambassador in Berlin wrote, "If the Poles would have lost, not only would Christianity have experienced a dangerous reverse, but the very existence of Western civilization would have been imperiled."[33]

Why would he have written that? Wasn't it a bit much? Well, keep in mind that this was an ambassador in war-torn Berlin. He clearly realized that in the depressed stupor following World War I, Western Europe could easily have given in to the temptation of Marxist ideology, an ideology that often appeals to people when they're down and out, broken, and poor. He also realized that a million-man Red Army of liberated peasants could be particularly inspiring — not to mention intimidating — to Europe's suffering people. Amazingly, miraculously, the Poles bore the brunt of that full fighting force and then routed it. Once again, God used Poland to save the Western world.

Collapse of the Commie Dominoes, 1989. I spent a year living in Poland, and one of my most vivid memories had to do with falling dominoes.

It was November 9, 2009. I was watching TV with a Polish family, and because my Polish wasn't very good, I could barely understand what was going on. It looked like an important event or ceremony. Several European leaders were there. I remember Angela Merkel, chancellor of Germany, being one of them.

My host explained to me in English that this was the anniversary of the fall of the Berlin Wall. I did the math: Yep — 1989, 2009 — 20 years. Okay. I settled into my seat to try to enjoy the program, which centered on the successive fall of 1,000 giant styrofoam dominoes that snaked along the path where the Berlin Wall once stood.

The dominoes represented the Wall, and their cascading collapse was deeply moving. But most moving of all for me and my Polish friends was our surprise at seeing who got to topple the first domino: Lech Wałesa, former president of Poland and leader of the Solidarity labor movement. We shouldn't have been surprised. It was that labor movement and Wałesa's leadership that began another kind of domino effect: the collapse in Eastern Europe of the Soviet, totalitarian, Communist regime — what Ronald Reagan rightly called the "Evil Empire."

As I now picture Wałesa pushing that first domino, I can't help but think back to the words of Adam Mickiewicz's famous poem:

> For the Polish Nation did not die. Its body lieth in the grave; but its spirit has descended into the abyss, that is into the private lives of people who suffer slavery in their country ... . But on the third day the soul shall return again to the body, and the Nation shall arise, and free all the peoples of Europe from slavery.

That's precisely what happened. After being slaves in their own country under their godless Communist masters, after enduring so much brutality, hardship, and humiliation, the Polish people rose again in Solidarity and freed the peoples of Europe in a relatively bloodless revolution.

But one more thing: As I now picture Wałesa pushing that domino, I also can't help but think back to the words of Słowacki's poem about a "Slavic Pope" who "comes to the rescue":

Now he approaches, the one who distributes
    Global new might,
He who can make blood circulate backwards
    Inside our veins.
Now in our hearts the pulsation starts flowing,
    Heavenly light ... .

These words come to mind because it wasn't just Wałesa who was pushing that domino, distributing "global new might." Everyone in Poland knew there was a hidden hand *pushing Wałesa*, giving him strength, encouragement, and making the blood of courage circulate in his veins. Of course, it was the hand of Pope John Paul II. The Poles all knew it, and Wałesa knew it, too.[34] The truth is that Wałesa was but one man among millions of Poles who had been fired with new life and courage by the Slavic Pope who can "make blood circulate backwards inside our veins."

And they could all point to the exact time when it happened, when John Paul made "the pulsation start flowing" in their hearts. It was June 2, 1979, in Warsaw's Victory Square, Communist Poland's epicenter of atheism. Just eight months earlier, John Paul had been elected the first Slavic Pope and the first non-Italian Pope in 450 years. Then, right there under the watchful eyes of their Communist oppressors, the Poles were thinking, in the words of Słowacki, "Here comes the Slavic Pope to the rescue."

John Paul didn't let them down. With earth-shaking power, during the massive outdoor Mass, he proclaimed the Gospel to 300,000 Poles packed into the square and to 10 million more watching on television — and then everything changed. Of course, I wasn't there, but my fellow Marian priest, Fr. Kazimierz Chwalek, MIC, a native of Poland, witnessed it and remembers it well:

We will never forget it. It was like we were barely alive. Communism had beaten us down so badly. And then John Paul came to us, carrying the Good News, and we came alive. He helped us remember who we were, and we weren't afraid. We belonged to Christ, and we wanted God. In fact, that was the rhythmic chant that rose from the crowd, "We want God, we want God ... ." And he spoke to our hearts. It was electric.

But there was one moment, one moment when we knew that everything was different, everything had changed. It's when John Paul proclaimed with power, "... And I cry from all the depths of this millennium, I cry on the vigil of Pentecost: Let your Spirit come. *LET YOUR SPIRIT COME*, and renew the face of the earth, *this* earth [the land of Poland]."

As the Slavic Pope, John Paul had come with global might and the power of the Spirit to make new blood pulse and circulate in the hearts and veins of those who would push the domino that would set Europe free. And that's exactly what happened. The 10 million Poles who heard the Pope's homily led to the 10 million-member labor union, called Solidarity, that had the power to bring the entire Polish economy down to its knees. Wielding such power of peaceful persuasion, Solidarity brought the entire Communist Polish leadership to the bargaining table. Then Solidarity won big. It was legalized, its membership exploded, and its candidates went on to sweep the 1989 election. Then Europe won big as other Communist governments fell to democracy. Then the free world won big in a giant, global, domino effect.

God had used Poland to save the world — again. We'll hear more about this story in Chapter 6, specifically about the hidden, motherly hand that pushed *John Paul II* to push Walesa to push the rest of the Soviet bloc to freedom. But we're getting ahead of ourselves. We first need to begin the story.

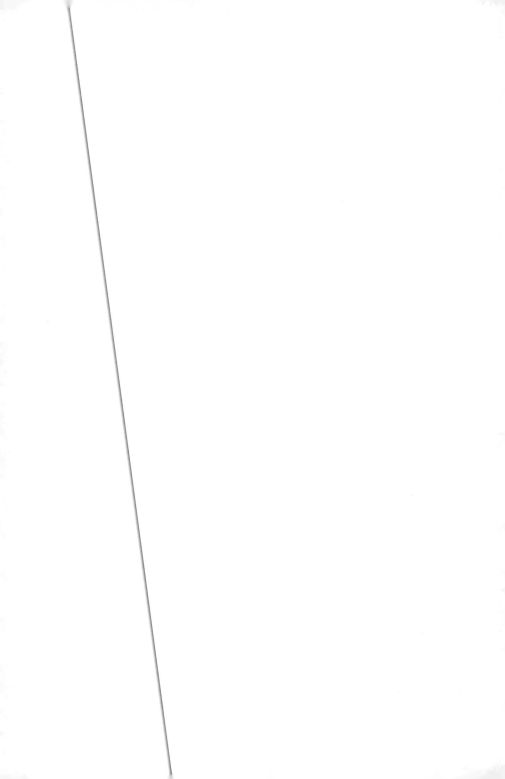

CHAPTER 4

The Story Begins

*I feel certain that my mission will not come to
an end upon my death, but will begin.*

~ St. Faustina

The three previous chapters have led up to this moment.
Finally, we arrive at the second greatest story ever told. With
this story, we will (1) return to the heart of the "school of
trust" revealed in the first greatest story; (2) discover the most
important lesson of this school during the age of the Church;
and (3) be amazed by how God is once again using Poland,
now more powerfully than ever before, for his saving mission.
Let's begin.

*D*IVINE DRAMA. The second greatest story unfolds as the
most violent war in human history is getting ready to
explode, in the country that would see the largest number of
its citizens slaughtered in that war, and during the bloodiest
century in human history. Whew! That's heavy — and fitting.
After all, during a time of incredible evil, we need an incredibly
powerful story to remind us of the goodness of God. In the
darkest era, we need the brightest light to keep us from giving
up and losing heart. In the time of greatest desperation and
despair, we need a most convincing message and witness to
hope. That's what God has been up to. That's why, in our
time, he's giving us the second greatest story ever told. *It's
because we need it.*

And this isn't the first time God has done something like
this. I mean, remember when God's people were slaving away
in the darkness of Egyptian oppression and cried out to God?
What did God do? Something dramatic. He sent 10 plagues,
parted the Red Sea, and manifested his saving glory. And
remember when, immediately afterward, the Israelites slapped
God in the face and showed the greatest ingratitude? What did
God do in the midst of that darkness? He dramatically revealed

his mercy, "The Lord, the Lord, a God merciful and gracious, slow to anger, and abounding in mercy and faithfulness, keeping merciful love for thousands, forgiving iniquity and transgression and sin" (Ex 34:6-7). And remember when Jansenism was destroying God's school of trust and causing so much horrible heartache in the Church? What did God do then? Again, he did something dramatic. He revealed his Sacred Heart through St. Margaret Mary in France. Well, now the second greatest story begins with something just as dramatic. In the face of some of the greatest darkness in human history, God reveals his Merciful Heart, his Divine Mercy, through St. Faustina Kowalska in Poland.

Really. He did. We shouldn't be surprised that God acts in history. We shouldn't be surprised that he acts dramatically during the darkest of times.

SAINT FAUSTINA. The second greatest story is not primarily about St. Faustina Kowalska, the Polish nun from the Sisters of Our Lady of Mercy. However, she's closely related to our hero, St. John Paul II. In a sense, they're like Clare and Francis or, better yet, like Monica and Augustine. She's the prayerful woman behind the great man. And it's important to know a bit of her story so as to better understand his.

Now, right off the bat, I want to address something that may be bothering some readers after reading the last section. There are some people who get really uncomfortable with the idea that God reveals himself or speaks to people. I don't know why this is the case. He did it in the Old Testament. He did it in the New Testament. He continues to do it now. Maybe the problem is with "false prophets," those people who tell everyone that God is speaking to them but who are really just being deceived, hungering for attention, or nuts. Don't worry. Saint Faustina was not being deceived, nor hungering for attention, and she certainly wasn't nuts. She's a saint, a great saint. In other words, she's been vetted and tested by the Church, and God is using her as a prophet to speak a powerful word of mercy for our time, as he explains in her *Diary*:

> In the Old Covenant I sent prophets wielding
> thunderbolts to My people. Today I am sending
> you with My mercy to the people of the whole
> world. I do not want to punish aching mankind,
> but I desire to heal it, pressing it to My Merciful
> Heart. ... Before the Day of Justice I am sending
> the Day of Mercy.[35]

Now, don't get hung up on the word "prophet." A
prophet is someone who has had a powerful experience of God
that he is then called to share at a given time for the strength-
ening of other people's faith, hope, and love.[36] Sometimes a
prophet's experiences of God come through extraordinary
mystical experiences, such as in the case of St. Faustina. At
other times, their experiences come through the silent, hidden
action of the Holy Spirit, such as in the case of St. Thérèse
of Lisieux. Whatever the nature of his experience of God, if
a prophet is authentic — of which only the Church has the
authority to make a final, definitive determination — then his
experience becomes a gift for the people of his time.

By the way, I just mentioned that St. Thérèse was
a prophet. Yes, she is, too. In fact, she represents part of a
whole prophetic stream in the life of the Church. In other
words, sometimes God has a message that's so important that
he uses not just one, not two, but a whole series of prophets
to make sure people get the message. In chapter two, we saw
that the modern "stream of mercy" began with St. Margaret
Mary and the Sacred Heart, ran through St. Alphonsus de
Liguori, and then into St. Thérèse of Lisieux. Now, we'll be
learning that it goes on to Saints Faustina and John Paul II.
Wait, is John Paul a prophet as well? Absolutely, and I'll say
more about that later. For now, though, let's just focus on
Thérèse and Faustina.

Did you know that St. Thérèse actually appeared to St.
Faustina? She came to her in a dream and "passed the torch,"
so to speak, of teaching the message of God's school of trust
for our day. Here's Faustina's own account of what happened:

I want to write down a dream that I had about Saint Thérèse of the Child Jesus. I was still a novice at the time and was going through some difficulties which I did not know how to overcome. .... . I made novenas to various saints, but the situation grew more and more difficult. The sufferings it caused me were so great that I did not know how to go on living, but suddenly the thought occurred to me that I should pray to Saint Thérèse of the Child Jesus. I started a novena to this Saint, because before entering the convent I had had a great devotion to her. Lately I had somewhat neglected this devotion, but in my need I began again to pray with great fervor.

On the fifth day of the novena, I dreamed of Saint Thérèse, but it was as if she were still living on earth. She hid from me the fact that she was a saint and began to comfort me, saying that I should not be worried about this matter, but should trust more in God. She said, "I suffered greatly, too," but I did not quite believe her and said, "It seems to me that you have not suffered at all." But Saint Thérèse answered me in a convincing manner that she had suffered very much indeed and said to me, "Sister, know that in three days the difficulty will come to a happy conclusion." When I was not very willing to believe her, she revealed to me that she was a saint. At that moment, a great joy filled my soul, and I said to her, "You are a saint?" "Yes," she answered, "I am a saint. Trust that this matter will be resolved in three days." And I said, "Dear sweet Thérèse, tell me, shall I go to heaven?" And she answered, "Yes, you will go to heaven, Sister." "And will I be a saint?" To which she replied, "Yes, you will be a saint." "But, little Thérèse, shall I be a saint as you are, raised to the altar?" And she answered, "Yes, you will be a saint just as I am, *but you must trust in the Lord Jesus.*"[37]

Now, notice a couple of key points here. First, it's hard not to miss that St. Faustina certainly had her priorities straight. She clearly wanted to become a saint! Good. So should we all.

Second, notice Thérèse's counsel to Faustina about how she could become a saint: *Trust.* The heart of the message of God's school of trust is TRUST! It's part of the Sacred Heart devotion, "Sacred Heart of Jesus, I place my trust in Thee." It's a key part of St. Alphonsus's moral theology, to trust in the merciful God. It's at the center of St. Thérèse's Little Way of humble confidence.

Trust is the main theme of the message of Divine Mercy given to the world though St. Faustina. Not only is it a constant refrain in her *Diary*, but it's enshrined on the main icon of the devotion, the Image of Divine Mercy, which reads, "Jesus, I trust in you." Could the Lord have made it any more obvious? Clearly, he wants to continue his school of trust and heal the distorted image we have of him as a result of the fall. This latter point is precisely why he had Faustina paint an image of him as the Merciful Savior. Through her, he's saying to us, "Look! This is who I am! I am love and mercy itself. Trust in me!"

In a sense, this describes St. Faustina's entire mission, namely, completing God's school of trust for our time, even from heaven! She herself explains it:

> I feel certain that my mission will not come to an end upon my death, but will begin. O doubting souls, I will draw aside for you the veils of heaven to convince you of God's goodness, so that you will no longer continue to wound with your distrust the sweetest Heart of Jesus. God is Love and Mercy.[38]

Oh, and I also said her mission is to "complete" God's school of trust for our time. I mean that. It's her message — crazy as it might sound — that will prepare the world for the Lord's final coming. Bear with me here. I know this may sound a bit much, and I'll have more to say on it later. But for now, read and consider what Jesus said to the great apostle of mercy for our time:

> When I became aware of God's great plans for me, I was frightened at their greatness and felt myself quite incapable of fulfilling them, and I began to avoid interior conversations with Him, filling up the time with vocal prayer. I did this out of humility, but I soon recognized it was not true humility, but rather a great temptation from the devil. When, on one occasion, instead of interior prayer, I took up a book of spiritual reading, I heard these words spoken distinctly and forcefully within my soul, **You will prepare the world for My final coming.** These words moved me deeply, and although I pretended not to hear them, I understood them very well and had no doubt about them.[39]

The Lord spoke similar words to St. Faustina on several other occasions.[40] Also, in a related passage from her *Diary*, we read of the Lord telling Faustina that her native land of Poland will have a special role in fulfilling this awesome mission:

> **I bear a special love for Poland, and if she will be obedient to My will, I will exalt her in might and holiness. From her will come forth the spark that will prepare the world for My final coming.**[41]

Clearly, we're dealing with an extraordinary saint here, a saint with a truly remarkable mission that involves both her and her native land. But that shouldn't surprise us. After all, we're also dealing with the second greatest story ever told.

*E*ARLY SPREADING OF THE MESSAGE. St. Faustina died at the age of 33 on October 5, 1938. Less than a year later, on September 1, 1939, the terrible war that Faustina had foreseen and warned others about came crashing down on Poland, beginning with the Nazi invasion and occupation.[42] It's hard to overstate the death, destruction, and devastation that World War II inflicted on Poland. Out of a pre-war population of 35 million people, six million of its citizens were killed in combat or, in most cases, murdered outright. That is an 18-percent casualty rate, the highest of any country during World War II. Poland also became home to many of the Nazi death camps during the Holocaust, the vast majority of whose victims were God's chosen people, the Jews. Needless to say, with so much unheard of violence and bloodshed, Satan was having a field day.

During this time of hell on earth, a circulation of pamphlets and prayercards bearing the Divine Mercy Image, Chaplet, Litany, and Novena gave comfort to countless numbers of brutalized Polish souls. That the message spread throughout Poland on the cusp of the war is largely thanks to the efforts of St. Faustina's spiritual director, Blessed Fr. Michael Sopocko, who personally funded this apostolate of mercy.

Less than a year before her death, while suffering from the tuberculosis that would eventually take her life, Faustina was shown some of the prayercards Fr. Sopocko had had printed. She records her reaction in her *Diary*:

> When Mother [Irene] showed me the booklet with the Chaplet, the litany, and the novena, I asked her to let me look it over. As I was glancing through it, Jesus gave me to know interiorly: **Already there are many souls who have been drawn to My love by this image. My mercy acts in souls through this work.** I learned that many souls had experienced God's grace.[43]

A few months later, in a letter to Fr. Sopocko, Faustina speaks of the effects of the Divine Mercy prayercards and the way they are spreading:

> People have started buying them and many a soul has already obtained God's grace which flows from this source. ... They are being purchased by those

who are attracted by God's grace, and it is God himself who acts here. Our Congregation has already purchased enough of them. Mother Irene distributes these holy cards and the booklets. We have even decided to hand them out at the gate. Mother Irene gave as many as 50 booklets to one of the Jesuit Fathers who goes on missions all over Poland.[44]

"All over Poland." Granted, Faustina is only talking here about 50 booklets, but Fr. Sopocko was also going throughout the country, distributing many more. Unfortunately, practically speaking, the Nazi invasion of Poland put a stop to the further printing and distribution of such materials. But Fr. Sopocko came up with another idea for spreading the message of Divine Mercy upon meeting a priest from my community, Fr. Joseph Jarzebowski, MIC.[45]

In 1940, a number of priests and seminarians had told Fr. Jarzebowski about a holy, learned priest from Vilnius who had been spreading the "devotion to Divine Mercy" all over the country. Father Jarzebowski went to meet him. During their meeting, Sopocko learned of Jarzebowski's plans to make the perilous journey to his community's religious house in Washington, D.C., where his superiors in Rome had assigned him. Sopocko gave Jarzebowski pamphlets on the Divine Mercy message, which included the chaplet, litany, and novena as well as a document that he had written, presenting the reasons for instituting the Feast of Divine Mercy. Father Jarzebowski, who was skeptical of any private revelations not yet approved by the Church, nevertheless, accepted the documents from Fr. Sopocko, who added, "When you arrive in the States, notify the bishops and spread the message." Jarzebowski replied, "*If I arrive safely, I will count it a miracle, and I will spread this message and devotion until the end of my life.*"

Despite the fact that his American visa had expired, Fr. Jarzebowski went ahead and tried to get an exit permit from the Soviets. Amazingly, he received the permit, obtained the needed funds from the Marian Fathers in the U.S., and got a train ticket across Russia, through Siberia, to the port city of Vladivostok, where he planned to take a boat to Japan. (The trip to Japan was made possible by St. Maximilian Kolbe's Franciscan brothers in Nagasaki, Japan, who helped Fr. Jarzebowski obtain necessary transit documentation.) Everything was falling into place, which Fr. Jarzebowski attributed to his growing devotion to Divine Mercy.

Just before he left on his journey, Fr. Jarzebowski went to visit Fr. Sopocko again in Vilnius. The next day, while still in Vilnius, he celebrated Mass before the original Divine Mercy Image that had been painted under the direction of St. Faustina and entrusted his journey to Divine Mercy. He departed by train for Japan the following day, Ash Wednesday, February 26, 1941, at 3:00 p.m., the Hour of Great Mercy.

On Fr. Jarzebowski's train, every coach had two members of the NKVD (the old KGB), and they bothered the priest about not having a Japanese transit visa. He told them it was waiting for him at a later train stop. Amazingly, they allowed him to continue on. At the last stop, Vladivostok, he still needed to get a Japanese visa, which would require him to present his expired American visa. Father Jarzebowski prayed to the Merciful Jesus and gave the consulate his American visa without the sheet containing the expiration date. Thankfully, the consulate didn't notice and pressed it with the stamp for the Japanese visa. But the danger was not yet over.

As he was boarding the ship for Japan, Fr. Jarzebowski realized that the customs agents were confiscating crosses and books. He prayed to Jesus to save his Divine Mercy materials. One agent took Father's breviary out of a bag and looked through it. He wasn't sure what to make of it but found the prayercards charming and let it all go. He marked that bag with chalk and then marked a second bag containing the Divine Mercy materials. He didn't even bother to look inside.

The ship to Japan had accommodations for only 80 people but carried more than 500. Needless to say, it was a long two days and two nights at sea — but Fr. Jarzebowski didn't mind; he was on his way to freedom.

Father Jarzebowski's ship pulled into the Japanese port on March 13, 1941. Soon thereafter, he met up with the Franciscans who had aided his passage. Perhaps because of his extraordinary joy and amazing story, they invited him to give them a retreat. He did so at their Mugenzai no Sono (Garden of the Immaculate) Monastery in Nagasaki.

Of course, the theme of the retreat was Divine Mercy. And what a retreat it must have been! By that point in his trip, Fr. Jarzebowski's gratitude to Jesus, The Divine Mercy, could hardly be contained. Unfortunately, the monastery's founder, St. Maximilian Kolbe, couldn't attend. He was in the midst of another sort of spiritual exercise, this one at the Auschwitz concentration camp. There, five months after Jarzebowski's arrival in Japan, Kolbe would not be preaching mercy but rather living it to the full — he'd be freely giving up his life that another prisoner might live.

While God did not ask Fr. Jarzebowski to become a martyr of merciful love like Maximilian Kolbe; nevertheless, the Lord did choose to pass the torch of Divine Mercy to this Marian priest, making him a great apostle of his mercy. And Fr. Jarzebowski's work of mercy, as we'll learn in later chapters, is just as important as Kolbe's. What? I say that because, as we'll later discover, their two works are really one.

So, in May of 1941, seven months before the Japanese attack on Pearl Harbor, Fr. Jarzebowski arrived in Seattle, Washington, and from there, made his way to Washington, D.C. On his arrival at the Marian's religious house in D.C., he knew that the Merciful Savior had brought him safely home to his brothers in America — and he kept his promise to Fr. Sopocko. He and the Marians of the Immaculate Conception, taking advantage of the environment of freedom in the United States, spread the Divine Mercy message throughout the country. Eventually, from their printing presses in Stockbridge, Massachusetts, that message would go out to all the world.

But we're getting ahead of ourselves. Despite such initial successes, the message of Divine Mercy would have to go through a period of darkness.

THE BAN. During the war years, many people received great graces and comfort from the Divine Mercy booklets and prayercards that Fr. Sopocko had distributed. Then, after the war, as the testimonies to these graces spread, more and more people wanted to get the Divine Mercy literature for themselves. Recognizing this growing interest in Sr. Faustina's writings, Mother Michaela Moraczewska, the superior General of Sr. Faustina's community, had one of the sisters type out the six handwritten notebooks that comprise Sr. Faustina's *Diary.*

Unfortunately, the transcription process was not done carefully, and the final typescript was full of errors and omissions. Making matters worse, this faulty typescript was then made available to anyone who wanted to print prayercards and spread the Divine Mercy devotion. For instance, an Italian woman with a religious bookstore in Rome visited the sisters' convent in Krakow, made copies of the typescript, and then proceeded to print and sell erroneous Divine Mercy booklets in Italian. Something similar happened in France.

Even with the errors, these foreign translations were a hit in their home countries. People were still suffering the effects of the war, and the message of Divine Mercy brought them great comfort and amazing graces. However, as the devotion grew in popularity, the errors in the literature were brought to the attention of various priests and theologians who then wrote to the Holy Office in Rome (the present-day Congregation for the Doctrine of the Faith). After getting several of these complaints and then going through the literature, the Holy Office prepared a decree in 1958 that would have forever prohibited the Divine Mercy devotion as presented by Sr. Faustina. However, because the Pope at the time, Pius XII, was so ill, the Holy Office didn't submit this decree until after his death, slipping it under a large pile of papers for the next pope to deal with.

The next Pope, St. John XXIII, was unexpectedly elected after 11 ballots at the relatively old age of 76. The faithful called him "Good Pope John" and loved him like a grandfather. Many of the Vatican bureaucrats surely wanted him to act like a grandfatherly Pope. In other words, they hoped he'd just go into semi-retirement mode as a kind of interim or caretaker Pope and keep business as usual until the next papal election.

Having worked at the Vatican before being elected Pope, John XXIII knew what "business as usual" meant. For instance, he was well aware that certain members of the curia would sometimes slip important papers at the bottom of piles with the hope that a tired, overworked Pope would just glance over them and rubber stamp his approval. Well, when John XXIII first arrived at his office and saw his new desk with the tall pile of papers awaiting his signature, he proceeded to sit down, make the Sign of the Cross, and *flip* the whole pile over! Thus, the *very first* thing he dealt with as Pope was the decree that had been slipped in at the bottom of the pile, the decree prepared by the Holy Office regarding Sr. Faustina, the decree that would have forever forbidden the spread of the Divine Mercy devotion and the hanging of Divine Mercy Images in the churches.

According to one of his personal secretaries, the Pope read this decree carefully, shook his head, and said, "No, no, no. This must be looked into further. The bishops of Poland need to be consulted."[46] But they couldn't be consulted because of the religious suppression under the Communists. (At the conclusion of the war, the Poles passed from Nazi tyranny to Communist oppression.) So, instead of a decree forever forbidding the message, Pope John only approved a notification that prohibited "spreading of the devotion to Sr. Faustina, pending clarification of [the Vatican's] concerns."[47] That notification was published on March 6, 1959.

Of course, this notification was not as bad as the decree of prohibition, but it still put the brakes on the propagation of the message of Divine Mercy and forms of devotion based on Sr. Faustina's revelations. This was deeply disappointing to the many people who had benefitted from it, and it caused difficulties for communities that had been spreading the devotion, such as the Marian Fathers in Stockbridge.[48]

For many, the Holy Office's notification was met with great surprise: "How could something that has borne so much fruit be banned?" For anyone who might have read St. Faustina's *Diary*, however, this notification shouldn't have come as a surprise. After all, Faustina had clearly prophesied that such a thing would happen. Nevertheless, again, it caused great suffering for many people, not the least of whom was Blessed Michael Sopocko, who had done so much to spread the message. Faustina predicted his turmoil, too:

> Once, as I was talking with my spiritual director [Fr. Sopocko], I had an interior vision — quicker than lightning — of his soul in great suffering, in such agony that God touches very few souls with such fire. The suffering arises from this work. There will come a time when this work, which God is demanding so very much, will be as though utterly undone. And then God will act with great power, which will give evidence of its authenticity. It will be a new splendor for the Church, although it has been dormant in it from long ago. ... When this triumph comes, we shall already have entered the new life in which there is no suffering. But before this, your soul [Fr. Sopocko] will be surfeited with bitterness at the sight of the destruction of your efforts.[49]

The ban did indeed seem to "destroy" and "undo" Fr. Sopocko's efforts, who in the years after Faustina's death was frequently mocked by bishops and clergy alike for being "carried away" by "that crazy mystic." Moreover, Fr. Sopocko, whom Jesus considered to be a true and faithful friend, suffered the added bitterness of passing away just three years before the work of mercy rose again.[50]

*L*IFTING OF THE BAN. By now, we all likely realize that the ban was eventually lifted, but how did it happen? First and foremost, we should probably thank the Polish laity, who can be quite determined (and stubborn) when it comes to pursuing God's glory. After the announcement of the ban, they never let up on giving the poor Archbishop of Sr. Faustina's Archdiocese of Krakow a piece of their mind. In a journal entry for August 22, 1965, that Archbishop, Karol Wojtyła, wrote about the Polish laity's cause: "They are bombarding me with requests to begin the process."[51] By "the process," he meant the steps required to prepare for Sr. Faustina's beatification and eventual canonization. The people were convinced of her holiness and the authenticity of her message, and this was one way to reopen the discussion. Actually, Wojtyła didn't need a lot of prodding from the laity. The previous day, after meeting with Fr. Sopocko, he had written in his journal regarding the process, "This matter is foremost on my mind, maybe we will still be able to begin it this year."[52]

Less than a month later, Wojtyła was in Rome for the last session of Vatican II. As he was exiting St. Peter's Basilica in the recessional procession after the opening Mass, he was speaking with his friend, Monsignor Andrew Deskur, who had introduced him to the Divine Mercy message when the two were in the seminary together. Suddenly, the two of them spotted Cardinal Ottoviani, who was the prefect of the Holy Office and knew the matter of Faustina very well. The two friends went up to the Cardinal and asked him whether it were still possible to begin the process of Faustina's beatification given the fact of the notification of prohibition from Ottoviani's office. Ottoviani replied, "What? You haven't started it yet? Hurry and start it before the witnesses die."[53] That's all the encouragement Wojtyła needed.

The next month, on October 21, 1965, Wojtyła began the informative process relating to the life and virtues of Sr. Faustina Kowalska in the Archdiocese of Krakow and delegated his auxiliary bishop Julian Groblicki to oversee it. From this moment, Sr. Faustina received the title "Servant of God." Less than two years later, in June of 1967, Archbishop Wojtyła became Cardinal Wojtyła. Then, in September that same year, the new Cardinal officially closed the first informative stage in the process for the beatification of the Servant of God, Sr. Faustina Kowalska. Finally, in January of 1968, by a decree of the Sacred Congregation of the Causes of Saints, the process of beatification of the Servant of God Sr. Faustina Kowalska was formally inaugurated.

During the years of the informative process and subsequent beatification process of Sr. Faustina, thousands of pages of documents relating to the life and virtues of Sr. Faustina were sent to Rome, and the Vatican became much better acquainted with her. This deeper knowledge and appreciation of Faustina by Vatican officials eventually led to what took place on April 15, 1978: In response to inquiries from the Marian Fathers of the Immaculate Conception in Stockbridge and from prelates in Poland, such as Cardinal Wojtyła, regarding the "Notification" of 1959 (which effectively banned the spreading of the message of Divine Mercy through Sr. Faustina), the Sacred Congregation for the Canonization of Saints issued a new "Notification":

> This Sacred Congregation, having now in [its] possession the many original documents, unknown in 1959; having taken into consideration the profoundly changed circumstances, and having taken into account the opinion of many Polish Ordinaries, declares no longer binding the prohibitions contained in the quoted "Notification" [of 1959].[54]

In other words, by this document, to the great rejoicing of the faithful, the Vatican lifted the ban on spreading the message of Divine Mercy through Sr. Faustina. Then, less than six months after this momentous document was issued, the Cardinal Archbishop who had done so much behind-the-scenes work to accomplish this task *was elected Pope John Paul II*. With his election, the "new splendor" in the Church, prophesied by Sr. Faustina, began. Let's close this chapter by reading that prophecy once again:

There will come a time when this work, which God is demanding very much, will be as though utterly undone. And then God will act with great power, which will give evidence of its authenticity. It will be a new splendor for the Church.

Mercy Pope

Today is the happiest day of my life.

~ Pope John Paul II
after St. Faustina's canonization

Commenting on coincidences, Pope John Paul II once said that "in the designs of providence," *there aren't any.*[55] It's no surprise, then, that he clearly recognized the hand of God's providence in the fact that his election as Pope came *just six months* after the lifting of the ban on the message of Divine Mercy (which resulted from his efforts, as we read earlier). He further recognized that this blessed rebirth of Divine Mercy had come right as he was about to mount the largest pulpit in the world, the pulpit of the papacy. And from that papal pulpit, throughout his time as Pope, he would announce the good news of God's mercy to the ends of the earth, truly making Divine Mercy a "new splendor" in the Church.

The story of how Pope John Paul II proclaimed that message of mercy with power and how God himself confirmed it is the climactic lesson of God's school of trust in Church history, the most dramatic moment of Polish history, and the fulfillment of Faustina's amazing mission. It's the culmination of the second greatest story ever told.

*N*OW IS THE TIME OF MERCY. John Paul II's powerful proclamation of mercy begins with his second encyclical letter, *Dives in Misericordia* (*Rich in Mercy*), published in November of 1980. (Encyclical letters are important papal documents that help form the identity of a papacy.) This second encyclical, which, according to papal biographer George Weigel, "is the clearest expression of [John Paul's] pastoral soul"[56] was deeply influenced by St. Faustina. The Pope himself said he felt spiritually "very near" to Faustina and had been "thinking about her for a long time" when he began writing it.[57]

Arguably, the deepest insight into John Paul's "pastoral soul" revealed in *Dives in Misericordia* comes in the famous last chapter of the encyclical, which is a sustained meditation on the importance of *calling out for God's mercy even "with loud cries."*[58] The Pope says that "These 'loud cries' [for mercy] should be the mark of the Church of our times."[59] Why in our times? Because, again, we are in such great need of mercy! Clearly, John Paul was not blind to the great and unprecedented evil present in the modern world. He knew from his own experience of World War II in Poland and from Faustina's testimony that *now more than ever* is a time of mercy. Now more than ever does the world need mercy!

And what is mercy? John Paul II defines it in *Dives in Misericordia* as "love's second name,"[60] as "the specific manner in which love is revealed and effected in the face of the reality of the evil that is in the world, affecting and besieging man."[61] In other words, mercy is love when it meets poverty, weakness, brokenness, and sin. It's the power of love to bring good out of such evil. And because our time is marked by more suffering and sin than any other, for this very reason, now is the time of mercy; now is the time when mercy must be proclaimed more than ever before. This was John Paul's belief and the insight at the core of his "pastoral soul" as he witnessed the unprecedented and growing darkness of our time.

In fact, precisely because of the evils of the modern world, John Paul II saw the message of Divine Mercy as the special task that God had entrusted to him for our time. He said exactly this when he visited the Shrine of Merciful Love in Covalenza, Italy, on November 22, 1981:

> Right from the beginning of my ministry in St. Peter's See in Rome, I considered this message [of Divine Mercy] my special task. Providence has assigned it to me in the present situation of man, the Church and the world. It could be said that precisely this situation assigned that message to me as my task before God.[62]

So, it's clear that John Paul II did not leave Faustina and Divine Mercy in Poland when he became Pope. Rather, he took the message of Divine Mercy with him to Rome and proclaimed it with power. And to his delight, the message began to spread. For instance, when he had the joy of beatifying Sr. Faustina in 1993, he exclaimed, "It is truly marvelous how [Faustina's] devotion to the merciful Jesus is spreading in our contemporary world and gaining so many hearts!" He went on to describe this as "doubtlessly a sign of the times," and remarked, "Where, if not in the Divine Mercy, can the world find refuge and the light of hope?"

Later, in 1997, during his visit to the tomb of then-Blessed Faustina, in Krakow-Łagiewniki, Poland, John Paul declared, "The message of Divine Mercy has always been near and dear to me." He went on to say, "[I took it] with me to the See of Peter and ... in a sense [it] forms the image of this pontificate. ... I pray unceasingly that God will have 'mercy on us and on the whole world.'" Clearly, the Pope had internalized his famous call to the whole Church to "cry out for mercy," as he himself cries out for mercy "unceasingly," using the words of the Chaplet of Divine Mercy, given by the Lord to St. Faustina.

MERCY SUNDAY DURING THE YEAR OF MERCY. While Pope John Paul II proclaimed mercy throughout his whole pontificate, a particularly special moment of grace happened on Divine Mercy Sunday during the Great Jubilee Year of the Incarnation, 2000, the Year of Mercy. Before getting to what happened on that day, I should first say something about the significance of the Jubilee Year to the Pope.[63]

After Karol Wojtyła's election to the papacy on October 16, 1978, the head of the Church in Poland, Cardinal Stefan Wyszynski, said to him, "The task of the new Pope will be to lead the Church into the Third Millennium."[64] John Paul took these words very much to heart. After all, he had witnessed how Cardinal Wyszynski prepared Poland for her 1966 celebration of 1,000 years of Polish Christianity, which led to an immense outpouring of grace for the entire country. With this powerful memory firmly fixed in his mind, from the beginning of his pontificate, John Paul saw his task as that of preparing the whole Church for an even greater event: the 2,000-year commemoration of the most important moment in history, the Incarnation of the Lord. The Pope himself eagerly looked forward to this time of grace as a *"new springtime of Christian life,"* which, he hoped, "would be revealed by the Great Jubilee."[65]

That Great Jubilee, inspired by the jubilee tradition of the Old Testament,[66] would truly be a year of great grace and favor from the Lord, a year of reconciliation and forgiveness, a year overflowing with superabundant mercy.[67] But for all its blessings, the key moment of grace, the heart of the "new springtime of Christian life" that the Great Jubilee did indeed reveal, fittingly happened on April 30, 2000, the Second Sunday of Easter, Divine Mercy Sunday.

On that Divine Mercy Sunday of the Year of Mercy, John Paul II canonized St. Faustina as the first saint of the new millennium, an act, he said in his homily, that has a "particular eloquence." He revealed its particular eloquence as follows: "By this act, I intend today to pass on this message to the third millennium."

Now, what message was he talking about? The message of God's merciful love: a message that will help all people discover, he said, "the true face of God," a message that overcomes the false image of God that results from original sin, a message that gets to the heart of God's school of trust. In his homily, John Paul called it a "consoling message" that is

> addressed above all to those who, afflicted by a particularly harsh trial or crushed by the weight of the sins they committed, have lost all confidence in life and are tempted to give in to despair. To them the gentle face of Christ is offered; those rays from his heart touch them and shine upon them, warm them, show them the way and fill them with hope. How many souls have been consoled by the prayer,

"Jesus, I trust in you," which Providence intimated through Sr. Faustina! This simple act of abandonment to Jesus dispels the thickest clouds and lets a ray of light penetrate every life. Jesus, I trust in you.[68]

John Paul then ended his homily with a moving prayer to the new saint who, for the third time, he calls a "gift of God" to our time:

> And you, Faustina, a gift of God to our time, a gift from the land of Poland to the whole Church, obtain for us an awareness of the depth of divine mercy; help us to have a living experience of it and to bear witness to it among our brothers and sisters. May your message of light and hope spread throughout the world ... . Today, fixing our gaze with you on the face of the risen Christ, let us make our own your prayer of trusting abandonment and say with firm hope, "Christ Jesus, I trust in you! Jesus, I trust in you!"[69]

Saint Faustina seems to have heard this prayer not only from heaven but, one might say, even during her own lifetime! I say this because it appears that Faustina experienced a mystical vision of that great Divine Mercy Sunday of the year 2000. To help us understand how profoundly important that day was for the Church and the world, let's read Faustina's own description of that vision:

> Suddenly, God's presence took hold of me, and at once I saw myself in Rome ... . And I took part in the solemn celebration simultaneously here [in the convent in Krakow] and in Rome, for the celebration was so closely connected with Rome that, even as I write, I cannot distinguish the two but I am writing it down as I saw it. ... The crowd was so enormous that the eye could not take it all in. Everyone was participating in the celebrations with great joy, and

many of them obtained what they desired. The same celebration was held in Rome, in a beautiful church, and the Holy Father, with all the clergy, was celebrating this Feast, and then suddenly I saw Saint Peter, who stood between the altar and the Holy Father. I could not hear what Saint Peter said but I saw that the Holy Father understood his words.

Then suddenly, I saw how the two rays, as painted in the image, issued from the Host and spread over the whole world. This lasted only a moment, but it seemed as though it had lasted all day ... and the whole day abounded in joy.

Then suddenly I saw on our altar the living Lord Jesus, just as He is depicted in the image [of Divine Mercy]. ... Jesus looked with great kindness and joy at the Holy Father, at certain priests, at the entire clergy, at the people and at our Congregation.

Then, in an instant, I was caught up to stand near Jesus, and I stood on the altar next to the Lord Jesus, and my spirit was filled with a happiness so great that I am unable to comprehend it or write about it. A profound peace as well as repose filled my soul. Jesus bent toward me and said with great kindness, **What is it you desire, My daughter?** And I answered, "I desire worship and glory be given to Your mercy." **I already am receiving worship by the institution and celebration of this Feast; what else do you desire?** I then looked at the immense crowd worshiping The Divine Mercy and I said to the Lord, "Jesus, bless all those who are gathered to give glory to you and to venerate Your infinite mercy." Jesus made a sign of the cross with His hand, and this blessing was reflected in the souls like a flash of light. My spirit was engulfed in His love. ...

I am immensely happy. ... I am happy with everything You give me.[70]

Let's look at four key points from this remarkable vision. First, notice that St. Peter appears in Faustina's vision and speaks with the Holy Father, who "understood" what the Apostle was saying. This is significant, because it seems to indicate that heaven was specially united with and authoritatively confirming this momentous occasion for the Church and the world. Also, as we'll see, it will prove to be the pinnacle of John Paul's ministry as the successor of St. Peter and the great Mercy Pope.

Second, notice that in Faustina's vision, the celebration in Rome was somehow simultaneously experienced at her convent in Krakow. She writes it as she saw it, but couldn't explain how the two could be experienced at the same time. Well, the organizers of the Divine Mercy Sunday 2000 event had set up giant TV screens in St. Peter's Square as well as at the sisters' convent in Krakow. Those screens did simultaneously broadcast the event such that the sisters in Krakow could see the people in Rome and the people in Rome could see the sisters in Krakow, which is exactly what Faustina describes in her vision. It seems that Faustina got a glimpse of modern technology!

Third, notice the conversation between Jesus and Faustina. Jesus asks her what she desires. She replies that she desires that worship and glory be given to his mercy. He responds, **"I already am receiving worship by the institution and celebration of this Feast."** Jesus' words here imply that the Feast of Divine Mercy had already been instituted. But when did that happen? It happened during the homily Pope John Paul gave at the canonization Mass! That was perhaps the greatest gift of the Great Jubilee Year. The Pope surprised everyone by stating in his homily, "It is important, then, that we accept the whole message that comes to us from the word of God on this Second Sunday of Easter, *which from now on throughout the Church will be called 'Divine Mercy Sunday.'"* By those words, the Great Mercy Pope instituted a feast that, according to the *Diary of St. Faustina*, Jesus deeply desired. For instance, we read this frank conversation between Faustina and Jesus regarding the Feast:

Today, Jesus, I offer You all my sufferings, morti-fications and prayers for the intentions of the Holy Father, so that he may approve the Feast of Mercy. But, Jesus, I have one more word to say to You: I am very surprised that You bid me to talk about this Feast of Mercy, for they tell me that there is already such a feast and so why should I talk about it? [There was a Feast of Mercy in the early Church, but it had been forgotten.] And Jesus said to me, **And who knows anything about this feast? No one? Even those who should be proclaiming My mercy and teaching people about it often do not know about it themselves.**[71]

Fourth, notice the joy and happiness that Faustina describes in her vision. She says that everyone was participating in the celebration "with great joy," that "the day abounded with joy," that Jesus "looked with great kindness and joy" on the people, and that Faustina herself was filled with an incomprehensible happiness and was "immensely happy." Even the Pope began his homily by saying, "*Today my joy is truly great in presenting the life and witness of Sr. Faustina Kowalska to the whole Church as a gift of God for our time.*" But most amazing of all: At the banquet following the canonization ceremony, Pope John Paul II shared with the doctor who had investigated the canonization miracle, Dr. Valentin Fuster, a startling revelation. He said to him, "*Today is the happiest day of my life.*"[72]

Wow! But why was there so much joy?

Well, for one, the greatest joy comes in our lives when we have accomplished our God-given mission. John Paul II, who believed that divine providence had assigned to him the task of spreading the message of Divine Mercy, accomplished his mission on that day. He canonized St. Faustina, passed her message on to the new millennium, and declared that the Second Sunday of Easter was to be celebrated as Divine Mercy Sunday, in fulfillment of the Lord's desires.

Also, the joy comes because of the very nature of the message. It proclaims Divine Mercy, a love more powerful than evil, a love that can even bring good out of evil. This is a profoundly joyful, hopeful, and consoling message that counteracts the often sad and depressing situation of the modern world. It's a message that announces God's particular closeness to us in our time, which is, in fact, the time of mercy. It's a message that shares the very good news that God is pouring out unprecedented mercy on the people of our time, because "where sin abounded, grace abounded all the more" (Rom 5:20). When we realize all this, when we see the true face of God, that he is love and mercy itself, that his love is more powerful than evil, and that he is pouring it out in a unprecedented way in our time, we cannot help but be filled with indescribable happiness and joy.

DEDICATION OF POLAND'S MERCY SHRINE, 2002. Divine Mercy Sunday, 2000, could have seemed enough Mission accomplished. Now, John Paul could just ease into a well-deserved retirement. Right? Wrong. He continued to lead the Church even more deeply into the mystery of mercy. He did so probably most profoundly in 2002 when he dedicated the Shrine of Divine Mercy in Krakow-Łagiewniki, Poland, and entrusted the whole world to Divine Mercy.

That shrine was particularly significant to John Paul. During the war, while he was working at the Solvay rock quarry and studying for the priesthood in secret, he learned about the mystic, Sr. Faustina. Her message deeply moved the young Karol Wojtyła, and so, he often stopped by her community's chapel on his way back to the seminary from a long day of hard work. With tears in his eyes, John Paul reminisced about this during some off-the-cuff remarks at the end of the Mass for the Shrine's dedication.

> At the end of this solemn liturgy, I desire to say that many of my personal memories are tied to this place. During the Nazi occupation, when I was working in

the Solvay factory near here, I used to come here. Even now I recall the street that goes from Borek Falecki to Debniki that I took every day going to work on the different turns with the wooden shoes on my feet. They're the shoes that we used to wear then. How was it possible to imagine that one day the man with the wooden shoes would consecrate the Basilica of the Divine Mercy at Łagiewniki of Krakow?[73]

While this dedication event featuring John Paul II was surely impossible "to imagine," it may have been possible to *foresee*. I say this because of a mysterious passage from the *Diary of St. Faustina*:

Today, I saw two enormous pillars implanted in the ground; I had implanted one of them, and a certain person, S.M., the other. We had done so with unheard-of-effort, much fatigue and difficulty. And when I had implanted the pillar, I myself wondered where such extraordinary strength had come from. And I recognized that I had not done this by my own strength, but with the power which came from above. These two pillars were close to each other, in the area of the image. And I saw the image, raised up very high and hanging from these two pillars. In an instant, there stood a large temple, supported both from within and from without, upon these two pillars. I saw a hand finishing the temple, but I did not see the person. There was a great multitude of people, inside and outside the temple, and the torrents issuing from the Compassionate Heart of Jesus were flowing down upon everyone.[74]

The certain person that St. Faustina describes as "S.M." is likely her spiritual director, Michael Sopocko. But who is the other person whose hand was finishing the temple? Could it have been St. John Paul II, who dedicated the shrine? It sure seems likely, because his words on that occasion not only finished the *physical* building of the Shrine by dedicating it, but they also finished the *spiritual* building of the Divine Mercy message.

In my opinion, the words of mercy that John Paul spoke during his homily of dedication were some of the most profound of his entire pontificate. You might say he chose the best for last. For, indeed, this was his last pilgrimage to his beloved homeland, and he knew it. Many had advised him not to make the trip, because of his ill health, which knew was getting worse. But he wanted to go. He had a message to give. He had a spiritual work to "finish."

Before we look at the homily itself, which put a kind of "cap" on the message of Divine Mercy, I should point out that I'm not the only one who took note of it. For instance, the homily caused Cardinal Christoph Shönborn of Vienna to have a kind of "conversion" to Divine Mercy and inspired him to organize the World Apostolic Congresses of Mercy, attended by dozens of cardinals and bishops.[75] Also, Pope Benedict XVI later described the homily of dedication as a "synthesis" of John Paul's entire papal teaching, which showed that devotion to Divine Mercy is not some "secondary" devotion but rather "an integral dimension of a Christian's life and prayer."[76] Let's read the homily's stirring conclusion now, which includes an act of entrustment of the whole world to Divine Mercy:

> How greatly today's world needs God's mercy! ...
>
> Today, therefore, in this Shine, I wish *solemnly to entrust the world to Divine Mercy.* I do so with the burning desire that the message of God's merciful love, proclaimed here through Saint Faustina, *may be made known to all the peoples of the earth* and fill their hearts with hope. May this message radiate from this place to our beloved homeland and throughout the world. May the binding promise of the Lord Jesus be fulfilled: from here there must go forth "the spark which will prepare the world for [the Lord's] final coming" (*Diary*, 1732).

This spark needs to be lighted by the grace of God. This fire of mercy needs to be passed on to the world. *In the mercy of God the world will find peace and mankind will find happiness!*[77]

For me, the most astonishing part of this remarkable statement is when John Paul actually cites the passage from the *Diary of St. Faustina* that we read in chapter 4:

I bear a special love for Poland, and if she will be obedient to My will, I will exalt her in might and holiness. From her will come forth the spark that will prepare the world for My final coming.[78]

It's astonishing to me because that's the *last* passage from the *Diary of St. Faustina* I ever would have expected John Paul to repeat. I mean, it talks about *the end of the world*. But nobody knows when that will be (see Mt 24:36). Still, the Pope not only repeated this apocalyptic passage, he strengthened it, saying, "May the *binding promise* of the Lord Jesus be fulfilled." And he identified the "spark" and subsequent fire that will prepare the world for the Lord's final coming as Divine Mercy. What's going on here? Has John Paul lost it?

Obviously, the Pope was not saying we know the day or the hour when the Lord is coming. He wasn't speculating about that. What he was proclaiming, though, is that *now is the time of mercy*, now is a time of *particular urgency* for the message of Divine Mercy. And while we do not know the day or the hour of the Lord's final coming, this is the message that prepares the world for it.

Underscoring this point that now is the time of great mercy for the Church and the world, John Paul expressed the following in a homily he gave the very day after his dedication of the shrine and entrustment of the world to Divine Mercy:

... *[W]e today have been particularly called* to proclaim this message [of Divine Mercy] before the world. We cannot neglect this mission, if God himself has called us to it through the testimony of Saint Faustina. God has chosen our own times for this purpose . ... [I]t is as if Christ, using the testimony of a lowly Sister, entered our time in order to indicate clearly the source of relief and hope found in the eternal mercy of God. *The message of merciful love needs to resound forcefully anew.* The world needs this love. The hour has come to bring Christ's message to everyone ... . The hour has come when the message of Divine Mercy is able to fill hearts with hope and to become the spark of a new civilization: the civilization of love.[79]

"*It is as if Christ has entered our time.*" That is indeed what he has done through the prophetic witness of St. Faustina. Through her, he is saying to the Church and to the world of our day: "The hour has come: Now is the time of mercy!" He's saying that in the midst of the prevailing "culture of death," God is pouring out the grace and mercy needed to build up the "culture of life" and the "civilization of love." Will we make use of this time of mercy? Will we recognize this special gift that God is giving to us?

*D*IVINE CONFIRMATION, *2005.* Even after hearing John Paul's powerful words of mercy at the shrine in Krakow in 2002, many clergy still did not believe that "now is the time of mercy." They felt that all this Divine Mercy stuff simply stemmed from the fact that John Paul was Polish. They'd imply that in his old age, the Pope was just becoming more and more (unreasonably) obsessed with a Polish devotion. They pointed out, for instance, that the Image of Divine Mercy has red and white (pale) rays and would comment, "Look, those are the colors of the Polish flag. This is just a case of Polish nationalism. We don't need to listen to all this stuff about Divine Mercy."

In the face of such dismissive attitudes, God himself did something dramatic to confirm that now *really is* the time of mercy. Let me preface this story by sharing one of my own.

When I was in the seminary, Pope John Paul II was one of my biggest inspirations and role models. Pictures of him covered my walls, his books lined my shelves, and the story of his life often occupied my thoughts. It's that latter part, his remarkable life, that most captivated me. Let me put it this way: I never got tired of reading the latest John Paul biography, and even back then, I was convinced that his story was probably the second greatest story ever told. But there was just one problem: The story wasn't over, and this caused me a bit of distress.

To understand that last point, I should mention that I have a pretty melancholic temperament. In other words, it doesn't take much to get me down-in-the-dumps and depressed. So, when I would reflect on the amazing life of John Paul II, I'd think to myself, "There can be no fitting end to such an amazing life. No matter what happens, it's going to be anti-climactic. So, if the Pope just dies of a heart attack in the bathtub, I'm going to be so depressed. And because that's probably what's going to happen — some mundane and uneventful demise — I might as well get depressed about it beforehand." And so I would.

Bizarre? Yes. But that was me.

Well, when April 2, 2005, rolled around, and John Paul the Great breathed his last, it was the most beautiful, fitting, and perfect ending to his amazing life that I ever could have imagined … *almost.*

What do I mean by "almost"? I mean that April 2, 2005, was the day *before* Divine Mercy Sunday. *He was so close! Why couldn't he have held on for just one more day?* If he'd have died on Divine Mercy Sunday, then it would have been the perfect ending! It truly would have been the second greatest story ever. But the ending ruined it. So, of course, I got depressed — but not for long. I soon learned that it *was* the perfect ending. Let me explain.

John Paul II had a longtime personal secretary, Archbishop Stanislaw Dziwisz, who was in the room with the Pope during his final hours. Dziwisz reports that on the night of April 2, as John Paul was nearing his death, he, Dziwisz, suddenly felt a strong imperative in his heart, telling him to celebrate Mass right away. Obediently, Dziwisz began to set up for Mass right then and there in John Paul's room, by his bedside.

As he was setting up for Mass, Dziwisz realized that it was well after sundown on a Saturday, and so he set up the vigil Mass for the Sunday, which of course, was the Sunday of Divine Mercy. Dziwisz celebrated the Mass as the Pope was going in and out of consciousness. At the time of Communion, John Paul was able to receive the Eucharist, doing so through a droplet of the Precious Blood. Less than half an hour after receiving the Lord, John Paul went home to his eternal reward.[80] As Pope Benedict XVI would later describe it, John Paul went to the Father, "in the arms of mercy."[81]

Wow. Of all the days for John Paul to go, what better day than Divine Mercy Sunday?[82] That was the very feast that he himself had established during the Great Jubilee Year, the year of mercy, an event that led him to say, "Today is the happiest day of my life." But maybe that statement was no longer accurate. I say this because I believe April 2, 2005, became the happiest day of all. I mean, John Paul surely realized what was happening. As he was slipping into eternity on that great day, he knew that God himself was confirming him in Divine Mercy, confirming his life as a witness to Divine Mercy, confirming him as a great prophet of mercy for our time. I can't imagine the inner joy John Paul must have felt as he received his last Eucharist at the very beginning of that great feast. In his heart of hearts, he must have been singing the Canticle of Simeon:

> Lord, now you let your servant go in peace; your word has been fulfilled: my own eyes have seen the salvation which you have prepared in the sight of every people: a light to reveal you to the nations and the glory of your people (Lk 2:29-32).

John Paul truly could go in peace. He had passed on to the people of the new millennium the consoling message of hope for our time, the message of Divine Mercy. He had passed on not some new Gospel but rather the very heart of the Gospel, which is God's mercy for sinners. In our unprecedentedly debauched times, when there seem to be so many reasons to get discouraged and to despair, John Paul left us a message of hope and strength: *now is the time for mercy.* And if his death on the vigil of Divine Mercy Sunday doesn't prove the divine authenticity of that proclamation, I don't know what else will — maybe his final words?

JOHN PAUL'S FINAL WORDS. It's reported that Pope John Paul II's final words were actually one word, spoken with great effort immediately before he died: "*Amen.*"[83] But, actually, that's inaccurate. John Paul delivered his final words the day *after* he died. What? Here's how it happened.

Although he died on Saturday, April 2, 2005, the vigil of Divine Mercy Sunday, John Paul had already prepared his *Regina Caeli* message for Divine Mercy Sunday itself. Obviously, he couldn't give that message — he had died the night before. However, an archbishop of the Vatican, Leonardo Sandri, read John Paul's final message before the people gathered in St. Peter's Square. That message communicates his last words to humanity, with the last part being a kind of "icing on the cake" of the second greatest story ever told, a story of Divine Mercy for our time. Let's ponder deeply the final words of the Great Mercy Pope, St. John Paul II:

As a gift to humanity, which sometimes seems bewildered and overwhelmed by the power of evil, selfishness, and fear, the Risen Lord offers his love that pardons, reconciles, and reopens hearts to love. It is a love that converts hearts and gives peace. *How much the world needs to understand and accept Divine Mercy!*

Lord, … we believe in you and confidently repeat to you today: Jesus, I trust in you, have mercy on us and on the whole world.[84]

Once again, *wow!* John Paul's final words to humanity repeat the main message of his life, a witness to hope that proclaims, "*How much the world needs to understand and accept Divine Mercy!*" Further, in the form of a prayer, he includes the words that appear on the Divine Mercy Image ("Jesus, I trust in you") along with the words of the Divine Mercy Chaplet ("have mercy on us and on the whole world"), which he said he prayed unceasingly when he visited the tomb of then-Blessed Faustina in 1997. All this is a fitting conclusion to what he'd said on so many other occasions:

> There is nothing that man needs more than Divine Mercy. ... We have a greater need than ever for a regenerating experience of mercy. ... Apart from the mercy of God there is no other source of hope for mankind. ... How greatly today's world needs God's mercy![85]

Yes, truly, how much the world needs to understand and accept Divine Mercy! Going back to the Pope's final words, notice that he concludes by telling us how to *understand* the message: "Jesus, I trust in you." Then he tells us how to *accept* the message: "Jesus, have mercy." Trusting in Jesus and asking for his mercy: This is the way forward in the time of mercy. This is how we prepare the world for the Lord's final coming — not with fear and trembling but by putting our trust in God's infinite mercy and calling out for mercy on ourselves and on the whole world.

John Paul's last words, together with some of his first words, provide fitting "bookends" to the second greatest story ever told. The first bookend is based on the key words of his first papal homily: "Be not afraid!" The last bookend is drawn from the key words of his final message: "Jesus, I trust in you!" Mixing metaphors, here, you might say these are really two sides of the same coin. How are we to "be not afraid"? The answer is simple: Trust in Jesus. "Jesus, I trust in you."

How fitting it is that God's school of trust, that long lesson through the ages, ends with the second greatest story pointing us back to the center of the first greatest story — Jesus — and a call to trust in him. That's really everything that God has been trying to get us to do since the fall. He just wants us to trust in him. His message for the "end times" is really the same message from the beginning of time to fallen humanity: *Trust in me! I am Love and Mercy itself.*

But how do we trust? Well, truth be told, trusting is not easy. We're still fallen. We're still broken. And even with the testimony of the such great mercy saints as Margaret Mary Alacoque and Thérèse of Lisieux, even with the amazing drama of the second greatest story ever told, which is based on the remarkable lives of Saints Faustina Kowalska and John Paul II, we *still* have a hard time trusting. So what do we do now?

Well, there's actually more to the story. (Believe it or not, the second greatest story gets *even better.*)

CHAPTER 6

Fatima

If what I say to you is done,
many souls will be saved and there will be peace.

~ Our Lady of Fatima

I've often thought about what other story might be a contender for the title, "the second greatest story ever told." In fact, I haven't just thought about it. Through intense study and research, I've endeavored to find the best, most dramatic, and most amazing stories in Church history. I've done this not only because I love history but because ... well, let me put it this way: If I'm going to go around claiming that this story, the story surrounding John Paul II as a prophet of mercy, is the second greatest story ever told, then I'd better have done my homework.

Well, after doing my homework, I believe I've found a story that gives John Paul's story a run for the money: It's the story of Our Lady of Fatima, and its amazingly powerful. I realized its power when I first shared it with my dad. Now, my dad, who was not known for having a very deep faith (nor, like his son, a long attention span), amazingly, not only listened to me tell him the full story but reacted to it by exclaiming, "Mike, if people heard that story, they'd believe!"

It really is an amazing story. And what's even more remarkable is that *it's part of the second greatest story ever told.* I realized this well after John Paul II's death in 2005, and when I saw the connection, it absolutely knocked my socks off. In this and the following chapter, I'd like to make that connection, showing how the second greatest story *gets even better.* Of course, you've probably heard much of the story of Fatima before, but probably not the key connections, and that's the part, I bet, that will knock *your* socks off.

P͟OOR P͟OPE B͟ENEDICT XV. In a certain sense, the story of Fatima begins with Pope Benedict XV. Elected Pope on

September 3, 1914, just over a month after the beginning of World War I, Benedict literally had the weight of the world on his shoulders, a world that was blowing itself up. He famously called the war "the suicide of civilized Europe"[86] and poured himself out in an effort to end the carnage.

Immediately after his election, Benedict declared Vatican neutrality in the war, and from that position, labored to negotiate peace with the warring countries. Unfortunately, both sides viewed him with suspicion, or worse. The German Protestants, for example, viewed a "papal peace" as insulting, while many of the French saw Vatican involvement as being anti-French. Still, the Pope made every effort for peace.

His first encyclical letter, *Ad Beatissimi*, issued on November 1, 1914, was a stirring appeal for an end to the conflict. Then, again and again, he called for peace, tried to negotiate peace, and prayed for peace. Yet nothing seemed to be working. Through 1915 and 1916, the war raged on as millions upon millions of soldiers marched to their deaths in a terrible war of attrition, where the strategy became the grinding down of the enemy through sheer loss of life.

Despite the unprecedented horrors of "The Great War," as it was called at the time, despite his failed efforts for peace, Pope Benedict didn't get discouraged. Why not? Because he had a secret weapon, a weapon he describes in a letter to Cardinal Pietro Gasparri, his secretary of state, on May 5, 1917:

[My] earnestly pleading voice, invoking the end of the vast conflict, the suicide of civilized Europe, was then and has remained ever since unheard. Indeed, it seemed that the dark tide of hatred grew higher and wider among the belligerent nations, and drew other countries into its frightful sweep, multiplying ruin and massacre. Nevertheless [my] confidence was not lessened. ... Since all graces which the Author of all good deigns to grant to the poor children of Adam, by a loving design of His Divine Providence are dispensed through the hands of the most holy Virgin, [I] wish that the petition of her most afflicted children, more than ever in this terrible hour, may turn with lively confidence to the august Mother of God.[87]

So, Benedict's secret weapon was not the poison gas that suffocated soldiers in the trenches on the Western Front. It wasn't the merciless spray of machine gun bullets that tore into the soft flesh of charging infantry. Nor was it the newly invented massive metal tanks that crushed men into the blood-soaked earth. Rather, his secret weapon was she who crushes the proud head of Satan: the Blessed Virgin Mary. More specifically, Pope Benedict decided to invite all the sons and daughters of the Church to pray a solemn novena to Mary, our "Mother of Mercy," asking her for peace:

To Mary, then, who is the Mother of Mercy and omnipotent by grace, let loving and devout appeal go up from every corner of the earth — from noble temples and tiniest chapels, from royal palaces and mansions of the rich as from the poorest hut — from every place wherein a faithful soul finds shelter — from blood-drenched plains and seas. Let it bear to her the anguished cry of mothers and wives, the wailing of innocent little ones, the sighs of every generous heart: that her most tender and benign solicitude may be moved and the peace we ask for be obtained for our agitated world.[88]

On the eighth day of the novena, May 13, 1917, the Pope's plea for peace was finally answered — not by a prime minister, president, or king, but rather, by a queen, the Queen of Peace herself.

OUR LADY APPEARS. The Queen of Peace, Our Lady of Fatima, did not travel to the Vatican in Rome. Rather, she showed up at a place in Europe that was about as far away as possible from the horrors of the war. She appeared near the town of Fatima, Portugal, which is located at the far western end of the Iberian Peninsula.[89] Also, she didn't go there to have a formal meeting with the Vicar of Christ on Earth, the Pope. Rather, she went to three simple shepherd children — Lucia dos Santos (age 10) and her two younger cousins Francisco and Jacinta Marto (ages 9 and 7, respectively) — who were tending their flocks at a place called the Cova de Iria.

When the beautiful Lady appeared to the children, she asked them to return to the Cova on the 13th of each month. They did so, except for one time, on the 13th of August, when they couldn't go because they'd been unjustly incarcerated by the local authorities. (After they were freed, she appeared to them on the 20th of that month.) Anyway, during each apparition, Mary asked the children to pray the Rosary daily for world peace and to do penance for sinners, who had no one to pray for them and who were going to hell in such great numbers. At its heart, the message was not just for the children but for everyone as a call to repentance and reparation for the many sins being committed in the modern world.

Among the six apparitions from May to October, those of July and October were particularly important and deserve our special attention as part of "the second greatest story ever told."

JULY 13, 1917: THREE SECRETS. The core of the July 13th apparition can be divided into three parts or "secrets." (They were called "secrets," because Mary didn't want them to be revealed right away.)

The First Secret. The First Secret helps us understand why Our Lady of Fatima so often appeared to the children looking serious and sad. In fact, in a sense, you might say that the First Secret is really the secret of Mary's suffering, revealing why she is Our Sorrowful Mother. More specifically, this secret consists of a terrible vision of hell that Mary revealed to the three children and that Lucia describes for us:

Our Lady showed us a great sea of fire which seemed to be under the earth. Plunged in this fire were demons and souls in human form, like transparent burning embers, all blackened or burnished bronze, floating about in the conflagration, now raised into the air by the flames that issued from within themselves together with great clouds of smoke, now falling back on every side like sparks in a huge fire, without weight or equilibrium, and amid shrieks and groans of pain and despair, which horrified us and made us tremble with fear. The demons could be distinguished by their terrifying and repellent likeness to frightful and unknown animals, all black and transparent. This vision lasted but an instant. How can we ever be grateful enough to our kind heavenly Mother, who had already prepared us by promising, in the first Apparition, to take us to heaven. Otherwise, I think we would have died of fear and terror.[90]

This vision of hell had a profound effect on the children. They became more serious and their hearts were filled with a burning zeal to save sinners by praying and making sacrifices for them.

Reading the description of this vision should also make us more serious and zealous for the salvation of souls as we realize the terrible consequences of the unprecedented evil of the modern world: Souls are going to hell in massive numbers. As one contemporary saint, Thérèse of Lisieux, put it, "Souls are being lost like flakes of snow [on a winter's day], and Jesus weeps."[91] Yes. Jesus weeps, Mary weeps, and we also should weep. But as we've learned earlier, our situation is not hopeless, the weeping need not lead to despair. In fact, there's good news: God is not outdone by evil, and as we learned earlier, he is offering unprecedentedly great graces in this our time, which, in fact, is the time of mercy. We'll soon learn how these graces of mercy come to us through the Immaculate Heart of Mary, but first, let's turn our attention to the other two secrets.

The Second Secret. The Second Secret explicitly points to future events of the second greatest story ever told, which involves World War II and Communism. Lucia recounts the Second Secret for us, which comes from the lips of Our Lady, following the vision of hell:

> You have seen hell where the souls of poor sinners go. To save them, God wishes to establish in the world devotion to my Immaculate Heart. If what I say to you is done, many souls will be saved and there will be peace. The war is going to end; but if people do not cease offending God, a worse one will break out during the Pontificate of Pope Pius XI. When you see a night illumined by an unknown light, know that this is the great sign given you by God that he is about to punish the world for its crimes, by means of war, famine, and persecutions of the Church and of the Holy Father. To prevent this, I shall come to ask for the Consecration of Russia to my Immaculate Heart, and the Communion of reparation on the First Saturdays. If my requests are heeded, Russia will be converted, and there will be peace; if not, she will spread her errors throughout the world, causing wars and persecutions of the Church. The good will be martyred; the Holy Father will have much to suffer; various nations will be annihilated. In the end, my Immaculate Heart will triumph. The Holy Father will consecrate Russia to me, and she shall be converted, and a period of peace will be granted to the world.[92]

Let's unpack several of the more remarkable points from this passage.

First, Our Lady says that the war (World War I) will end, and it did, in fact, end the following year.

Second, she warned of a "worse" war that would break out during the pontificate of Pope Pius XI. That war, World

War II, was certainly worse than World War I on account of the number of people who were killed (50 million to 20 million, respectively), on account of the fact that God's chosen people, the Jews, were nearly annihilated, and on account of the high ratio of civilian to military deaths. Now, regarding the statement that the war would begin during the pontificate of Pope Pius XI, that needs a little explaining.

Pope Pius XI died on February 10, 1939, and while many people would say that World War II started on September 1, 1939, with the German invasion of Poland, fighting had already begun when Japan invaded Manchuria in 1937 and then Russia the following year, which both happened during the pontificate of Pius XI. Also, according to Lucia, the war began not with the German aggression against Poland but against Austria when, on March 12, 1938, Nazi Germany annexed Austria, occupying it with troops.

Third, Our Lady mentioned "a night illumined by an unknown light." Well, on January 25 and 26, 1938, an extraordinary, five-hour-long aurora borealis lit up the night skies of Europe and America. Lucia, who, by then, was Sr. Lucia, interpreted this light as the sign that the war would soon begin. Recall that, for her, the outbreak of the war began with the annexation of Austria, which took place less than two months after the January aurora borealis.

Fourth, Our Lady speaks of a divine punishment because of the earth's crimes that will include war, famine, and persecution. Of course, we all know about the horrors of World War II, the "worse war" that Mary spoke of, which surely included famine and persecution of the Church. But she is also referring to the great suffering that would be caused by the Soviet Union, led by Russia. She makes this point explicit when she continues, saying, "If my requests are heeded, Russia will be converted, and there will be peace; if not, she will spread her errors throughout the world, causing wars and persecutions of the Church."

Now, we who are reading this in the new millennium clearly recognize the fulfillment of this prophecy. We need only think of the Cold War and how the Soviet Union spread its errors of atheistic Communism to countries throughout the world and how this led to so many conflicts and "proxy wars" between the United States and the Soviet Union on nearly every continent. Also, we need only think of how, in every country where the Soviets gained power or influence, the Church was always persecuted. This was especially true in those countries that were either part of the Soviet Union or its satellite states. Such Soviet persecution was by far the largest contributor to the fact that there were more Christian martyrs in the 20th century *than in all other centuries combined.*

Again, we who are living in the third Christian millennium can clearly see the fulfillment of the "Russia" prophecy. But what about the people who were living in July of 1917? What would they have thought? I suggest that they likely would have been highly skeptical of such a prophecy. First of all, Russia at the time was still known as "Holy Russia," because of the deep piety of the people, who practiced Russian Orthodox Christianity. So, what sense did it make to speak of Russia's "conversion"? Moreover, what were the "errors" that she would spread? Even though a revolution was taking place within Russia, the Bolsheviks (a political faction that adopted a strict, atheistic, Communist ideology) would not rule the country until October of 1917. Second of all, Russia was still thought of as "Poor Russia," which was far behind the economically and technologically advanced countries of Western Europe. How could such a second-rate power influence the world with her errors? In July of 1917, this all seemed highly unlikely, which shows all the more the remarkable nature of the Fatima prophecy.

Fifth, and most importantly, Our Lady said that all these horrors could be prevented by turning to her Immaculate Heart. More specifically, she asked for two things: (1) that Russia be consecrated to her Immaculate Heart and (2) that people embrace the Five First Saturdays devotion to her Heart, which she spelled out in detail in an apparition to Sr. Lucia in 1925.[93] (Also, it's worth repeating that in every one of the six apparitions, Our Lady emphasized the importance of praying the Rosary daily for world peace, even revealing herself in the last apparition as "the Lady of the Rosary.")

Why is the Immaculate Heart so important for the world peace described by Our Lady? Sr. Lucia specifically asked Jesus why the consecration of Russia to Mary's Immaculate Heart was so important. Here is his reply:

> Because I want my whole Church to acknowledge that consecration as a triumph of the Immaculate Heart of Mary, in order to later extend its [following] and to place devotion to this Immaculate Heart alongside devotion to my Sacred Heart.[94]

These words of Jesus make a key point for the second greatest story ever told: It is Jesus' desire to join together in the minds and hearts of the faithful the connection between the Immaculate Heart and the Sacred Heart. But what is that connection? We'll discover it in the next chapter. First, however, we need to cover the Third Secret.

The Third Secret. The Third Secret, like the Second, points to future events. This time, however, the future events are not spoken of by Our Lady, but, rather, they're *shown* to the children in a prophetic vision. Also, while the first two secrets were made public in 1941, the Third Secret was not revealed until the year 2000. Sr. Lucia presents the Third Secret as follows:

> After the two [secrets] which I have already explained, at the left of Our Lady and a little above, we saw an Angel with a flaming sword in his left hand; flashing, it gave out flames that looked as though they would set the world on fire; but they died out in contact with the splendor that Our Lady radiated towards him from her right hand: pointing to the earth with his right hand, the Angel cried out in a loud voice: "Penance, Penance, Penance!" And we saw in an immense light that is God: "something similar to how people appear in a mirror when they

pass in front of it" a Bishop dressed in White "we had the impression that it was the Holy Father." Other Bishops, Priests, men and women Religious going up a steep mountain, at the top of which there was a big Cross of rough-hewn trunks as of a cork-tree with the bark; before reaching there the Holy Father passed through a big city half in ruins and half trembling with halting step, afflicted with pain and sorrow, he prayed for the souls of the corpses he met on his way; having reached the top of the mountain, on his knees at the foot of the big Cross he was killed by a group of soldiers who fired bullets and arrows at him, and in the same way there died one after another the other Bishops, Priests, men and women Religious, and various lay people of different ranks and positions. Beneath the two arms of the Cross there were two Angels each with a crystal aspersorium in his hand, in which they gathered up the blood of the Martyrs and with it sprinkled the souls that were making their way to God.[95]

It is widely accepted that this prophetic vision, which, according to the Vatican, should be understood in a "symbolic key,"[96] refers primarily to the events that have occurred during the Second World War and Cold War. It paints a symbolic picture of the suffering of the Church in the midst of those wars, a suffering that happened because the directives of Our Lady of Fatima were not sufficiently followed. We'll have more to say about the contents of the Third Secret in the next chapter.

OCTOBER 13, 1917: THE MIRACLE OF THE SUN. I shared earlier that when I told the story of Fatima to my dad, he responded, "If people heard that, they'd believe!" While the prophetic aspects that we covered in the last section were certainly impressive to him, what knocked his socks off was *the great solar miracle*. That's the part he especially thought would get people to believe. He was right. What is known as the Miracle of the Sun came as a gift from Our Lady to confirm the message of Fatima in a dramatic way. And such a miracle was important. After all, it would take decades before the prophecies of Our Lady of Fatima would be fulfilled, but the Miracle of the Sun was immediate and left little room for doubt. As part of the second greatest story, God worked one of the most awesome and dramatic public miracles in the history of the Church to confirm the story. In what follows, we're going to find out what this great miracle was by reading firsthand, eyewitness accounts.

Eyewitness Accounts. The Miracle of the Sun happened during the last apparition of Our Lady of Fatima and was witnessed by a gathering of about 75,000 people. So many people came because Our Lady had told Lucia during the July 13 apparition that she would perform a miracle in October, "for all to see and believe."[97] The word about this promised miracle quickly spread. Even the secular, anti-Catholic newspaper, *O Seculo*, helped get the word out, although it did so in a mocking tone.

All morning long on October 13, 1917, the day of the promised miracle, a steady rain saturated the Cova de Iria as well as the tens of thousands of people gathered there At midday, Our Lady appeared to the children, who were kneeling in mud at the front of the crowds. As usual, Lucia engaged the Lady in conversation, who in this instance, revealed herself as "the Lady of the Rosary." The conversation concluded with a particularly somber tone as the Lady repeated the heart of the Fatima message with a sorrowful plea, recorded by Lucia: "Looking very sad, Our Lady said: 'Do not offend the Lord our God anymore, because he is already so much offended.'"[98]

After speaking these words, Mary opened her hands, and the reflection of her own glorious light was reflected on the sun as she disappeared into the distance. The children then beheld a series of visions: St. Joseph with the Child Jesus, Our Lady robed in white with a blue mantle, and then Our Lady again, first appearing as Our Lady of Sorrows and then as Our Lady of Mount Carmel. As the children beheld these visions, the people who had gathered saw something very different, as is described by one of the eyewitnesses, Mary Allen:

> As we approached the hillside upon which the appearances were supposed to have taken place, I saw a sea of people. (Some newspapers said there were 70,000 people there.) I didn't count, but it was more people than I have ever seen in my life, even to this day. ... We had just arrived there when suddenly my attention was drawn by a sudden bright light from the heavens, lighting up the whole countryside. Suddenly the rain ceased, the clouds separated and I saw a large sun, brighter than the sun, yet I could look at it without hurting my eyes, as if it were only the moon. This sun began to get larger and larger, brighter and brighter until the whole heavens seemed more brilliantly lighted than I have ever seen it. Then the sun started spinning and shooting streams of light, which changed it to all colors of the rainbow. ... At the same time, it started getting bigger and bigger in the sky as though it were headed directly for us, as though it were falling on the earth. Everyone was frightened. We all thought it was the end of the world. Everyone threw themselves on their knees praying and screaming the Act of Contrition. Suddenly the sun stopped spinning and returned to its place in the sky. Everyone started shouting: "Miracle! This is a miracle!" Just then I noticed that both the ground and my clothes were bone dry. Everyone seemed to rush forward to see the children. Unfortunately I was only able to see them at a distance.[99]

The dancing and then falling sun that could be looked at without pain to the eyes; the exclamations of tens of thousands of people, "Miracle!;" the drying up of the clothes and ground — truly, a great miracle occurred on that October 13th afternoon. But lest it be said that the massive crowd was just made up of gullible and pious peasants who simply saw what they wanted to see, we have the following testimony from Alfredo da Silva Santos, a business professional from Lisbon who, by his own admission, was not the most fervent believer and something of a skeptic:

> We made our arrangements, and went in three motorcars on the early morning of the 13th. There was a thick mist, and the car which went in front mistook the way so that we were all lost for a time and only arrived at the Cova da Iria at midday by the sun. It was absolutely full of people, but for my part I felt devoid of any religious feeling. When Lucia called out: "Look at the sun!," the whole multitude repeated: "Attention to the sun!" It was a day of incessant drizzle but a few moments before the miracle it stopped raining. I can hardly find words to describe what followed. The sun began to move, and at a certain moment appeared to be detached from the sky and about to hurtle upon us like a wheel of flame. My wife — we had been married only a short time — fainted, and I was too upset to attend to her, and my brother-in-law ... supported her on his arm. I fell on my knees, oblivious of everything, and when I got up I don't know what I said. I think I began to cry out like the others. An old man with a white beard began to attack the atheists aloud, and challenged them to say whether or not something supernatural had occurred.[100]

This testimony gives us a hint of what the atmosphere must have been like in Portugal leading up to the apparitions. We know that the atheists and anti-Catholics enjoyed mocking the children of Fatima and those who followed them. Surely, many of them showed up to continue their mockery, but the old man with the white beard confronted their disbelief.

Here's another testimony, this time from a priest, Fr. Ignacio Lorenco, who witnessed the miracle from 11 miles away and saw the reaction of one of the atheists who had mocked the believers:

> I feel incapable of describing what I saw and felt. I looked fixedly at the sun, which seemed pale and did not hurt the eyes. Looking like a ball of snow revolving on itself, it suddenly seemed to come down in a zigzag [motion], menacing the earth. Terrified, I ran and hid myself among the people, who were weeping and expecting the end of the world at any moment. Near us was an unbeliever who had spent the morning mocking at the simpletons who had gone off to Fatima "just to see an ordinary girl." He now seemed to be paralyzed, his eyes fixed on the sun. Afterwards he trembled from head to foot and lifting up his arms fell on his knees in the mud, crying out to Our Lady.[101]

Even more remarkable than the reaction of this unbeliever-turned-believer is the response from the largest newspaper in the region, *O Seculo*, that had done so much to mock the occurrences at the Cova. Despite its atheistic and anti-Catholic positions, it couldn't help but report the truth of the phenomenon. The following excerpt from the article about the Miracle of the Sun was written by Avelino de Almeida, the reporter who had previously written negative articles about the apparitions:

> From the road, where the vehicles were parked and where hundreds of people who had not dared to brave the mud were congregated, one could see the immense multitude turn toward the sun, which appeared free from clouds and in its zenith. It looked like a plaque of dull silver, and it was

possible to look at it without the least discomfort. It might have been an eclipse which was taking place. But at that moment a great shout went up, and one could hear the spectators nearest at hand shouting: "A miracle! A miracle!" … Before the astonished eyes of the crowd, whose aspect was biblical as they stood bareheaded, eagerly searching the sky, the sun trembled, made sudden incredible movements outside all cosmic laws — the sun "danced" according to the typical expression of the people. … Standing on the step of an omnibus was an old man. With his face turned to the sun, he recited the Creed in a loud voice. I asked who he was; I saw him afterwards going up to those around him who still had their hats on, and vehemently imploring them to uncover their heads before such an extraordinary demonstration of the existence of God. … People then began to ask each other what they had seen. The great majority admitted to having seen the trembling and the dancing of the sun; others affirmed that they saw the face of the Blessed Virgin; others, again, swore that the sun whirled on itself like a giant wheel and that it lowered itself to the earth as if to burn it in its rays. Some said they saw it change colors successively.[102]

Our Lady had kept her promise: a miracle "for all to see and believe," and what a remarkable miracle it was! Apart, perhaps, from Our Lady's apparition in Zeitoun, Egypt, which drew crowds of upwards of 250,000 people in the late 1960s and early 1970s — most of whom were Muslims — and which was captured on video,[103] I know of no other miracle in the whole history of the Church that was so dramatic and witnessed by so many people as it happened. No wonder it's part of the second greatest story ever told! But what are the remarkable connections between the Fatima story and that of John Paul II? We'll discover that in the next chapter.

CHAPTER 7

Fatima and the Mercy Secret

*Though the Witch knew the Deep Magic,
there is a deeper magic still.*

~ Aslan, the Great Lion of Narnia

*A**SPECIAL ANNIVERSARY*. Our Lady of Fatima first appeared to the three shepherd children on May 13, 1917, at about 5 p.m. Exactly 64 years later on May 13, 1981, at 5 p.m., a small, open-air jeep rode out into St. Peter's Square, carrying Pope John Paul II, who warmly greeted pilgrims gathered in the square. At one point, the jeep stopped so the Pope could take a little girl into his arms. After he gave her back to her jubilant parents, the jeep continued on its way through the sea of waving, cheering faithful. Suddenly, a gunman fired two shots at the Pope from close range. The first bullet grazed his elbow. The second struck him in his abdomen and ricocheted inside him, shredding intestines and piercing his colon, which caused massive internal bleeding. The Pope slumped back into the arms of his secretary, Stanislaw Dziwisz, and was raced to the hospital. Unfortunately, the loss of blood was too great. He was pronounced dead at 5:45 p.m.

Of course, that's not true! The Pope didn't die in the hospital from his gunshot wounds. But why not? Didn't the "Third Secret" of Our Lady of Fatima reveal that "a bishop dressed in white," understood to be the Pope, would be shot *and killed*? Yes it did. Well, it must have meant some other pope then, right? Not according to John Paul II. He firmly believed that the vision referred particularly to himself. Alright, then, was the vision wrong? Did Lucia write it down incorrectly? No. Commenting on the Third Secret's imagery, Cardinal Ratzinger, the future Pope Benedict XVI, explains:

> The future is not in fact unchangeably set, and the image which the [Fatima] children saw is in no way a film preview of a future in which nothing can be

changed. Indeed, the whole point of the vision is to bring freedom onto the scene and to steer freedom in a positive direction. The purpose of the vision is not to show a film of an irrevocably fixed future. Its meaning is exactly the opposite: It is meant to mobilize the forces of change in the right direction.[104]

Put differently, paying attention to the Fatima message is not like going to a psychic or a palm reader. (By the way, please don't ever do that![105]) One of the great dangers of such people, whose powers often come from demons, is that they erroneously present the future in a fatalistic, "irrevocably fixed" way. They make it seem as if what they say will absolutely happen, leaving the person feeling discouraged or even in despair if what's said is unpleasant. But this denies us the power of human freedom, one of the greatest gifts that God has given us in creating us. Through freedom, we can turn to God in prayer, and by his grace, move mountains or change the course of history. The life of the Church gives countless examples of the power of such prayer, often involving the Blessed Virgin Mary's intercession.[106]

So, yes, in the vision from 1917, the Pope is shot and killed — but in reality, it didn't have to turn out that way. In fact, it *didn't* turn out that way. The Pope's life was spared in 1981. He did not die. But why not? Why was his life spared? Three reasons: the power of human freedom we just spoke about, Our Lady, and Divine Mercy.

Human Freedom. Describing the *human freedom* aspect, Cardinal Ratzinger states that the fact that John Paul survived the assassination attempt "only shows once more that there is no immutable destiny, that faith and prayer are forces that can influence history, and that, in the end, prayer is more powerful than bullets, and faith more powerful than armies."[107] Yes, faith and prayer are that powerful. When human freedom is steered in *this* positive direction, when people choose to pray to God with a living faith, it has the power to change the course of history.

And, again, it did change history: John Paul's life was spared. Surely, all the Rosaries, penances, and First Saturday devotions inspired by the message of Our Lady of Fatima had something to do with it. I say this because of John Paul's own explanation of why his life was spared: "One hand fired, and another guided the bullet."[108] He believed the hidden hand guiding the bullet was that of Our Lady of Fatima. And I suggest that, yes, she spared his life, *thanks to so many of the faithful who had been inspired by and responded to her message of prayer and penance.* Unfortunately, though, it seems that *not enough people* were inspired to convert and pray, and the horrors of World War II and Communism did come — but maybe that's not *completely* unfortunate after all. What? I'll say more about this in the coming sections on Divine Mercy, but first, let's turn to Our Lady.

Our Lady. Why did John Paul conclude that Mary had saved his life? Well, consider the facts.

First, John Paul recalls that "at the very moment I fell ... I had this vivid presentiment that I should be saved."[109]

Second, the Pope later learned that even though the bullet ricocheted inside him, it missed all his major organs and spinal cord. Also, it missed the main abdominal artery by only a tenth of an inch. Had that artery been struck or even grazed, John Paul certainly would have bled to death on his way to the hospital. It seemed that something had redirected the bullet's path, so it wouldn't have a lethal effect.

Third, and most importantly, while in the hospital recovering from the shooting, John Paul reflected on the date: May 13. He knew it was the anniversary of the first apparition of Our Lady of Fatima. Therefore, he asked that the document containing the Third Secret, which he had never read, be brought to him. (He also asked his friend from the seminary, Archbishop Andrew Deskur, who had introduced him to Divine Mercy, to read to him the newly published *Diary of St. Faustina*[110] — so both Fatima and Divine Mercy were on his mind after he was shot!) His personal secretary records the Pope's reaction after reading the Third Secret:

When he was finished, all his remaining doubts were gone. In Sr. Lucia's vision, he recognized his own destiny. He became convinced that his life had been saved — no, given back to him anew — thanks to Our Lady's intervention and protection. ... It's true, of course, that the "bishop dressed in white" is killed in Sr. Lucia's vision, whereas John Paul II escaped an almost certain death. So? Couldn't that have been the real point of the vision? Couldn't it have been trying to tell us that the paths of history, of human existence, are not necessarily fixed in advance? And that there is a Providence, a "motherly hand," which can intervene and cause a shooter, who is certain of hitting his target, to miss? ... "One hand shot, and another guided the bullet" was how the Holy Father put it.[111]

The Pope's conviction that his life had been "given back" to him by Our Lady of Fatima grew when he later met with the man who shot him, Mehmet Ali Ağca, to personally forgive him. On that occasion, Ağca spoke words that had a profound impact on the Pope. He said to the Holy Father: "I know I was aiming right. I know that the bullet was a killer. So why aren't you dead?"[112] According to Dziwisz, John Paul "carried [these words] around with him for years, pondering [them] over and over again." Such pondering nourished his feeling of gratitude to Our Lady.

But why did Our Lady save the Pope? Was it because he had consecrated his life to her from the time he was 18 years old? Was it because of all the prayers and sacrifices of those who had been inspired by the message of Fatima? I'm sure these things had something to do with it. But a deeper reason, I believe, has to do with Divine Mercy — more specifically, a deep secret of Divine Mercy. Let's cover this point in its own section.

*T*HE DIVINE MERCY SECRET. There's a hidden, little-known truth about Divine Mercy. It involves what C. S. Lewis calls in his book *The Lion, the Witch, and the Wardrobe* the "Deeper Magic from before the dawn of time."[113] Of course, it's not really magic. In the allegorical story, it's called "magic," but this magic in the story represents the reality of grace, a very *deep* grace, a hidden and secret grace. Let me say more about this.

In Lewis's story, the White Witch (who represents Satan) is aware of a Deep Magic, an unwritten law of the land, that gives her the right to kill traitors: "[E]very traitor belongs to me as my lawful prey and ... for every treachery I have a right to a kill."[114] In view of this, she claims her right to kill Edmund, one of the four children (who are the main characters), because Edmund had betrayed his family and friends (and thus he represents each one of us, poor sinners who betray each other and Christ with our sins). But the leader of all those who oppose the White Witch, a stately lion named Aslan (who represents Christ), makes a deal with her. He will take Edmund's place — the White Witch may kill him instead.

With wicked delight, the evil woman accepts the opportunity to destroy her powerful rival and so publicly renounces her right to take Edmund's life. Aslan then hands himself over to her, and that very night, placing Aslan on a massive stone table, the witch and her evil minions mock, torture, and kill him.

Two of Aslan's friends — two of the other children, Susan and Lucy — witness his violent death from a hiding place and spend the night weeping. Then, as the first rays of dawn appear, they hear a deafening "crack," find the stone table broken in half, and Aslan's body gone. Suddenly, their hero appears, alive, larger and more majestic than before, and he tells his surprised friends what has happened, teaching them the meaning of the *Deeper* Magic:

> It means that though the Witch knew the Deep Magic, there is a magic deeper still which she did not know: Her knowledge goes back only to the dawn of time. But if she could have looked a little further back, into the stillness and the darkness before Time

dawned, she would have read there a different incantation. She would have known that when a willing victim who had committed no treachery was killed in a traitor's stead, the Table would crack and Death itself would start working backwards.[115]

The divine mysteries represented in Lewis's book by the "Deep Magic" and the "*Deeper* Magic" have been unfolding since the beginning of time. After Adam and Eve's sin, Satan had rights over them. For instance, they had to pay "the wage of sin," which is death (Rom 6:23). In other words, Adam and Eve had to die, and this was simply part of the "Deep Magic" of *Divine Justice*, which basically says, "If you, a creature, dishonor your Creator by disobedience, you have severed your relationship with God and must die."

But to Satan's surprise, they did not have to go to hell, the "second death," a permanently severed relationship with God. Why not? Because thousands of years later, an action of the "*Deeper* Magic," *the Divine Mercy* of Christ's sacrifice on the Cross, would make "death work backwards." In other words, when the Innocent Victim who is Life itself allowed himself to be killed through satanic action, his divine life was given to all those who had lost their lives through the devil's lies. Like the White Witch, Satan found himself tricked into viciously taking Christ's life, which unleashed the torrent of grace and mercy that saves the world from sin and death. The devil knew the Deep Magic of Divine Justice, but his inordinate pride did not allow him to understand the *Deeper Magic* of Divine Mercy.

Maybe Satan should have known. After all, God had told him, the serpent, after the fall: "I will put enmity between you and the woman, between your seed and her seed; he shall bruise your head, and you shall bruise his heel" (Gen 3:15). The woman is Mary and her seed (who with her, will crush the serpent's head) is Christ Jesus, our Savior. We will say more about Mary's cooperative role with Christ in the work of Divine Mercy in the next section, but first we need to realize the main point about the Secret of Divine Mercy.

Here is that point: Divine Mercy is the power of God's love to bring not only good out of evil but *an even greater good out of evil*. This is why Satan hates it so much. It not only cancels out his gains, but it reverses them, making them into losses. The most classic expression of this remarkable reality, referring to the fall itself, is expressed in song during the *Exsultet* of the most solemn liturgy of all, the Easter Vigil:

> O truly necessary sin of Adam,
>> destroyed completely by the Death of Christ!
> O happy fault,
>> that earned so great, so glorious a Redeemer!

The sin of Adam was necessary to bring us so great, so glorious a Redeemer as Christ Jesus, our Lord! The sin is called "O happy fault!" And its evil is "destroyed completely" by the Savior. This is the wonder of wonders of Divine Mercy. It has the power not only to bring good out of evil but *an even greater good*. In fact, according to St. Thomas Aquinas, the graces of salvation that we receive through Christ's death on the Cross are even greater than the salvation that would have come to us had there been no fall and no Cross.[116] Truly, as St. Paul says, "where sin increased, grace abounded all the more" (Rom 5:20).

Of course, as St. Paul further explains, this does not mean that we "continue in sin that grace can abound." By no means! But it does reveal an amazing secret of Divine Mercy, something that proves that God's ways are not our ways. After all, how, in human terms, can loss be gain? Yet in the realm of Divine Mercy, it can be so. In the realm of Divine Mercy, if we repent and trust in the power of God's mercy, then nothing is lost when his mercy brings an even greater good out of our evil. This "Deeper Magic" of Divine Mercy is a mystery that boggles the mind, yet it is so beautiful, deserving of our praise and adoration!

Perhaps the best expression of this mystery of mercy and the praise it deserves comes again from St. Paul, who writes of how we, the Gentiles, have received mercy through the Jews' disobedience and how the Jews will also receive mercy through our former disobedience:

Just as you [Gentiles] were once disobedient to God but now have received mercy because of [the Jews'] disobedience, so they have now been disobedient in order that by the mercy shown to you they may receive mercy. For God has consigned all men to disobedience, that he may have mercy upon all.

O the depth of the riches and wisdom and knowledge of God! How unsearchable are his judgments and how inscrutable his ways! For who has known the mind of the Lord, or who has been his counselor? Or who has given a gift to him that he might be repaid? For from him and through him and to him are all things. To him be glory for ever. Amen (Rom 11:30-36).

So, here again, we see the secret of Divine Mercy at work: God can bring not only good out of our evil but an even greater good. He saves both the Jews and the Gentiles through their mutual disobedience! Praise the Lord! Now let's apply this secret of Divine Mercy to Fatima and Pope John Paul II.

THE SECRET APPLIED TO FATIMA. Quite frankly, Fatima seemed like a failure. As World War I raged, Our Lady had said that the war would end but warned of "a worse war" to come and sufferings of the Church by Russia if people didn't do as she asked. Well, what she asked for was not fully done, and those terrible punishments came. So Fatima failed, right? Wrong. While Mary warned of war and suffering, she also left us with a message of hope: "In the end, my Immaculate Heart will triumph."

What? How can one speak of a "triumph" in the face of such epic world catastrophe? How can one enjoy the taste of victory with the stench of tens of millions of burnt and rotting bodies filling the air? How can one win when so many have lost? Because of the secret of Divine Mercy. In fact, the triumph of Mary's Immaculate Heart is really the triumph of *Divine Mercy*, which through Mary, has the power to bring an even greater good out of the evils that have already come.

And the greater good is this: *Now is the time of mercy.* Now is a time of great, extraordinary, and unprecedented grace and mercy for the Church and the world. Now is a time when God is making it easier than ever before to become saints. Now is the "end time" when, by calling out for mercy, we can prepare the world for the Lord's final coming. And this time of grace *wouldn't have been possible* without the great evils of the 20th century.

Now, don't get me wrong. God certainly did not want World War II nor the godless, totalitarian regime of the U.S.S.R. In fact, to prevent these evils, he sent his own mother, Our Lady of Fatima, on one of the most dramatic peace-keeping missions in the history of the world. But we didn't listen, and so God allowed the evils. (I purposely say "allowed" not "caused.") Yet through these very evils, by the power of his mercy, God is drawing out not only good but an *even greater good.* Thus, we can proclaim with St. Paul, "O the depth of the riches and wisdom and knowledge of God! How unsearchable are his judgments and how inscrutable his ways!" Thus, we can truly sing a modified *Exsultet*: "O happy punishments, O necessary sufferings, that brought us so great a time of mercy!"

That last line is really not so far-fetched. I say this because the original *Exsultet* joyfully inaugurates the Easter season, the time when we rejoice in the power of mercy to bring good out of evil — the *evil* being Christ's suffering and death during his hour of darkness, the *good* being Christ's resurrection, which puts an end to death and bathes the world in the light of God's love. Moreover, this Easter mystery is precisely what is taking place now: death to life, darkness to light, hate to love. This time, however, the suffering Christ is not Jesus but *his Body, the Church,* and the Resurrection is *this present time of grace and mercy* being given to the Church. From this perspective, the haunting vision of the Third Secret of Fatima makes perfect sense. Let's read the most relevant part once again:

Other Bishops, Priests, men and women Religious going up a steep mountain, at the top of which there was a big Cross of rough-hewn trunks as of a cork-tree with the bark; before reaching there the Holy Father passed through a big city half in ruins and half trembling with halting step, afflicted with pain and sorrow, he prayed for the souls of the corpses he met on his way; having reached the top of the mountain, on his knees at the foot of the big Cross he was killed by a group of soldiers who fired bullets and arrows at him, and in the same way there died one after another the other Bishops, Priests, men and women Religious, and various lay people of different ranks and positions. Beneath the two arms of the Cross there were two Angels each with a crystal aspersorium in his hand, in which they gathered up the blood of the Martyrs and with it sprinkled the souls that were making their way to God.

Do you see, then, where the graces of the time of mercy come from? *They come from the blood of the martyrs.* Recall that the 20th century was the bloodiest century in human history. There were more martyrs in that century than in all other centuries combined. But, again, as the early Church Father Tertullian said, "The blood of the martyrs is the seed of the Church." And what did the angels do in the vision? "They gathered up the blood of the Martyrs." And what did they do with the blood? They "sprinkled the souls that were making their way to God."

Truly, now is the time of mercy, because we're the ones being sprinkled with that blood! And if the blood of the martyrs in the early Church brought the grace of conversion to the Roman Empire and to the barbarian hordes that became Christian Europe, then it looks like we're *super-primed* for a new springtime in the Church. Now more than at any other time in history, we're awash in the blood of the martyrs, and so, there is more grace and mercy available to us today than ever before in the history of the Church.

As we read earlier, Pope John Paul II was spared a martyr's death by Our Lady of Fatima so he could lead the Church to the triumph of mercy. Or was he spared? While the Pope didn't die after the May 13th shooting, it seems that he was, nevertheless, a martyr. In other words, the "deeper magic," that is, the *deeper mercy* somehow both saved John Paul's life *and* allowed him to still be a martyr. How did that happen? Let's find out now.[117]

Notice how in the Third Secret, "the Holy Father passed through a big city half in ruins and half trembling with halting step, afflicted with pain and sorrow, he prayed for the souls of the corpses he met on his way; having reached the top of the mountain, on his knees at the foot of the big Cross he was killed by a group of soldiers who fired bullets and arrows at him … ." Does this description of the Pope as "half trembling with halting step" point to the tremors and poor balance that plagued John Paul II in his old age — symptoms of Parkinson's disease? And does John Paul, in a very real sense, suffer a white martyrdom as he stretches out his arms in his final days on the cross of his advanced Parkinson's disease and other ailments, which contributed to his death? Is this white martyrdom being hinted at in the Third Secret as the Holy Father dies in a hail of "bullets and arrows"?

Indeed, on his final Good Friday, John Paul cannot lead the Church on the Way of the Cross in the Colosseum in Rome; he can only embrace the corpus of Christ on the crucifix in his papal apartments. And on his final Easter Sunday, he cannot even speak to the faithful gathered in St. Peter's Square for his Easter message; all he can do is bless them silently. Then, notice how John Paul chooses to die serenely before the eyes of all the world in his papal apartments in St. Peter's, instead of remaining at Gemelli Hospital. Here, it's instructive that papal biographer George Weigel calls John Paul's last months and then his death his last and greatest encyclical.[118]

So, is the grace and mercy, the "deeper magic" at work in the sparing of John Paul's life through Our Lady's intercession, the greater good of his whole pontificate that is, then, sealed by the white martyrdom of his heroic death for the good of the whole Church? In this vein, it's fascinating to note here that just as the blood of the martyrs is gathered up by the angels and then sprinkled upon the faithful making their way to God, as depicted in the Third Secret, so the Church has gathered up or preserved the blood of John Paul II (which had been kept on hand in case he needed a transfusion in his final days) as the principal relic for his beatification and canonization. And now the Church is in a sense sprinkling the faithful with the blood of St. John Paul II by staining drops of his blood on cloths and making them available as relics for the faithful to venerate at churches and shrines throughout the world. For instance, we have one of these blood-stained relics here at the National Shrine of The Divine Mercy in Stockbridge, Massachusetts.

But there's still more to John Paul's death when it comes to Fatima. As Pope Benedict XVI pointed out in his *Regina Caeli* message on Divine Mercy Sunday in 2008:

> In the evening of the unforgettable Saturday, April 2, 2005, when [Pope John Paul II] closed his eyes on the world, it was precisely the eve of the Second Sunday of Easter, and many people noted the rare coincidence that combined the Marian dimension — the first Saturday of the month — and the dimension of Divine Mercy.

So John Paul II didn't just die in the arms of Divine Mercy; he died in the arms of Our Lady as well.

Thus, while Our Lady of Fatima's pleas were not sufficiently heeded and the world experienced more suffering than ever before, God is bringing an even greater good out of that great evil, through Mary Immaculate. She spared the life of John Paul II (but did not spare him from martyrdom), so he could go on to lead the Church, with Mary, to the triumph of her Immaculate Heart, the triumph of Divine Mercy. But how does she do this precisely? We will learn about that in the next section, but let's close this one by reflecting on how the first and last apparitions of Fatima point to the secret of Divine Mercy, that Fatima is really about God bringing good out of evil.

Fatima's First and Last Mercy Apparitions. The apparitions of Fatima did not actually begin on May 13, 1917. That was the beginning of *Our Lady's* apparitions to the children. But the previous year, in 1916, an angel appeared to the young shepherds to prepare them for what was to come. And what did he say to them? He taught them to pray and then encouraged them to pray *a lot.* Why? Because, as he put it, "The most holy Hearts of Jesus and Mary have *designs of mercy* on you."[119] Designs of mercy. Yes, the mission of Fatima is a mission of mercy.

And what was the last vision of Fatima? It happened in 1934 while Sr. Lucia was praying in the chapel at a convent in Tuy, Spain. First I'll give an artist's rendition of her vision, and then we can read Lucia's description of it:

Suddenly the whole chapel was illumined by a supernatural light, and above the altar appeared a cross of light, reaching to the ceiling. In a brighter light on the upper part of the cross, could be seen the face of a man and his body as far as the waist; upon his breast was a dove of light; nailed to the cross was the body of another man. A little below the waist, I could see a chalice and a large host suspended in the air, on to which drops of blood were falling from the face of Jesus Crucified and from the wound in His side. These drops ran down on to the host and fell into the chalice. Beneath the right arm of the cross was Our Lady and in her hand was her Immaculate Heart. (It was Our Lady of Fatima, with her Immaculate Heart in her left hand, without sword or roses, but with a crown of thorns and flames). Under the left arm of the cross, large letters, as if of crystal clear water which ran down upon the altar, formed these words: "Grace and Mercy."[120]

Grace and mercy. What is the time of mercy but a time of great and extraordinary grace and mercy? That is where the Immaculate Heart wants to lead us. She wants to bring us to the grace and mercy that flow from the wounds of Christ crucified. See it in the image? That's what God the Father wants to give us through the blood of his Son and the blood of the martyrs, who are also his sons and daughters. And, again, it is Mary who, with her divine Spouse, the Holy Spirit, takes us there. As we'll see in the next section, she takes us there by means of the consecration.

*T*HE CONSECRATION AND THE POPES. Earlier, I put the blame for the horrors of World War II and Communism on the fact that people did not adequately heed the message of Fatima. They didn't pray enough, didn't amend their lives enough, and didn't do enough penance. Still, that's only part of the story. Some of the blame — perhaps the greater amount — also falls on the shoulders of the popes and bishops who didn't consecrate Russia to Mary's Immaculate Heart in a timely fashion, as she had requested. This, at least, according to Sr. Lucia, is Jesus' own judgment on the matter. In August of 1931, just weeks after the Nazis became the most powerful political party in Germany and while Russia suffered through the fourth year of Stalin's first five-year plan to implement Communism, the Lord told Sr. Lucia:

> [The leaders of the Church] did not wish to heed my request. Like the King of France, they will repent and do it, but it will be late. Russia will have already spread her errors throughout the world, provoking wars, and persecutions of the Church; the Holy Father will have much to suffer.[121]

The mention of the King of France adds salt to the wounds. On June 17, 1689, St. Margaret Mary had written a message from Jesus to the King of France, Louis XIV, requesting that he publicly consecrate France to the Sacred Heart. The King ignored the request, as did his son, Louis XV, and grandson, Louis XVI. That grandson and all the Church of France would have to suffer terribly for this total disregard of the Lord's wishes.

On June 17, 1789, exactly *100 years to the day* that Margaret Mary had written her letter to the King, the Third Estate declared itself the National Assembly of France, taking upon itself legislative power apart from the King. This began a cascade of events that ultimately led to the beheading of King Louis XVI in 1793, the near destruction of the French Church, and the rise of an anti-Christian secular order and mentality that holds sway in France even to this day. Yet all this could have been avoided had the King of France simply heeded the Lord's requests.

Sadly, after his arrest, King Louis XVI vowed to consecrate himself, his family, and his kingdom to the Sacred Heart of Jesus if he regained his freedom — but, by then, it was too late. The King remained in bondage while murderous, anti-Christian forces ran free.

A similar scenario was unfolding with regard to Our Lady of Fatima's 1917 request that the Pope and bishops consecrate Russia to her Immaculate Heart. Even by 1931, her request had still not been heeded. Yet, with the election of Pius XII on

March 2, 1939, things seemed to be changing for the better. Not only had the new Pope been consecrated a bishop on May 13, 1917, the date of the first apparition of Fatima, but he was deeply Marian and devoted to Our Lady of Fatima — the coincidence of his May 13th consecration had not been lost on him. So, he seemed like the perfect Pope to fulfill Our Lady's request, even though the "worse war," World War II, had already begun.

Sister Lucia wrote to the new Pope in 1940:

> If Your Holiness would deign to make the consecration of the world to the Immaculate Heart of Mary, making special mention of Russia, and would order at the same time that in union with Your Holiness all the bishops should also make it, the days would be shortened by which God has decided to punish the nations for their crimes through war, famine and persecutions against the Church and Your Holiness.[122]

Notice that the promise here is no longer that war, famine, and persecution will be avoided but rather *shortened.* That's because, unfortunately, by 1940, World War II's wheels of destruction had already begun to turn. Nevertheless, having the suffering shortened would be a great and welcome blessing.

Thankfully, on October 31, 1942, in Portugal, Pope Pius XII heeded Our Lady's request and consecrated the world to her Immaculate Heart while making a special reference to Russia. Six weeks later, in Rome, he repeated the consecration on December 8, the solemnity of the Immaculate Conception. Unfortunately, only a small number of bishops participated in these two consecrations, so Russia was not converted. But, fortunately, the consecrations did seem to affect the course of the war. One sign of this came through Sr. Lucia's report that, in the spring of 1943, Jesus appeared to her and expressed his great delight over the consecration.[123] A second sign came through the fact that in early 1943, the Allies began winning important battles, whereas, before they had been losing almost every one. For instance, in February that year, the Nazis lost the key battle of Stalingrad, which changed the course of the war, particularly on the Eastern front.

Eventually, in 1945, World War II ended, but the Cold War between the Soviet Union and the West immediately followed. Knowing this, and well aware of the terrible persecution of the Church in Communist lands, Pius XII wrote an apostolic letter, *Sacro Vergente Anno*, that explicitly consecrated the people of Russia to Mary's Immaculate Heart. Unfortunately, the bishops of the world were not involved, so Russia remained unconverted. Since that effort of Pius XII, no other pope even attempted to explicitly consecrate Russia to Mary's Immaculate Heart — until St. John Paul II.

PARALLELS BETWEEN FATIMA AND DIVINE MERCY. We'll hear about John Paul II's attempts at making the consecration of Russia in the next chapter, but before we do, as we close this last chapter on Fatima, let's briefly take note of some of the striking parallels between Fatima and Divine Mercy with John Paul II as our hero:

1. *Assassination Attempt.* Not only did Our Lady of Fatima spare John Paul's life, but the Pope demonstrated remarkable mercy by then visiting his would-be assassin in prison and personally forgiving him. Also, as he recovered in the hospital from his gunshot wounds, John Paul asked to see the Third Secret of Fatima and had his friend from the seminary, Archbishop Andrew Deskur, read to him from the newly published *Diary of St. Faustina.*[124]

2. *Bold Papal Acts.* As the Great Mercy Pope, John Paul gave us the universal feast day of Divine Mercy Sunday (2000); as the Pope of Fatima, he gave us the Luminous Mysteries of the Rosary (2002) — more on this later.

3. *Message for the New Millennium*. John Paul II placed Divine Mercy and Fatima front and center during the Great Jubilee Year, 2000, which was a crucial event of his papacy.

Regarding Divine Mercy, he canonized Sr. Faustina on Divine Mercy Sunday, April 30, 2000, as the first saint of the new millennium. He also established Divine Mercy Sunday as a universal feast day and identified Divine Mercy as the message of the third millennium.

Regarding Fatima, he decided to beatify the shepherd children Jacinta and Francisco on May 13, 2000, the feast of Our Lady of Fatima, in Fatima, Portugal. He also took the occasion to disclose the Third Secret and to emphasize the timeliness of the message of Fatima, with its urgent call for prayer, conversion, and consecration.

4. *Prophetic Connection*. John Paul II is both the Pope of the Third Secret of Fatima and is certainly part of the spark that would come from Poland, as prophesied by St. Faustina and as quoted by John Paul himself when he made the Act of Entrustment of the world to Divine Mercy in 2002. (See *Diary*, 1732.)

5. *Death*. John Paul II died on both the vigil of Divine Mercy Sunday and a First Saturday, which is part of the Fatima devotion. (As Pope Benedict XVI noted, it's a rare coincidence for a First Saturday to coincide with the vigil of Divine Mercy Sunday.)

In the next chapter, we'll see how, through his efforts to consecrate Russia and the world to the Immaculate Heart, John Paul makes even more explicit the amazing connections between Mary (especially as Our Lady of Fatima) and Divine Mercy.

CHAPTER 8

World Consecration and the Triumph

*Let there be revealed, once more, in the history of
the world ... the power of merciful Love!*

~ Pope John Paul II, Act of Consecration

John Paul II first made his own personal Marian consecration
(as Karol Wojtyła) when he was 18 years old after reading the
book, *True Devotion to Mary*, by St. Louis de Montfort. He
later described that spiritual act of entrusting himself totally to
Jesus through Mary as a "decisive turning point" in his life.[125]
In fact, after making his consecration, he never forgot it as he
renewed it daily and placed it at the very heart of his personal
spirituality. Perhaps the fact that he had lost his own biological
mother at a young age contributed to the fervor with which
he lived out this crowning of Marian devotion. Whatever the
reason, the consecration touched him deeply, and he explicitly
chose the Mother of God as his own adoptive mother, entrusting
himself to her motherly care as he prayed:

> *Totus tuus ego sum et omnia mea tua sunt. Accipio
> te in mea omni. Praebe mihi cor tuum, Maria.*
> (I belong totally to you, and all that I have is yours.
> I take you for my all. O Mary, give me your heart.)[126]

When Wojtyła became a bishop, he adopted a shortened
version of the above prayer as his episcopal motto, "*Totus
Tuus*" (Totally Yours), which appeared below his episcopal
coat-of-arms. That coat-of-arms, consisting of a golden cross
with the letter "M" on the lower right, also emphasized his
personal consecration to his mother, Mary, because it captured
that iconic moment from the Gospel of John (19:26-27) when
Jesus, dying on the Cross, entrusts his mother to us ("Behold,
your mother") and us to his mother ("Behold, your son").
When Wojtyła became Pope, he kept this same episcopal
Marian motto and coat-of-arms.

Seeing that Wojtyła had such an extraordinary Marian devotion, it's not surprising that this "most Marian Pope," as many have called him, would be the one to fully and successfully consecrate Russia to Mary's Immaculate Heart. We'll see how he did so in the sections that follow.

FIRST TWO ATTEMPTS. Recall that after his election, Pope John Paul II very much had Divine Mercy on his mind. He'd been elected just six months after having worked for 10 years to get the ban lifted on the Divine Mercy message and devotion. Then, in his second encyclical letter, *Dives in Misericordia,* published in 1980, he had written at length about Divine Mercy and its importance for our time.

Of course, in the background of this mission of mercy was his deep devotion to Mary, the mother to whom he had entrusted his life. But suddenly, in 1981, after being shot on the anniversary of the first apparition of Our Lady of Fatima and after reading the contents of the Third Secret, he discovered that this same mother, Our Lady of Fatima, was more deeply involved in his mission of mercy than he had realized. He clearly saw that she was no longer to remain in the background.

Immediately after coming to these realizations, John Paul thought of consecrating the world and Russia to Mary's Immaculate Heart, and he soon began composing an act of consecration for this purpose. Less than a week after the shooting, in a recorded address to the pilgrims in St. Peter's Square, he repeated his own personal consecration to Mary, saying, "To you, Mary, I repeat, *Totus tuus ego sum.*" (I am totally yours.) Then, less than a month after the shooting, on June 7, 1981, the solemnity of Pentecost, the Pope prayed the Act of Consecration of the world and Russia. Because he was still recovering from his wounds, again, his prayer had to be recorded and then broadcast for the people. Since few bishops were present, this first attempt at the consecration of Russia did not completely fulfill Our Lady's request at Fatima. No matter. John Paul would attempt to make the consecration two more times.

The second attempt came on the one-year anniversary of the shooting, May 13, 1982, during a pilgrimage to Fatima. Unfortunately, the Pope's written invitation to all the bishops of the world to join him for this consecration arrived too late, and so they were not able to participate. Therefore, again, it did not fulfill Our Lady's request. Nevertheless, the consecration on that occasion was deeply significant because, through it, *John Paul began to make explicit the connection between Fatima (especially with regards to Marian consecration) and Divine Mercy.*

Now, we've already seen how the Fatima messages themselves allude to this connection with the angel's words about "designs of mercy" and Sr. Lucia's last vision that included the words, "grace and mercy," but in 1982, John Paul made this connection much clearer. He did this especially during his homily at Fatima when he explained the meaning of a personal consecration to Jesus through Mary.

The homily's context is the widespread, "almost apocalyptic" evil of our time, an evil that "menaces," that is "spreading," and that gathers "like a dark cloud over mankind." The Pope confesses that this evil causes "trepidation" in his own heart. Despite this, he finds hope in "a Love more powerful than evil" that no "sin of the world can overcome." This love he identifies as "merciful Love."[127]

And what about this *merciful love?* What does it have to do with Marian consecration? Everything. It has everything to do with it, *because Mary is the one who brings us to the source of merciful love.* Mary is the one who brings us to the love that is more powerful than evil. Indeed, as John Paul says in his homily, consecration to the Immaculate Heart means "drawing near, through the Mother's intercession, to the very Fountain of Life that sprang from Golgotha."[128] And what is this fountain of life? The Pope identifies it as "*the Fountain of Mercy,*"[129] the pierced side of Christ from which blood and water flowed as a source of grace and mercy (see Jn 19:34).

The Pope goes on to explain that consecration to the Immaculate Heart of Mary means "returning to the Cross of the Son." It means bringing the world and all its problems and sufferings to "the pierced Heart of the Savior" and thus "back to the very source of its Redemption." It means bringing the world, through Mary, to Divine Mercy! According to the Pope, the power of the Redemption, the power of merciful love "is always greater than man's sin and the 'sin of the world'" and is "infinitely superior to the whole range of evil in man and the world."

Now, Mary knows the power of the Redemption, the power of merciful love, better than anyone. In fact, John Paul says she knows it "more than any other heart in the whole universe, visible and invisible." And she knows it so intimately because, in her Immaculate Conception, she is the greatest recipient of God's mercy. Moreover, she did nothing to deserve the grace of being conceived without any stain of sin. Rather, it was a totally free gift from God, merited by the sacrifice of Jesus on the Cross. Therefore, intimately knowing the powerful gift of Christ's sacrifice, Mary calls us not only to conversion but "to accept her motherly help to return to the source of Redemption." For, again, her task is to draw us to the Fountain of Mercy, to the pierced side of Christ, to his Merciful Heart.

Essentially, then, consecrating ourselves to Mary "means accepting her help to offer ourselves and the whole of mankind"[130] to the infinitely Holy God. It means entrusting ourselves to her, the one who was most united to Christ's own consecration: "Hail to you who are wholly united to the redeeming consecration of your Son!"[131] It means entrusting ourselves to Mary's prayers, that she may "help us live with the whole truth of the consecration of Christ for the entire human family of the modern world."[132] In other words, consecrating ourselves to Mary means relying on her motherly intercession to help us consecrate and offer ourselves more fully to Christ in his Divine Mercy.

As if this weren't enough to make explicit the connection between Fatima, the consecration, and Divine Mercy, John Paul made sure that we didn't miss his point when, the following week, during his May 19, 1982, general audience in Rome, he said:

> Last week I myself went on pilgrimage to Portugal, especially to Fatima, in order to give thanks that *the mercy of God* and the protection of *the Mother of Christ* had saved my life last year. The message of Fatima ... is more urgent than ever, when evil is threatening us through errors based on denial of God. The message of Fatima ... invites us to approach anew *the Fountain of Mercy* by an act of consecration. Mary wishes us to draw near to [this fountain]: each one of us, each nation, and the whole world.[133]

Notice that he describes his pilgrimage as one of thanksgiving to "the mercy of God" and "the Mother of Christ." Moreover, he tells us that Mary, through the message of Fatima, wants to draw "each one of us, each nation, and the whole world" to "the Fountain of Mercy." Thus, the end and goal of the message of Fatima is *to bring us to God's mercy*. And so, the "triumph" of Mary's Immaculate Heart is really when we allow her to wash us in the Fountain of Divine Mercy, which she is especially free to do when individuals and nations are consecrated to her.

In the next chapter, we'll look more closely at how an individual, personal Marian consecration leads us to the triumph of Divine Mercy. Here, however, let's finish learning how John Paul's consecration of Russia and the world leads to that triumph.

THIRD TIME'S THE CHARM. Recall that John Paul's second attempt to consecrate the world and Russia failed because the invitations to the world's bishops arrived too late. The Pope didn't make the same mistake twice. For his third attempt at the consecration on March 25, 1984, he was meticulous in his preparations.

First, more than three months beforehand, he sent out his invitations to all the Catholic bishops of the world, asking them to join him in making the consecration — the letter was dated December 8, 1983, the solemnity of the Immaculate Conception. Second, he invited the patriarchs of the Orthodox Church to participate, and five of them actually came. Third, he carefully studied all the pertinent texts from the Fatima apparitions as well as previous consecration texts. Fourth, he personally consulted with Sr. Lucia. Fifth, he had the statue of Our Lady of Fatima from the Fatima Chapel of the Apparitions in the Cova da Iria flown to Rome for the occasion, the same statue that, in its crown, contains one of the bullets that had struck the Pope.[134] With these unprecedented preparations made, all that was left was to wait for the day that heaven had already been awaiting for so long.

On March 25, 1984, in St. Peter's Square, with a crowd of about 200,000 of the faithful, with numerous bishops and cardinals present, in union with all the bishops throughout the world, and before the Fatima Shrine statue of Our Lady, Pope John Paul II solemnly consecrated the world and Russia to Mary's Immaculate Heart as had been requested by Our Lady of Fatima. However, unfortunately, because the Pope did not explicitly say "Russia" in his public prayer, choosing instead to use veiled references as Pius XII had done, some have argued that it did not count.

But it did count because the Pope clearly implied Russia when he said, "In a special way we entrust and consecrate to you those individuals *and nations* that particularly need to be thus entrusted and consecrated." He clearly intended to consecrate Russia, as did the bishops, who undoubtedly understood the implication.

After the ceremony, when he was thanked for consecrating "the world," John Paul himself added, "and Russia."[135] This point of including Russia was deeply meaningful to him, because his own home country, Poland, was still suffering behind the Iron Curtain. In fact, many have speculated that during the several pauses John Paul made while reciting the consecration prayer, he was probably bringing this intention of his heart even more directly to Our Lady, namely, his prayer for the collapse of Soviet Communism.

Still, the rumors persisted: "Did the consecration really count? Had the Pope actually done what was required?" To quell these rumors and set the record straight, Sr. Lucia gave her own opinion, in writing, on August 29, 1989:

> Afterward [Pope John Paul II] wrote to all the bishops of the world asking them to unite themselves to him. He had the statue of Our Lady of Fatima [from the Cova da Iria chapel] brought to Rome on March 25, 1984. Then publicly, in union with those bishops who wished to associate themselves with His Holiness, he made the consecration in the way in which the Blessed Virgin had wished that it should be made. Afterward people asked me if it was made in the way our Lady wanted, and I replied: "Yes." From that time, it is made![136]

Before reading this clear statement of Sr. Lucia, I still had questions of my own about the consecration, and so I asked one of the experts from the World Apostolate of Fatima why the 1984 consecration emphasized "the world" more than Russia. This was the insightful response I received:

> If Russia had been consecrated as Our Lady had asked back in 1917, then Communism would have been nipped in the bud and World War II never would have happened. Instead, because of the consecration's long delay, World War II did happen and Russia did spread her errors of atheism and Communism throughout the world. Therefore, by 1984, not just Russia but *the whole world* needed to be consecrated. So, John Paul explicitly consecrated "the world" as well as "nations that particularly need to be thus entrusted and consecrated," which would include nations such as China and North Korea that certainly needed to be consecrated as well.[137]

This response raises an important point: The consecration was made, *but it was made late*, as Mary herself had said. Therefore, we shouldn't expect things to turn out as they would have had the consecration been done back in the early 20th century. After all, our Lord wants the response of faith, and when faith isn't put into action, miracles don't happen, or they're lessened. Think, for example, of Our Lady of Fatima's words regarding the October 13th Miracle of the Sun, which was *lessened* because of the actions of the faithless civil authorities, who imprisoned Lucia, Francisco, and Jacinta. Mary told Lucia, "Had they not taken you to [prison], the miracle would have been greater."[138]

Alright then, does this mean that the conversion of Russia won't take place? No. Our Lady promised it would happen. However, just as it took a long time for Russia to be consecrated, it may now take a long time for it to be converted. But this isn't necessarily a bad thing. What? I say that because, as Pope Francis has often pointed out, our God, the God of mercy, is a God of *surprises*. And one of the ways he surprises us is that, through the power of his mercy, through the "secret of Divine Mercy," *he can make a "plan B" turn out even better than the original plan, "plan A."* So, for instance, in the case of the message of Fatima, even though "plan A" was that Russia be consecrated back in 1917 or so, the late consecration in 1984, the "plan B," if you will, could potentially bring about even greater grace. What? How can that happen? It can happen if we follow the Pope's lead. Read the closing words of John Paul's 1984 consecration prayer and see what I mean:

> Let there be revealed, once more, in the history of the world the infinite saving power of the redemption: the power of *merciful Love!* May it put a stop to evil! May it transform consciences! May your Immaculate Heart reveal for all the *light of hope!*[139]

What lead is the Pope taking here? The same lead that the Immaculate Heart of Mary always wants us to follow: the lead to Divine Mercy, the lead to merciful love. Our Lady and the Pope want to bring us from Mary's Immaculate Heart to the Sacred and Merciful Heart of Jesus. The Heart of Jesus. That is always the goal, *yet we get there best by going through the Immaculate Heart.* That is what Jesus wants us to see, the lesson he wants to teach us through Fatima. This is why, as we read earlier, Jesus told Lucia that he would not convert Russia without the consecration:

> [I will not do it without the consecration because] I want my whole Church to acknowledge that consecration as a triumph of the Immaculate Heart of Mary, in order to later extend its [following] and to place devotion to this Immaculate Heart alongside devotion to my Sacred Heart.[140]

So, Jesus had hoped to show the Church and the world the importance of the loving Heart of our Immaculate Mother and its intimate relation with his Sacred Heart *through the great victory she would have brought us by converting Russia and preventing World War II and Communism.* But that "Plan A" didn't work out because, apparently, not enough people turned to God and the consecration wasn't made soon enough.

Since we didn't cooperate with "Plan A," the Lord gave us "Plan B," which is *the second greatest story ever told,* a story of hope that arises from the ashes of World War II and from the bitter persecution at the hands of Communist oppressors, a story that not only includes the story of Fatima but makes it *even better.*

I'm talking about the story of St. John Paul II himself and how he gives testimony, how he gives solemn voice to the powerful connection between Mary and Divine Mercy for the world. It is *he* who fulfills the Lord's desire of placing devotion to "this Immaculate Heart alongside devotion to my Sacred Heart." He's the one who, in his very person, as the Great Marian Pope and the Great Mercy Pope, unites these two glorious themes. He's the one who, in his brilliant homily on

May 13, 1982, explicitly places these two devotions along-side each other. He's the one who, in his consecration prayer of 1984, in the part we just read, shows us how it is *Mary's Immaculate Heart* that reveals for all "the power of merciful Love" and "the light of hope." And what is the power of merciful love and the light of hope but the *rays of mercy* that shine forth from the Heart of Jesus?

God's "Plan B" is so glorious because it marvelously draws out of the evils of the 20th century — evils that "Plan A" was designed to avoid — an even greater good. Through the blood of millions of hidden martyrs, through nearly 100 years of people living the message of Fatima, a time of mercy has been granted to the Church and to the world, and that time of mercy is *now.*

So, as we still await and pray for the complete conversion of Russia and the world, with Mary, in this time of mercy, we can call down an ocean of mercy on ourselves and on the whole world as we place our trust in Jesus, our Savior. This, in fact, is the final message. As we learned in chapter 4, this is the way that we can prepare the world for the Lord's final coming. This is the way laid out for us by Jesus through the great, prophetic saints of our day, Faustina and John Paul II.

*E*FFECTS OF THE *1984* CONSECRATION. Even though I said earlier that it may take a long time for Russia to be converted because the consecration requested by Our Lady of Fatima was so late in coming (1984), still, Our Lady quickly got to work after her request was fulfilled. Specifically, she began by laboring to dismantle the atheistic, oppressive Soviet regime, setting her sights on its Achilles heel: its satellite state of Poland.

From the mid-1980s, the anti-Communist Solidarity labor union in Poland, which we read about in chapter 3 and which had been beaten down in 1981 through hundreds of arrests, assaults, and the imposition of martial law, *began to rise again.* A powerful dose of strength and courage for this rising came through the transfusion of a martyr's blood late in the year of the consecration.

Blessed Fr. Jerzy Popiełuszko, "the priest of Solidarity," had supported the labor movement from the beginning. Then, in the aftermath of the 1981 crackdown, he became the leading voice in Poland that supported and encouraged Solidarity through its sojourn in the darkness. His weekly sermons, which interwove spiritual principles with biting criticism of the Communist regime, were attended by tens of thousands of people and broadcast throughout Poland.

The Communist leaders were furious. They arrested Popiełuszko on the basis of trumped up charges, but he was soon released and returned to his preaching. He was threatened and intimidated, but he continued preaching. On October 19, 1984, the 37-year-old priest was apprehended, tortured, and beaten to death by government agents. Yet, afterward, his blood spoke more eloquently than his most stirring sermon. Amazingly, more than a quarter of a million people attended his funeral. Then, fired with an even more fervent faith and courage and in direct defiance of their Communist masters, the Polish people helped the beaten, broken body of Solidarity to regain its feet and fight again — in the spirit of Fr. Jerzy.

The next year, in 1985, less than a year after the consecration, Mikhail Gorbachev assumed power as the head of the Soviet Union. He introduced wide-ranging reforms — popularly associated with the Russian words "glasnost" (literally translated as "publicity," meaning openness and transparency) and "perestroika" (literally translated as "restructuring," meaning a restructuring of the political and economic systems) — that would help accelerate the downfall of the Soviet Union.

In 1986, a general amnesty was granted to Polish political prisoners, and more than 200 jailed leaders of the Solidarity movement were set free. Shortly thereafter, Lech Wałesa began to reestablish Solidarity as a legal entity in Poland.

In 1987, many of the local chapters of Solidarity came out of hiding and became active once again. Waves of debilitating strikes, led by Solidarity, then hit Poland for much of 1988 until the government expressed its willingness to negotiate in late August. In 1989, elections were held, and the rest you've already read in chapter 3. Suffice it to say that the dominoes of Communism came crashing down, and by 1991, the Soviet Union was officially dissolved.

By the way, it's worth noting the date on which Mikhal Gorbachev signed the document that ended the Soviet Union: December 25 — Christmas Day. Just as our Immaculate Mother gave us the gift of the Prince of Peace on Christmas, so also, on Christmas day, nearly 2,000 years later, she gave the world a gift of peace through the downfall of a menacing force that had caused the Church and the world inestimable suffering. Thus, she also helped us to better appreciate a gift she had already given: the worldwide consecration to her Immaculate Heart.

In the next chapter, we'll come to better appreciate the gift of making a *personal* consecration to Jesus through Mary, which is an important piece to completing the second greatest story ever told. Before we get to that chapter, though, by way of introduction to the role of personal consecration, let me first share another important contribution that John Paul II made as the Pope of Fatima: the Rosary.

Postscript on the Power of the Rosary. Recall that at the beginning of nearly every one of the monthly Fatima Apparitions, Our Lady asked the children to pray the Rosary for world peace. This idea that the Rosary could obtain peace wasn't something new. Indeed, many times throughout the Church's history, Our Lady's intercession through peoples' praying of the Rosary has led to peace, victory, and protection.[141] The most dramatic of these instances, the event that led Pope Pius V to declare the feast of the Holy Rosary, was the Christian naval victory over a vastly larger Muslim fleet at the Battle of Lepanto on October 7, 1571. That victory, like the Battle of Vienna in 1683, helped save Christian Europe from rape, death, and destruction at the hands of Muslim invaders.

Knowing the power of the Rosary and inspired by Our Lady of Fatima, Pope John Paul II promoted his "favorite prayer" not only by his own personal example (he prayed several Rosaries every day) but also by issuing in 2002 an apostolic letter *Rosarium Virginis Mariae*, through which he introduced the Luminous Mysteries to the faithful.

Regarding John Paul's example of praying the Rosary, Pope Francis described its effect on him when, as Fr. Jorge Bergolio, he prayed it together with the Pope in Buenos Aires, Argentina:

> If I remember well it was 1985. One evening I went to recite the Holy Rosary that was being led by the Holy Father. He was in front of everybody, on his knees. The group was numerous; I saw the Holy Father from the back and, little by little, I got lost in prayer. I was not alone: I was praying in the middle of the people of God to which I and all those there belonged, led by our Pastor.
>
> In the middle of the prayer I became distracted, looking at the figure of the Pope: his piety, his devotion was a witness. And the time drifted away, and I began to imagine the young priest, the seminarian, the poet, the worker, the child from Wadowice … in the same position in which he knelt at that moment, reciting *Ave Maria* after *Ave Maria*. His witness struck me. I felt that this man, chosen to lead the Church, was following a path up to his Mother in the sky, a path set out on from his childhood. And I became aware of the density of the words of the Mother of Guadalupe to Saint Juan Diego: "Don't be afraid, am I not [here who am] your mother?" I understood the presence of Mary in the life of the Pope.
>
> That testimony did not get forgotten in an instant. From that time on I recite the fifteen mysteries of the Rosary every day.[142]

In this experience of prayer with John Paul II, Pope Francis gets to the heart of why the Rosary is such a powerful instrument of peace: It unites us with our tender mother,

Mary. Like the soft rhythm of a lullaby, the Hail Marys of the Rosary tranquilly rock us in the arms of our sweet mother who says to us, as she said to St. Juan Diego, "My littlest child … do not be afraid."

As we'll see in the next chapter, a personal consecration to Jesus through Mary brings us even more deeply into this motherly peace, even in the midst of great suffering.

Chapter 9

Personal Consecration and the Triumph

Our Mom is the instrument of God's mercy.

~ St. Maximilian Kolbe

In the last chapter, we witnessed the power of worldwide Marian consecration for bringing about the triumph of the two Hearts of Jesus and Mary. Here we're going to look at how a *personal consecration* helps brings about that same triumph. But there's something else.

In this penultimate chapter, I'd like to do a favor for my readers — because you deserve it. I mean, you've hung in there with me through a fast-paced, wide-ranging overview of Biblical history, Church history, and Polish history, as well as an intense account of key events of the 20th century (spilling into the 21st) that surround the dramatic and blessed life of St. John Paul II. In short, you've stayed with me through the second greatest story ever told, and there's certainly been a lot to it.

So now, as we begin drawing things to a conclusion, I'd like to do you the favor of telling a part of the story *that gathers all the pieces together* before you're sent off in the final chapter. More specifically, in the sections that follow, we'll be examining some key moments in Polish history and Church history contemporary to John Paul II, and as we do, we'll continue to join his two great themes of Mary and Divine Mercy. To help us with this, we're going to trace the story of a saint, a great saint, who was deeply beloved by John Paul: St. Maximilian Kolbe.

THE GREAT APOSTLE OF MARIAN CONSECRATION. Most people know the Polish priest, Maximilian Kolbe (1894-1941), as the Saint of Auschwitz, the martyr of charity who freely gave up his life in a Nazi concentration camp for the sake of a fellow prisoner. However, this dramatic act of generosity is but the crowning of an entire life given totally to God *for a very specific purpose*, a purpose that, I believe, gets even more closely to the heart of St. Maximilian than his death at the hands of the Nazis. What was that central purpose of his life? How can we best describe Kolbe at his core? I suggest that, above all, Kolbe was *the Great Apostle of Marian Consecration for our time.*

Now, while it's true that Pope John Paul II did more than anyone in our time to make Marian consecration known, it was Maximilian Kolbe's mission and Marian apostolic spirit that inspired not only John Paul but the Poland that formed him. The Great Apostle of Marian Consecration preceded the Great Mercy Pope, and without the former we wouldn't have had the latter, as we'll soon see.

In view of all this and in light of the second greatest story, we might consider Kolbe as another Faustina for John Paul: a kind of background figure to his story without whom we likely wouldn't have had the Pope we did. Moreover, just as Faustina was the Great Apostle of Divine Mercy (with John Paul), so Kolbe is the Great Apostle of Marian Consecration (also with John Paul). Getting to the heart of it, you might say that Faustina and Kolbe are like two spiritual parents who helped pass on to John Paul (and to us) two of the most important spiritual weapons for the great battles of our time: Divine Mercy and Marian consecration.

So how is Kolbe the Great Apostle of Marian Consecration? To answer this question, let's unpack three key points about Kolbe: (1) his intensity, (2) the way his mission inspired others, and (3) how he prepared Poland for World War II.

KOLBE'S INTENSITY. To understand St. Maximilian Kolbe as the Great Apostle of Marian Consecration, we first need to get to know a key quality of his personality: his intensity. Kolbe was *intense* — and it showed. I remember the first time I saw a photo of him. My immediate reaction went something like this: "I don't like him." His face looked way too stern. I knew he was holy, but I thought to myself, "Well, I'm just going to have to stick with the gentler saints." It was only later, after reading a book about Kolbe, that I discovered that while, yes, he was very intense, his was a beautiful intensity — an intensity of love. A story from his time in the seminary gives us a wonderful snapshot of what I now see as perhaps his most endearing quality.

Kolbe wasn't always known as "Maximilian." Rather, his birth name was Raymond. His religious superiors gave him the name Maximilian, which roughly translated means "the greatest." Perhaps surprisingly, Kolbe happily accepted the name — what humility! But here's the reason for his joyful acceptance of it. He didn't think he was the greatest. Not at all. Rather, he simply wanted to give the greatest possible glory to God. *That* was his intensity. He loved God so much that he wasn't satisfied with simply being good and following the rules. He wanted to give God everything — the greatest possible glory. But how? At the time, he wasn't exactly sure.

When I think of the young Kolbe, still studying at the minor seminary in the Polish city of Lwow, I image him as a giant fire hose with tons of water pressure behind it. Unfortunately, the nozzle of that big hose is stuck on the "mist" setting, so the rushing water anticlimactically and harmlessly exits with a big "*poof*" of fine spray going off in a million different directions. That was Kolbe in the minor seminary. He was all over the place, applying his intensity to such varied projects as drawing up plans for a rocket that could reach the moon, designing a receiver that could pick up sound waves from outer space, and planning to leave the seminary to fight in the Polish army to liberate his country.

In the midst of his flurry of grandiose thoughts and ideas, he continuously repeated one question in his heart: "But how shall I give the greatest possible glory to God?" In other words, he wanted to find that target to which he could direct all of his prodigious energy and zeal. Well, he did find it during his time of further studies in Rome. There, in the Eternal City, the nozzle began to tighten, the "mist" setting switched to "jet stream," and Kolbe's great and *focused* energy started to become a massive force for good in the Church.

At least three big lessons helped to focus Kolbe's intensity and clarified for him how he could give the greatest possible glory to God, three lessons that came from reading about Guadalupe, Rattisbonne, and de Montfort's Marian way.

Guadalupe. During his studies in Rome, Kolbe read the story of the 1531 apparition of Our Lady of Guadalupe in Mexico City. He learned that the Spaniards, who had arrived in the new world more than a decade earlier, had had only meager success in their efforts to convert the natives. However, when Our Lady appeared on the tilma of St. Juan Diego, *all heaven broke loose.* Within 10 years, almost 10 million natives converted to Catholicism and were baptized, paving the way for the nearly complete conversion of Mexico. Amazingly, all this happened at the very same time that roughly the same number of people were leaving the Church in Europe because of the Protestant Reformation.

Kolbe's Lesson: Where Our Lady is, there is her Spouse, the Holy Spirit, who will bring massive graces of conversion.

Rattisbonne. Another story that deeply moved Kolbe during his studies in Rome involved the conversion of a Jewish atheist, Alphonse Ratisbonne, in 1842. Ratisbonne despised the Catholic Church and the Catholic faith, especially because his older brother, Theodor, had converted to Catholicism and become a Catholic priest. On a dare from a Catholic friend, Baron de Bussieres, Ratisbonne began to wear the "Miraculous Medal"[143] and recite the *Memorare* prayer to prove the fruitlessness of what he thought were just the ridiculous superstitions of the Catholic religion.

On January 20, 1842, Ratisbonne accompanied Baron de Bussieres into a church, what is now the Basilica of St. Andrea delle Fratte in Rome, where the Baron had some business to attend to. When the Baron returned, he found Ratisbonne weeping and kissing his medal, saying, "I saw her! I saw her!" Ratisbonne later recounted what happened in his diary:

> I had only been in the church a moment when I was suddenly seized with an indescribable agitation of mind. I looked up and found that the rest of the

building had disappeared. One single chapel seemed to have gathered all the light and concentrated it in itself. In the midst of this radiance I saw someone standing on the altar, a lofty shining figure, all majesty and sweetness, the Virgin Mary just as she looks on this medal. Some irresistible force drew me toward her. She motioned to me to kneel down and when I did so, she seemed to approve. Though she never said a word, I understood her perfectly.[144]

This encounter with Mary so profoundly affected Ratisbonne that he converted to Catholicism and was ordained a priest in 1847. He later moved to the Holy Land with his brother Theodor and founded a congregation of sisters to pray for the conversion of the Jews.

Kolbe was so moved by this story that he offered his first Mass at the very altar where Mary had appeared to Ratisbonne, frequently spoke to people about this remarkable conversion, and passed out Miraculous Medals to everyone, calling them his "bullets."

Kolbe's Lesson: When hardened sinners open their hearts to Mary, even the slightest bit, she obtains for them the grace of conversion to her divine Son, sometimes in dramatic ways.

De Montfort. The third insight that helped Kolbe discover how he could give the greatest glory to God came from his reading of the book *True Devotion to Mary* by St. Louis de Montfort (1673-1716), which describes the spirituality of Marian consecration. While de Montfort didn't invent Marian consecration, he summarized and popularized the various streams of teaching on the subject, making it more accessible to the masses. Anyway, Kolbe was particularly struck by the bold claim of de Montfort that a total consecration to Jesus through Mary is the "surest, easiest, shortest and the most perfect means" to becoming a saint.[145] If true, then here was Kolbe's answer as to how he could give the greatest possible glory to God: Marian consecration. After all, giving the greatest possible glory to God is all about becoming a saint, and if Marian consecration is the quickest and easiest way, then *this was it!* This was the secret weapon Kolbe had been looking for in his fight against evil.

Kolbe was also deeply moved by de Montfort's prophecy that these Marian saints would be particularly important during the "end times,"[146] which Kolbe believed had arrived, as he wrote:

> Especially in these last days ... God will raise up persons who through their special devotion towards the most Blessed Virgin will sanctify themselves and will not only oppose God's sworn enemies, but will sweep away from the face of the earth heresy, idolatry, impiety; they will build up the temple of the true God and will inspire all with genuine devotion to our Lady. ...
>
> In fact, "even as through Mary salvation began, so, too, through her, salvation will reach its accomplishment."
>
> Let us reflect seriously on all these points.[147]

Kolbe's Lesson (that he surely reflected on seriously): A total consecration to Jesus through Mary is the quickest, easiest, and surest way to become a saint — and that's a big deal. It's the key to giving the greatest possible glory to God. It's also the key to forming those saints of the "end times" who will prepare the world for the Lord's final coming.

Conclusion. So, in these three lessons gleaned from the stories of the apparitions of Our Lady of Guadalupe, Ratisbonne's conversion, and the teachings on Marian consecration of St. Louis de Montfort, Kolbe understood that Mary is the way to holiness in Christ that he would intensely follow. She is the way, especially through the consecration, that he could truly give the greatest possible glory to God. She's the way — the quickest and easiest way — for bringing about massive conversions, even of the most hardened sinners.

This was really his great mission: to take the secret weapon of Marian devotion, especially the consecration, and use it to bring the whole world to God. After all, what better way to conquer the world for God and establish his kingdom than through saints? It is the saints who give God the greatest glory. And what is better for God's glory, one saint or two? Two saints or 10? Ten saints or a thousand? A thousand saints or a million? Kolbe wanted to form millions of saints through Mary Immaculate as quickly as possible so as to win the whole world for God. This mission, as we'll see in the next section, inspired many other people.

KOLBE'S MISSION INSPIRED OTHERS. On February 17, 1917, while Kolbe was still in Rome for his studies, a troubling event took place in St. Peter's Square that intensified the young seminarian's already incredible intensity. He describes what happened as follows:

> [T]he Freemasons in Rome began to demonstrate openly and belligerently against the Church. They placed [a] black standard … under the windows of the Vatican. On this standard the archangel, St. Michael, was depicted lying under the feet of the triumphant Lucifer. At the same time countless pamphlets were distributed to the people in which the Holy Father was attacked shamefully.[148]

Suddenly, as Kolbe witnessed this disturbing scene, an idea came into his mind. Inspired by the Marian lessons he had learned in the seminary, he thought of founding an "active society" that would engage and conquer the kind of evil he saw in that square. He pondered this idea in his heart for many months, letting it mature and develop until the day of action arrived.

The Essence of the Militia Immaculata (MI). The day of action came on October 16, 1917, which was just three days after the Miracle of the Sun in Fatima and the same day that

Pope John Paul II would be elected 61 years later. On that day, Kolbe gathered together seven other men (three priests and four seminarians) and formed the *Militia Immaculata* (MI), a spiritual army for Our Lady whose goal is to convert sinners and win the whole world for God. In the following paragraphs, Kolbe describes its essence:

> [S]trictly speaking, [the essence of the MI] is our consecration to our Lady Immaculate ... according to the spirit of the MI, namely as one who is unconditionally and totally her instrument in life, death, and eternity, as one who is her property ... .
>
> [O]ur Mom is the instrument of God's mercy, not however of his justice. Our good God, in order not to punish us, has given us our Mom so that he could limit his justice as much as possible. We also through our consecration to her are instruments of God's mercy in her immaculate hands as she is an instrument [of Divine Mercy] in God's hands. Obedience is God's will; and for us it is God's will by means of the Immaculate, that is, it is the *merciful* God's will.[149]

For Kolbe, then, the essence of the MI is to live the consecration, and the essence of the consecration, for him, is to be Mary's instrument. More specifically, it's to be *an instrument of Divine Mercy* in her hands as she is an instrument of Divine Mercy in God's hands. It is to belong totally to her, to be used by her, for the work of Divine Mercy that God has entrusted to her. Elsewhere, Kolbe goes on to describe this sublime mission of mercy:

> The essence [of the MI] depends on belonging to [Mary Immaculate] without reservation. ...
>
> We belong to her, to the Immaculate. We are hers without limits, most perfectly hers; we are, as it were, herself. Through our [instrumentality] she loves the good God. With our poor heart she loves

her divine Son. We become the mediators through whom the Immaculate loves Jesus. And Jesus, considering us her property and, as it were, a part of his beloved Mother, loves her in us and through us. What a lovely mystery!

We know about the possessed [people] through whom the devil was thinking and acting. We want to be in her possession without any reservation. We want her to think, to speak, and to act through us. ... She belongs to God, having become his Mother. And we want to become the mother who would give the life of the Immaculate to every heart that exists and to those that will still come into existence. That is the MI — to bring [Mary] into every heart, to give her life to every heart. Thus entering these hearts and taking full possession of them, she may give birth to sweet Jesus, who is God, that he might grow in them in age and perfection. What a magnificent mission! True? ... Divinizing man to the God-Man through the Mother of the God-Man.[150]

If this seems a bit too much, like Kolbe is giving too much of a role to Mary or going too far in encouraging people to belong to her "without reservation," consider three things.

First, Mary Immaculate is the greatest saint, the perfect disciple, the only human being who loves Jesus perfectly. In fact, she's the one who loves him so much that it's not enough for her just to love him in heaven. She wants to continue, so to speak, to come down to earth and love him through the people on earth. And Jesus lets her! "In that case," Kolbe would say, "then why don't *we* let her?" If only *we* would! Then, through "our poor hearts," she could continue to love Jesus on earth with her perfect love. Not only that, but then through us, she could continue her primary work of love, through her Spouse, the Holy Spirit, which is to give birth to other Christs, to "sweet Jesus" — as Kolbe put it — in souls. Let's continue with this point.

Every member of the Body of Christ has a special mission. The Immaculata's just happens to be the most important, which is this: to give birth to and nurture Jesus in souls. In other words, it's to oversee the transformation, sanctification, and divinization of souls, through the power of the Holy Spirit, into the likeness of her divine Son. "So," Kolbe would ask, "why not let her continue this most important motherly mission in and through us by letting her take possession of us as her instruments?" If only we would, then, according to Kolbe, we would not only become great saints but also the most effective apostles.

Second, if Kolbe's words seem like "too much," just think of some of the lessons we've learned from Church history about Mary as the key to apostolic fruitfulness. For instance, think back to Jesus' words to Sr. Lucia of Fatima, that in this time of mercy, he desires to place the peace of the world and the "triumph" of Divine Mercy into his mother's hands. Also, think back to the lesson of Guadalupe, of how, when Mary appeared, there was an explosion of grace, resulting in millions of conversions. Finally, think back to the story of Alphonse Ratisbonne and how Mary herself conquered for Christ a man who seemed hopelessly lost.

In sum, the great work of mercy of our time, by the wise will of God himself, is the work of Our Lady. Yet this work, her work of moving the Heart of Christ to perform miracles of mercy for those in need, is nothing new. It goes back to her action at Cana in Galilee. There, she saw the need of the newly married couple and then moved Christ to perform a miracle of mercy (see Jn 2:1-11). So, Kolbe is not saying "too much" here. He's simply describing Mary's wonderful, God-given mission (which has a special urgency today).

Third, if Kolbe's words quoted above still seem a bit too much, we can also reflect on the teaching of sound theology, which tells us that, because Mary is without sin (immaculate), she does the will of God perfectly. Thus, *to do her will is to do God's will.* However, because she does God's will not as a robot but as a person — specifically, as a tender mother — there's an amazing little twist to the idea of doing God's will through her, a twist that Kolbe explains as he further describes the essence of the MI:

> The spiritual ideal [of the MI] is a surrender to the Immaculate without reserve ... according to the act of consecration. Therefore, we must accept and fulfill to perfection the will of the Immaculate ... . In other words, we must be the best possible instruments in her immaculate hands and let her lead us in everything. That is the perfect obedience through which she reveals her will and uses us as her instruments.
>
> I repeat: Because we surrender to her completely, she reveals her will to us and guides us. And it can be put this way: (If we can say this) the divine will and the will of the Immaculate are not altogether identical because the will of the Immaculate is a will of mercy, not of divine justice. The Immaculate is a personification of mercy. And we as instruments in her hands serve not to punish the world justly, but to convert and sanctify it. These fruits of grace or of divine mercy are handed down to us through the Mediatrix of all graces. And just as she is a most perfect instrument in the hand of God, of God's mercy and his most Sacred Heart, so we are instruments in her hands. And through her we are instruments of the most Sacred Heart or divine mercy. Hence our motto is this: "Through the Immaculate to the Heart of Jesus."[151]

Did you notice the twist? It may have been easy to miss because these paragraphs are so amazing. They show us the connections between the Sacred Heart, Divine Mercy, Mary, the consecration, and the present time of mercy. But the heart of those connections, the key little twist, is this: When we do the will of the Immaculata, we are doing "the *merciful* God's will." I know we just heard this a short time ago, but it's so important to understand Kolbe's vision that it doesn't hurt to hear it again: The essence of the MI is to live the consecration, which means to be an instrument in the hands of Mary, which means to allow her to do her will in and through us, and her will is "the *merciful* God's will." In short, *the MI is all about being instruments of Divine Mercy in the hands of our Immaculate Mother of Mercy.*

A Difficulty Leading to the Mission of the MI. Now, before moving on to the next point, I'd like to address one question that may have popped into your mind: "Isn't it unfair to God (and untrue) to make Mary into a kind of a figure of 'pure mercy' while God is painted as the 'mean guy' holding the justice bag?" This is a difficulty that often came into my mind when I would read certain passages in St. Louis de Montfort's writing. It seemed that, according to de Montfort, a central motive for making a Marian consecration is to shield ourselves from God's wrath, as if even our Savior can't put up with us because we're such wretched sinners, who should not dare to approach him on our own.[152] But that idea flew in the face of my understanding that God is Love and Mercy itself, that Jesus has come not for the righteous but for sinners, and that he wants us to not be afraid to approach him and to pray, "Jesus, I trust in you." Well, here's how I've tried to make sense of this difficulty.

The key idea is God's "school of trust," which we covered in chapter one. This school is God's effort to heal the wound caused by original sin that gives us a disordered image of God such that we tend to struggle with trusting him. Well, here's the main point about it: The wound that God's school of trust tries to heal *primarily has to do with our perception of God* (not of creatures). So, because Mary is not God, because she's a creature, the wound doesn't affect our relationship with her as much. In other words, we can trust Mary more easily. In fact, unless our image of Mary has become distorted by issues with our own mothers or by prejudice (such as often happens to Protestants and to Catholics who listen to certain Protestants talk about Mary), we naturally *do* trust her. After all, who's afraid of a tender mother? You might even say that it's sometimes easier to trust Mary than it is to trust Jesus. What? Well, it's like this: Even though Jesus *is* Love and Mercy itself, even though he's the main lesson in God's school of trust, *he's still God* — and it's our image of God that has become distorted through the wound of original sin.

Alright, now here's how Mary is *God's great secret weapon* in his "school of trust": This good mother who is so easy to approach *always* strives to lead us to the love of Jesus. As we learned from John Paul's amazing May 13, 1981, homily in Fatima, her whole being, her whole passion, her whole preoccupation is to bring us to the pierced side of Jesus, the "Fountain of Mercy." Her whole goal is to help us understand, accept, and believe in God's mercy. As Blessed Mother Teresa put it, "[Mary's] role is to bring you face to face ... with the love in the Heart of Jesus crucified."[153] Her whole role is to get us to hear Jesus' poignant cry of love from the Cross, "I thirst!"[154]

Yet, just as we tend to be afraid of God because of our wound of original sin, we also tend to fear suffering and the Cross. Therefore, it helps to have someone lead us to the suffering, crucified God-man, whose pierced Heart is the Fountain of Mercy. Because Mary is easy to approach and brings us there, she truly is the great secret weapon in God's school of trust, the great instrument of God's mercy leading us to the source of Divine Mercy. She herself is *not* the source. Rather, she's the instrument of mercy leading us to the source, to the Fountain of Mercy.[155]

But Mary is not the only secret weapon in God's school of trust. Her role points us to *our role*, which is also to be instruments of Divine Mercy (in her hands by virtue of the consecration), leading people to the source of Divine Mercy. The best way I can explain this is to anticipate a subject that will come up later.

In the next chapter and in Appendix Two, you'll read about an organization called the Marian Missionaries of Divine Mercy, which is composed of three levels. The first level consists of young men who give a year of service, doing the works of mercy where the need is greatest and where few others want to go. Living their Marian consecration is the key aspect of how they go about this work.

Let me explain this point.

When the Marian Missionaries begin their day, for instance, on the streets of New York City, they offer a fervent prayer to Mary Immaculate, asking her to use them as instruments of Divine Mercy in her hands by leading them to those who are most in need of the love of Christ — and she does it. Like a good mother, deeply concerned for her lost children, she always does it.[156] I can testify that every time the men return from their missions, they are filled with the most amazing stories of how Our Lady brought them to people who had given up on God, rejected God, or falsely believed that God had rejected them. Through a simple ministry of love and presence, the most rejected by society discover in these young men's faces the true face of God who is love and mercy itself.

So, like Mary, and with Mary, the Marian Missionaries aim to heal peoples' distorted image of God, so they can discover him as Love and Mercy itself. They truly are God's secret weapon, with Mary, in his school of trust. But it's not just their mission. *All of us* are God's secret weapon in his school of trust (especially if we've been consecrated to Jesus through Mary), because, well, *we're not God* — and that's perfect! After all, it's God himself whom we often don't understand because of our original wound that gets us to focus on God's justice as if that changes the truth that he is Love and Mercy itself.[157] Through us, through our acts of love and mercy, God gets to approach his lost sheep "in disguise," so they don't run away. Indeed, it's through our acts of mercy that they get a glimpse of the true face of God, who is the source of Mercy.

This brings us to another point about the *kind* of instruments those in the MI are called to be — along with being instruments (or "missionaries") of mercy. Specifically, they're called to be not passive but *active instruments*. This is why Kolbe, in referring to the members of the MI, likes to call them

"Knights." He preferred the term "Knight" to de Montfort's language of "slave" because, as one Kolbean scholar puts it:

> "Holy Slavery" ... has implications and overtones our age finds repugnant. Further, such words may obscure the liberating aspect of Kolbe's total consecration — the "freedom of the children of God." "Slave" conjures up the notion of passive and mindless beings, whereas a Knight is to be active, even aggressive, creative and apostolic within the context of obedience, using every technology and skill of this world to evangelize. ... The Knight does not wait passively for orders, but assuming the will and intentions of the Immaculate, acts vigorously for the Kingdom, either singly (first degree of the MI) or in concert with others (second degree).[158]

In other words, Kolbe's style of consecration emphasizes a *radically apostolic dimension.* The MI is ultimately about the apostolic task of winning the *whole world* for God under the generalship of Mary Immaculate as she labors to bring all souls to Christ. With this in mind, we can better understand the last sentence of the above citation, which refers to different "degrees" in the MI.

The MI itself is an army (open to everyone in any state of life) that is primarily made up of *solitary members* who live the consecration in their daily lives (the first degree). Of course, there are no completely solitary members of the MI, for all members are part of the MI organization. But the first degree refers to living the consecration in the Kolbean spirit, so to speak, "on one's own." Describing such a Knight of the first degree, Kolbe writes:

> [Such a person] cannot fail to exert an influence on the milieu surrounding him, even without realizing that he does. He does not, however, feel satisfied with this, but consciously makes every effort and does all he can to win others to the Immaculate.[159]

In other words, because a Knight gives himself over to Mary as her instrument of mercy, she acts in and through him for good, even if he doesn't notice. That's great, but Kolbe says it's not enough. Each Knight also feels a need to be *active* in winning everyone to Jesus through Mary. To this end, he says that each first-degree Knight is "ready to make use of all legitimate means which his state of life, his circumstances, and his vocation put at his disposal."[160] So, for instance a priest, religious sister, or layperson can be a first-degree Knight by offering him or herself as an instrument of Divine Mercy in Mary's hands and following her lead in bringing everyone to her Son. Concretely, a priest might do this by preaching about the consecration, or a layperson may do it by handing out Miraculous Medals.

But Kolbe knew that greater apostolic good can be done when Knights band together as special units or groups (the second degree) for specific apostolic activities. For instance, a group of Knights studying at the same college might come together to organize a campus-wide Marian consecration movement, culminating on a particular Marian feast day. Kolbe himself founded a particularly important group of Knights, an MI second-degree initiative that was the most important in his day. They were the Knights of Niepokalanow, and their specific mission, "to conquer all of Poland for the Immaculate,"[161] plays a crucial role in the second greatest story ever told. Let's hear their story now.

The Knights of Niepokalanow. The Knights of Niepoka-lanow were all Franciscan priests, brothers, or seminarians from Kolbe's own religious congregation, the Conventual Franciscan Order. In a sense, these Franciscan Knights were part of Kolbe's vision for the MI from the very beginning. Why? Well, as a prelude to describing the foundation of the MI, Kolbe describes the state of his own community:

> I remember speaking with my confreres about the poor condition of our Order and its future. It was then that this thought impressed my mind

very strongly: Either put it on a better footing, or
demolish it. I was feeling sorry for young men who
came to us with the greatest intentions, but who
soon lost the ideal of holiness they expected to find
in the friary. But the thought of either bettering the
Order or destroying it haunted me. How this was to
be accomplished, I had no idea.[162]

Kolbe had had these thoughts well before founding the
MI. However, after the idea of starting it came to him during
the demonstration of the Freemasons in Rome, he began to
make the connection: This was the way to renew the Order.
(Thus, the founding members of the MI were all friars from
Kolbe's own community.) Kolbe saw the MI as a seed of renewal
within his Order that could help rekindle zeal and apostolic
fruitfulness through the living of a complete consecration to
Mary Immaculate.[163]

A year and a half after the MI's founding, when he
presented his plan to the Superior General of his Order, the
Father General responded, "O, that there were at least twelve
of you!" and he gave his blessing in writing, saying that the
MI should be spread to the youth, presumably because that is
where renewal best takes root.[164]

At first, the growth of the MI within the Franciscans was
slow. Kolbe had many detractors, yet only a handful of dedicated
conferes. Nevertheless, with the blessing of their superiors, this
small group embarked on a bold mission of conquering all of
Poland for Mary Immaculate. How did they propose to do
it? Through a magazine called *Knight of the Immaculate*, for
which Kolbe had to raise the funds himself ... well, not entirely
by himself. He tells the story of how he paid for the first issue:

I remember a certain fact that happened in 1922,
when the first issue of the *Knight* was ready to
be sent to the printers. We had to make a down
payment of 500 marks. I had not been allowed to
contract debts nor to ask for a loan; I was, therefore,

seriously embarrassed. To get to the printing shop I had to pass through the church. There on the Immaculate's altar I found an envelope with "For the Immaculate" written on the outside. When I opened it, I found exactly 500 marks. Can one say that only by mere chance the offering happened to be just the amount I needed and had prayed for with such fervor?[165]

A key point here: The envelope said "For the Immaculate." This was not Kolbe's work. The whole thing was for her. It was her work. Kolbe and his friars were just instruments in Mary's immaculate and merciful hands. And what a work she did through them!

The original apostolate of the magazine began in January of 1922, in the city of Krakow, Poland, with a first print-run of 5,000 copies. But then, after complaints from his fellow Franciscans, Kolbe had to move the operation to another location in Grodno, Poland. Thankfully, by the end of the year, Kolbe and his Franciscan Knights were able to purchase their own printing press for the Grodno operation. It came from a convent of sisters in Krakow, the same convent where, four years later, a young woman named Helen Kowalska would begin her novitiate and take the name "Faustina." (Yes, *that* Faustina.)[166]

With the new printing press and more equipment that soon followed, the Knights' magazine apostolate continued and grew. By the end of 1926, *Knight of the Immaculate* expanded from 16 to 32 pages and had a monthly pressrun of 30,000 copies. The next year, it was up to 45,000 copies. But it wasn't just the number of pages and copies that increased. With the spread of the magazine, more and more young men began applying to the Conventual Franciscans with the intention of joining Kolbe in Mary's printing apostolate, and several of the friars in his Order also volunteered to help. By the end of 1927, the work had two priests and 18 brothers — as well as a new home 26 miles west of Warsaw called "Niepokalanow," meaning "City of the Immaculate."

At the new Niepokalanow location, vocations and the printing apostolate exploded. Men from every part of Poland came streaming to Niepokalanow in response to advertisements in the magazine such as this:

> The gates of the city of Mary Immaculate are always open! Enter by those gates all young men who seek to serve Mary without counting the cost! In work without end, in abandoning self, in penance — this is the way to that peace which the world cannot give.
>
> Whatever your skill, your trade, or talent — there is room within the City's gate. If you can strive after poverty and heroic chastity in a spirit of humility — your place is here. In return — the joy of Paradise, of the vision of the eternal God.[167]

Kolbe's vision truly inspired many. By the end of 1938, nine months before the Nazis invaded Poland, Niepokalanow was *the largest monastery in the world*. There were 11 priests, 660 brothers, 30 novices, and 129 seminarians (830 total). And the magazine they produced inspired even more people than that. By the end of 1938, *Knight of the Immaculate* reached a pressrun of *1,000,000 copies a month*. But they also produced a calendar (440,000 copies); a daily newspaper with a weekday pressrun of more than 100,000 copies a day and a weekend pressrun of 260,730 copies; a magazine for priests (12,000 copies every quarter); a magazine for children (170,000 copies each month); and they received an influx of mail reaching 835,586 pieces for the year 1938.[168]

Through the magazine and their other publications, nearly everyone in Poland had heard of Niepokalanow, millions of them had been inspired to dedicate themselves more fully to Our Lady, and hundreds of thousands had joined the MI. It certainly looked like Kolbe and his Knights had fulfilled their aim of conquering Poland for Mary Immaculate.

*K*OLBE *PREPARED POLAND FOR THE WAR.* One of the original Knights of Niepokalanow lives less than an hour drive from my home at the National Shrine of The Divine Mercy in Stockbridge, Massachusetts. Now in his 90s, Fr. Lucian Krolikowski, OFM Conv., spent his late teenage years with St. Maximilian Kolbe at the Niepokalanow monastery and saw the saint on a daily basis. After hearing that such a man lives so close by, of course, some of the seminarians from my community and I went to visit him and listen to his stories.

During one such visit, Fr. Lucian shared something that solved a mystery I had often pondered. The mystery had presented itself while I was reading some of Pope John Paul II's reflections on his experiences of World War II.[169] The Pope wrote that the war had been a profoundly formative experience for him, leading him to discern that he had a priestly vocation. More specifically, he highlighted two main factors that deeply influenced him: man's evil and man's goodness.

Having lived in the part of occupied Poland dubbed "Gestapo-land" by author James Michener (aptly named because of the intense presence of the Gestapo — the secret police of Nazi Germany), the future Pope, Karol Wojtyła, had firsthand knowledge of Nazi brutality. Not only did he himself experience hunger, hostility, and humiliation at their hands, but his own friends, neighbors, and coworkers were also daily tormented, arrested, and even killed. But while the evil certainly hit close to home, so did the goodness.

During the hellish years of the occupation, amid terrible suffering, the young Wojtyła witnessed many acts of kindness, generosity, and heroism among his friends and neighbors. For example, they courageously fought off despair with their lively faith, shared what little food they had with those who were worse off, and often risked their lives for God, neighbor, and country. Long after the war, as Pope, John Paul had the joy of raising to the honors of the altar several of his heroic countrymen, some of whom he had known personally. However, for every one of those publicly identified saints and blesseds, there were countless other hidden saints who will never be officially recognized as such. Wojtyła knew many of these unofficial saints, and he kept them in his heart till the end of his life, drawing strength and inspiration from their example.

This now brings us to the mystery that Fr. Lucian solved for me. After I read John Paul's testimony to the heroism of the Poles during the war, I often wondered, "How did they do it? Where did they find the strength?" I mean, if a similar tragedy were to happen today, would there be such widespread goodness in American cities? Would there be so many acts of kindness and self-sacrifice? When I read the news and learn of so many daily acts of cruelty and selfishness, I have my doubts.

So what made the Poles so extraordinarily great in the midst of their suffering? Fr. Lucian gave the answer with one simple statement: *"Father Maximilian prepared us for the war."* Yes. The Poles' heroic goodness was Kolbe's doing. Or, more accurately, it was Our Blessed Mother's doing. She used Kolbe, her faithful Knight, to accomplish her mission of helping her children.

And this makes sense. Imagine you're a mother with billions of children, and you clearly see that 35 million of them are citizens of a country (Poland) that will go through the worst suffering of any other country during the worst war (World War II). You can't stop it — although you surely tried (Fatima). So, what do you do? You gather up into your arms as many of these poor children as possible, so at least you'll be able to comfort them and give them strength as they pass through the fire. The only problem is that you're not living on earth anymore. You yourself can't go around, rounding up your children, bringing them into your consoling love. So what do you do?

First, you take one of your children (Kolbe) who has offered himself as a Knight in your service, who has given himself completely to you to be used as an instrument of your maternal love. Second, you fill him with a beautiful intensity of love and use him to inspire others to join him as dedicated Knights in your service (the Knights of Niepokalanow). Third, you use these faithful Knights to publish a magazine (*Knight of the Immaculate*) that will inspire all who read it to turn to you and accept your motherly love and tenderness. Fourth, you make your Knights grow in strength and number, so their magazine will conquer all of Poland for you, bringing your Polish children even closer to your Immaculate Heart, especially through a personal consecration to you. Fifth, when the terrible fire of war finally comes, because your children are in your arms and near your Heart, you give them strength to be heroic in suffering and valiant in death. Also, because the magazine has inspired hundreds of thousands of these children to consecrate themselves to you, you use them, too, as instruments of your tender love — through them, you reach out to those who still haven't drawn close to you.

All of that is precisely what Mary Immaculate did, through St. Maximilian Kolbe, to prepare Poland for the war. The whole story is really about a mother's compassion and mercy for her suffering children. Still, if this story is hard to believe, consider this: Mary sent her faithful Knight to another place, a place where Satan would unleash the hottest hell on her children. Think about it. If you were Mary, deeply concerned for the wellbeing of your children as the worst war in human history approached, and you only had this one great Knight, *where would you send him?* Probably to the place where hell would burn hottest, where there'd be the biggest explosion of evil. Well, that's exactly where she sent him.

In 1930, Mary sent her Knight to Nagasaki, Japan — yes, infamous Nagasaki. Of all the places in the world, she sent Kolbe to one of only two cities to ever be destroyed by an atomic bomb. (The other one was Hiroshima, Japan.) More specifically, she sent him to the city that bore the brunt of the biggest of the two bombs, the one called "Fat Man." Yes, she sent him there 15 years before the blast, so he and his Knights could prepare her children. If you were the mother of all humanity, knowing what she knew, wouldn't you have done the same? If you had a Kolbe, a most powerful instrument of your love, wouldn't you send him to the place that would soon suffer the most powerful instrument of destruction? Again, that's exactly what Mary did, and her faithful Knight quickly got to work.[170]

Within a month of arriving in Nagasaki, Kolbe and a few other Knights — without friends, without knowledge of the Japanese language, and with very little money — published 10,000 copies of *Knight of the Immaculate* in Japanese By the end of the year, the monthly circulation rose to 25,000 copies. By the close of the decade, it had increased to 70,000 copies and, thus, became the largest Catholic religious publication in Japan, a publication that drew both Catholics and pagans alike to Mary's Heart. (In fact, most of its readers were pagans.)

Within about a year of their arrival, Kolbe and his handful of friars, together with local workers, built a monastery in Nagasaki, "Mugenzai no Sono" (Garden of the Immaculate). Amazingly, despite being located in Nagasaki, the Mugenzai no Sono Monastery survived the atomic bomb blast of 1945. It survived because, inspired by Mary Immaculate, Kolbe had chosen to build the monastery behind a mountain. While this choice certainly made travel to the city center inconvenient — the Knights had to travel partway around a mountain — it nevertheless completely protected them and their monastery from the blast. Thus, after the mushroom cloud cleared, the dedicated friars of Mugenzai no Sono continued to be instruments of Mary's tenderness to the city's suffering survivors.

So, it makes sense that Mary would use the great instrument of her love and mercy (Kolbe) by sending him to the two places that would bear some of the worst suffering during the worst war: Poland and Nagasaki. Also, it makes sense that, as a final act, she would bring her faithful Knight back to Poland and send him charging right into *the heart of darkness*, to Satan's most diabolical stronghold: the Auschwitz death camp. There, Kolbe became a light in the darkness to countless prisoners through the witness of his faith and compassion. Finally, he drew unforgettable good out of evil by departing that place of hatred in a blaze of glorious self-giving love, giving his life for a fellow prisoner, and thus becoming the Church's first officially recognized "martyr of charity."

Okay, now let's get back to the main point in all this: Kolbe prepared Poland for the war. Specifically, he did this by means of a magazine, *Knight of the Immaculate*. The aim of that magazine was to draw everyone to Mary's Heart, especially through the consecration. In fact, with its circulation of a million copies a month, the magazine became *the largest, most intense promotion of Marian consecration in the history of the Church*. But why was the consecration so essential in all this? I mean, if Mary wanted to prepare the Poles for the war and help them in their suffering, why not emphasize the Rosary or some other Marian devotion? It's because in this case, unlike Fatima, Mary was not trying to prevent suffering but rather *to prepare for it* — and the consecration is particularly connected to the Cross.

The Consecration and the Cross. As we learned earlier, Pope John Paul II's papal coat-of-arms, with its big Cross and the letter "M" below one of its arms, echoes the Gospel of John, 19:26-27. That passage, which records some of Jesus' last words from the Cross, best summarizes what, according to the Pope, Marian consecration is all about. Let's read it now:

> When Jesus saw his mother and the disciple whom he loved standing near, he said to his mother, "Woman, behold, your son." Then he said to the disciple, "Behold, your mother." And from that hour, the disciple took her to his own home.

Who is the beloved disciple here? According to the Pope, it's *all of us*, because we're all the Lord's beloved disciples. And why does Jesus entrust his mother to us (and us to his mother) just before he dies on the Cross? I suggest he does this because he has called all of his disciples to take up their crosses daily and follow him, even unto Calvary. And as he was enduring his agony, he surely reflected that we, too, would have to go through times when we would not just have to carry our crosses but hang from them. He knew that we, like him, would sometimes have to endure excruciating darkness and suffering. So, for *this* reason, he gave us his mother as a parting gift of mercy as he was dying on the Cross. Let's look more closely at what this gift means.

Mary was a gift for Jesus as he suffered on the Cross. She was at least a drop of consolation in the midst of an ocean of bitterness. Knowing this, Jesus wanted to make sure his disciples would have no less a consolation than he himself had. In other words, he wanted to give us the gift of consolation, and he gives it through Mary for two reasons. First, she's the spouse of the Holy Spirit who's called *"The Consoler"* (Jn 16:7).[171] Doesn't it make sense, then, that, like her Spouse and with her Spouse, Mary would also be known as a great consoler of those who are suffering? In fact, the reality is deeper: Because Mary is the Mediatrix of all grace,[172] it's always through her that we receive and experience the consolation of the Holy Spirit. Second, the role of consoler is perfect for Mary because *she's the perfect mother*, and mothers tend to be the best consolers. Let's spend a bit more time on this point.

Mothers are geniuses when it comes to knowing how to comfort their suffering children. For instance, it was Mom who cleaned our bloody knees, kissed them, and made them feel better. It was Mom who knew how to dip the bitter pill in honey so it wouldn't taste so bad. It was Mom who sang us lullabies to calm our fears and help us find peace. In fact, it's because of this beautiful gift of motherly mercy that St. Louis de Montfort could say that a total consecration to Jesus through Mary is the *easiest* way to holiness. Of course, the Christian life is the way of the Cross, so by its nature, it's not easy, but our spiritual mother has a way of making our crosses into something sweet. This is part of the feminine genius, and it's why we all long for a mother's tender, comforting love during our times of greatest darkness.

I once watched a documentary on World War II that interviewed a veteran of the war. He shared that a soldier in his unit had been shot, but he and his fellow soldiers couldn't reach him because they were pinned down by enemy fire. All night long, they had to listen to that poor soldier dying of his gunshot wound. The veteran then shared a detail I will never forget: He said the soldier kept crying out for his mom. I had always thought that that was a cliché, something they just made up in the movies. But it's the reality. All night long, that dying soldier was calling out, "Mom! Mommy!"

Again, all of us in our heart of hearts long for a tender, motherly presence during times of great pain and suffering. We call out for Mom. And even if our biological moms can't be there, Jesus has made sure that we have a perfect, spiritual mother who will always be there for us: his loving mother, Mary. But to receive this gift, we have to respond to his invitation from the Cross to take her as our mother: "Behold, your mother" (Jn 19:27). For John Paul II, the consecration means to consciously accept that invitation. It's to imitate the beloved disciple who "took her to his own home," which the Pope interprets as the home of our hearts.[173]

This is Marian consecration. It's not only, as Kolbe says, to allow ourselves to be used as instruments of mercy in Mary's hands, but it's also to accept mercy from her. It means allowing Our Blessed Mother into our hearts, allowing her to be with us, especially in times of suffering, allowing her to show us her motherly tenderness. But we have to choose to allow her. After all, her mother love is certainly not "smother love." She won't impose her mercy on us. Indeed, she has great respect for human free will. (She knows what a "yes" to God can do!) So she waits for our yes. She waits for us to let her be the mother to us that we need in this valley of tears, the perfect mother that Jesus gave us as he was dying on the Cross. She waits for our gaze to behold hers because, since her time of suffering at Calvary, she is always lovingly beholding us, her dear children.

And this gets to the heart of the meaning of the statement, "Father Maximilian prepared us for the war." All of Kolbe's efforts to "conquer Poland" for Mary Immaculate were simply so that everyone there would accept and experience her tenderness and love. They surely needed it during the war, and she gave it. This is why so many Poles were very heroic in their suffering. They didn't have to endure it alone. The whole time, they had their sweet mother, Mary, holding their hands and guiding their steps as they passed through their trial by fire. Since she couldn't prevent the war, she drew good out of the evil by turning those who had to endure the worst of it into so many hidden saints and martyrs, whose suffering prepared the way for the present time of mercy in the Church.

That is how the personal consecration, inspired by St. Maximilian Kolbe as *the Great Apostle of Marian Consecration*, paved the way for and helps bring about the triumph of Mary's Immaculate Heart, which is ultimately the triumph of the Divine Mercy of her Son. Indeed, through the largest push for Marian consecration in the history of the Church, Kolbe helped form those saints whose merits have helped usher in the present time of mercy for the Church and the world. In light of all this, it should now be clear that there's so much more to Kolbe's story than his dramatic act of self-giving love at the Auschwitz death camp.

*C*ONCLUSION. Now, back to our story. While Kolbe is certainly not as directly related to the second greatest story ever told as is St. Faustina, his efforts surely influenced the life of St. John Paul II. And even if the future Pope never read *Knight of the Immaculate* magazine — though he very well could have, because it was first printed and distributed in his native Krakow — Kolbe still had a major impact on him.

After all, it was through Kolbe that all of Poland became enfolded in the Immaculate Heart of Mary, a Heart through which the graces and mercy of the Heart of Jesus flowed out to the whole country. Surely those graces touched the life of Karol Wojtyła, who discovered and accepted his vocation during the war years. Also, it's an interesting coincidence that during the very year when *Knight of the Immaculate* magazine was going out to a million Polish homes a month, Wojtyła was inspired to read *True Devotion to Mary*. That book moved him to consecrate himself to Jesus through Mary, an action that, again, he described as a "decisive turning point" of his life. Could that book have come to him from someone who had been inspired by *Knight of the Immaculate* or the "Marian buzz" it created in Poland? It's very possible. One thing is certain: Maximilian Kolbe became one of John Paul's very favorite saints and inspired the Pope to give his all as a Knight of the Immaculate, that is, as an instrument of God's mercy in the hands of Mary.

In the next chapter, we're going to look at how John Paul II's witness to Mary and Mercy, which we've now learned about through his story, can lead us to take up his mission. In other words, we'll see how the second greatest story can continue through me and through *you*.

CHAPTER 10
The Story Continues

I have come to set the earth on fire,
and how I wish it were already blazing!

~ Jesus, Gospel of Luke

In this last chapter, I have some good news. The second greatest story ever told can also be *your story.* That's because the story itself, in the end, isn't so much about a Polish Pope whom you may or may not have met. Rather, it's about the witness he gave to Divine Mercy and Mary for our time. It's his prophetic testimony that *now is the time of mercy*, a testimony that calls for our response. In other words, God didn't just give us the second greatest story so we could sit back and enjoy it. *He wants us to be part of it.*

For the remainder of this chapter, I'm going to do two things. First, I'll share some of my own personal testimony of how I myself have been caught up in this story. Second, I'll share how you can be caught up in it, too. But before we begin, lest you think this is just "my thing," I'd like to share a quote from someone else who also feels caught up in the story and who believes we're all called to be part of it. That someone is Pope Francis, and he spoke the following words to the priests of the Diocese of Rome — and to us all. (It's a longer quote, but well worth an attentive read.)

> [L]isten to the voice of the Spirit that speaks to the whole Church in this our time, which is, in fact, the time of mercy. I am certain of this. ... We have been living in the time of mercy for 30 or more years, up to now.
>
> It is the time of mercy in the whole Church. It was instituted by [St.] John Paul II. He had the "intuition" that this was the time of mercy. We think of the beatification and canonization of Sister Faustina Kowalska; then he introduced the feast of

the Divine Mercy. He moved slowly, slowly, and went ahead with this.

In the homily for the Canonization, which took place in 2000, John Paul II stressed that Jesus Christ's message to Sister Faustina was placed in time between two World Wars and is very linked to the history of the 20th century. How will the future of man be on earth, he says,

> It is not given to us to know it. It is true, however, that along with the new progresses we will not lack painful experiences. However, the light of Divine Mercy, which the Lord wished virtually to give again to the world through the charism of Sister Faustina, will illumine the path of the men of the third millennium.

It is clear. It was explicit in 2000, but it was something that had been maturing in [John Paul's] heart for some time. He had this intuition in his prayer.

Today we forget everything too hastily, also the Magisterium of the Church! It is inevitable in part, but we cannot forget the great contents, the great intuitions and the consignment left to the People of God. And that of the Divine Mercy is one of these. It is a consignment that [John Paul] gave us, but which comes from on High. It is up to us, as ministers of the Church, to keep alive this message … .[174]

So what's the message? What are the ministers of the Church and, in fact, all of us called to keep alive? I hope we haven't forgotten already! (Didn't the Pope say, "Today we forget everything so hastily"?) Well, here it is again: It's the good news that *now is the time of mercy*. This is the message that the "voice of the Spirit" speaks to us today. This is the "insight" that Pope John Paul II received in prayer for us. This is the "consignment left to the People of God" for our time, a kind of spiritual legacy or inheritance that "comes from on High." Pope Francis has heard this good news and is responding. Are we?

There's one last thing before I begin my testimony and share how each of us can be part of the second greatest story. It has to do with a key point we covered earlier.

*A*NOTHER *BIG PUSH.* In the last chapter, we learned that St. Maximilian Kolbe led the largest push for Marian consecration in the history of the Church and that *it was for an important historical reason.* Specifically, it was to prepare Poland for the horrors of World War II. Now, with this in mind, consider the following: We presently find ourselves in what is likely the *second largest push* for Marian consecration in the history of the Church. (Actually, this push may be even larger than Kolbe's.) But this time, this great push isn't happening in Poland. Rather, its epicenter is right here in North America.

Okay, so what does this mean for us? Does it mean that World War III is coming? Does it mean that the United States and Canada are going to suffer a trial by fire as bad or even worse than what befell Poland? I don't know. My hope is that this great push is a sign of a new springtime and spiritual renewal for the Church in America. My hope is that, with so many people consecrating themselves to Jesus through Mary, Our Blessed Mother is going to use us as instruments of mercy not only to convert the people of this land but those of the whole world.

But, again, I don't know what's coming. What I do know is that something *is* coming. Also, I do think that whether it will be good or bad depends on *our response.* I say this because, as we learned earlier from the story of Fatima, the future is not some irrevocably fixed reality. Prayer and conversion can avert war and destruction and change the course of history. Life or death, a blessing or a curse — it depends on us, on our free choice. Thankfully, we get to make our choice against the backdrop of the good news that *now is the time of mercy.* In other words, we have the encouragement that amazing graces are available to us today! So, *what will our response be?* Will we ignore the good news and miss out on this time of visitation? Or, rather, will we call out for mercy, receive mercy and, through Mary, be instruments of mercy? I hope it will be the latter.

What the Push Is Not. Again, just as Mary was on the move in Poland during the 1930s, bringing her children to her Heart to prepare them for the coming fire of war, so she's also on the move today, in America, preparing us for something big. In view of this fact, it's important to know exactly what she's doing, so we can better respond. To this end, let's explore what the second greatest push for Marian consecration is, beginning with what it's *not.*

First of all, this present push is not the only Marian con-secration movement since St. Maximilian Kolbe. In fact, there have been countless groups, faithfully laboring for decades, that have fruitfully spread the consecration in the spirit of St. Louis de Montfort, St. Maximilian Kolbe, and others. In fact, many of these groups are part of the present big push.

Second, the present push is not being led by great saints. In fact, it seems that Mary has chosen some of the weakest of souls to spearhead it. At least I speak for myself. (You'll soon see what I mean.) Yes, as embarrassing as this is to say and as much as I've dreaded saying it, I've had a particular role in this big push. I'm going to share that role in the next section as a prelude to explaining what the big push is. I decided to do so for two main reasons: First, I believe it will help others to better understand what Mary has been up to, so they'll be more ready to help her. Second, as you'll see, sharing my role really amounts to giving a personal testimony to the tenderness of our Mother of Mercy, who stooped down (and continues to stoop down) to raise a poor sinner from the dust. By giving this testimony, then, I not only pay a debt of gratitude to Our Blessed Mother but hope that others, by reading it, will better appreciate her goodness and, therefore, will not be afraid to help her.

*P*RELUDE TO THE *P*USH: *M*Y *T*ESTIMONY. I graduated from a university with a very strong Catholic identity. As strange as it may sound these days, the majority of the students had a deep and joyful faith. Of course, normally, that would be something to celebrate, but it got me depressed. I say that because, every day, I'd see the wholesome goodness of the students, and I'd think to myself, "There's *no way* I can be like them." Let me give some background to explain this.

I had a conversion back to my Catholic faith during my senior year in high school, not long before leaving for college. In fact, going to the Catholic university I mentioned was kind of a last-minute decision. My previous plan had been to attend a prestigious secular university in my home state of California. I'd been accepted and was all set to go, but something told me to give it up. I very reluctantly did, because I was still deeply attached to my worldly southern California ways. What helped push me to make the sacrifice, though, was a truth I'd only just recently accepted: *the meaning of life is to become a saint.* I was sure that if I stayed on my worldly path, not only would I not become a saint, but I'd probably end up in hell. So, I went to the Catholic school.

As I mentioned, the genuine holiness of the students both really impressed me and got me depressed. On the one hand, I was attracted to their sanctity. On the other hand, such sanctity seemed impossible for someone like me to attain. Then, things got worse when I started to read the lives of the saints for my theology classes. I thought to myself, "These saints are so awesome! But there's *no way* I can be like them." So, basically, I lost hope and resigned myself to the idea that I'd always be a failure in the one thing that mattered: becoming a saint.

Later that first semester, a friend of mine walked up to me and shoved a book in my face, saying, "Gaitley, you've gotta read this!" The book was *True Devotion to Mary* by St. Louis de Montfort, and I didn't want it. I had too many other books to read for my classes and told my friend as much. He persisted, and I finally took the book just to get him off my back — I didn't plan on reading it.

When I got back to my dorm room, I tossed the book on my desk, and it landed face down. On the back cover, some words caught my eye: "A total consecration to Jesus through Mary is the shortest, *easiest*, surest way to holiness." (The "easiest" part wasn't in italics, but that's certainly how I read it.) I said to myself, "Man! That's what I need. The *easiest* way to holiness!" I proceeded to devour the book in about a day and a half.

The book recommended making a 33-day preparation before the day of consecration. So, that's what I did. It wasn't easy, but I stuck with it and consecrated myself totally to Jesus through Mary on December 8, the solemnity of the Immaculate Conception. And that changed everything. For instance, I stopped chasing all the beautiful girls on campus and began to actually listen to a call to the priesthood, which I'd been ignoring. Because I'd invited Mary into my life, I felt I finally had the strength to hear that call. She seemed to be filling me with so much peace and joy that I thought to myself, "With Mary, this priesthood thing is going to be easy!" Best of all, I firmly believed that she could help even someone like me to become a saint.

The warm fuzzies lasted only a few months, and then it seemed that Mary's presence in my life disappeared. I was pretty sure I knew why. I figured she had finally discovered who I really was: a total knucklehead who couldn't keep up with the other guys on campus who were much more devoted to her as they prayed three Rosaries a day and fasted on bread and water several times a week. So that was that. I still pursued my priestly vocation, but Mary seemed far off, keeping her distance, and so I kept mine.

That dryness in my devotion to Mary lasted for more than 15 years. Of course, I went through the motions and said the prayers, but I had a hard time believing that Mary really loved me. Then came the summer of 2011.

Summer, 2011. By 2011, I'd already been ordained a priest, and I sometimes helped out with the formation of the new seminarians in my religious community, the Marian Fathers. In June of that year, I gave a talk to a group of them about our Marian charism, mission, and identity. I explained that as a particularly active community, our task is to spend ourselves in apostolic labor for the sake of Christ and the Church. Then, I asked them, "And where should our zeal for this task come from?" One of them answered, "From our love for Jesus." Of course, he was absolutely right, but there was more to it. I said, "As Marian Fathers of the Immaculate Conception, a prime source of our energy and zeal should also be a great love for Mary Immaculate." Next, I made a confession. I said, "Guys, please pray for me. I'm telling you this, but I myself need to grow here. I have a deep love for Jesus, and I'm sure Mary has a lot to do with this, but I need a jumpstart in my devotion to her." They promised their prayers.

Well, the grace of their prayers and the prayers of others who had been praying for me for years soon hit me in a most beautiful way.

Less than a month after giving the talk to the seminarians, I went on my annual retreat, and halfway through, I felt the inspiration to write a book on Marian consecration. It was a strange inspiration. After all, I should have been the *last person* to write about Mary. But there it was, right when I woke up in the morning: the idea for an entire Marian book, including the title: "*33 Days to Morning Glory.*" The inspiration was so strong that I got right out of bed and started writing. I wrote for the rest of the retreat. Then, because I'd already scheduled a week of vacation right afterward, I kept on writing. So, after just 10 days of writing, I'd finished a draft of the entire book! I believe this was a miracle because my first book, *Consoling the Heart of Jesus*, had taken me *10 years* to finish. I also believe the book was a miracle for another reason.

I already mentioned my 15-year dry spell in my devotion to Mary. Well, after writing *33 Days*, it went away — as in, *completely.* Mary was back, and I think I know why. Of course, it was the prayers of others, but it was also because of Saints Maximilian Kolbe and John Paul II.

The book, *33 Days to Morning Glory*, is divided into four parts or "weeks," where each week covers the consecration spirituality of a different Marian saint, two of whom are Maximilian Kolbe and John Paul II. Well, while I was researching and writing the chapters on Kolbe and John Paul, that's when the real breakthroughs and healing began. I'll now share what happened, starting with what I learned from Kolbe.

Kolbe Begins to Heal the Wound. Before reading St. Maximilian Kolbe's writings, I had pictured Mary as being larger than life, a huge queen perched on a massive pedestal, surrounded by a blaze of glory. Frankly — and I hate to say this — I also saw her as something of a nag. I got this impression from my readings of various Marian apparitions, where it seemed she was always saying, "Penance, penance, penance! Pray more Rosaries, fast ... and don't forget to clean your room!" Of course, she's not a nag. She's just a deeply concerned mother because so many of her children are being lost. Still, the way my mind works, I took what I read to mean that I could never do enough for her. I could never pray enough Rosaries or fast enough, and there she always was, looming large over my head, painfully reminding of this sad fact. Well, Kolbe changed this picture. He showed me a different Mary. Let me explain what I mean by quoting some of his own words to his friars at Niepokalanow:

> My dear, dear brothers, our dear little, little mother, the Immaculate Mary can do anything for us. We are her children. Turn to her. She will overcome everything.[175]

What I love about this is that Kolbe refers to Mary not as "Her Majesty the Queen" but as "mother," specifically our "*little* mother." This was revolutionary for me because I'd previously pictured her as *big*. I imagined her as so full of grace that all I saw was just a massive blaze of glory that was painful to the eyes. But here, Kolbe was going on about how she's our "dear little, little mother." He said "little" twice! That's what hit me: Mary's greatness is her littleness. Her power is her humility. I guess I should have known that, because she basically says as much in the *Magnificat*:

> My soul proclaims the greatness of the Lord; my spirit rejoices in God my Savior for he has looked with favor on his lowly servant. ... [T]he Almighty has done great things for me and holy is his name (Lk 1:46-55).

Yes, God is the Almighty, the one who "casts down the mighty from their thrones and lifts up the lowly." He's the Great and Holy One who bestows his greatness on those who are lowly and *little*. Mary, then, must be the littlest of all. For she is the one who was filled with God's grace and mercy more than any other creature. I realized, then, that I need not fear such a humble and little mother.

Kolbe also taught me something else about Mary that began to heal the wound. As we read earlier, he said that Mary is a kind of personification of God's mercy, not his justice. In other words, God gave her to us, so we could experience in a special way, through her, his tender, mother-like merciful love. We've all probably heard the saying, "He's got a face only a mother could love." Well, regarding our Mother of Mercy, we could also say, "He's got a *soul* only a mother could love." For Mary truly does love every soul, especially those going through great suffering and those who are in danger of being eternally lost. Truly, as our Mother of Mercy, her merciful Heart goes out to us the more weak, broken, and sinful we are. Thus, we should never doubt her love — as I did for 15 years.

Now, here's the Kolbe quote that helped heal my Mary-wound more than any other. In it, the saint speaks directly to all those who may still have doubts about Our Blessed Mother's love for us:

> Sometimes, my dear ones, the thought, a sad long-ing, as if a plea or a complaint may occur to you: "Does the Immaculate still love me?" Most beloved

children! I tell you all and each one individually, in her name (mark that: in her name!), she loves every one of you. She loves you very much and at every moment with no exception. This, my dearest children, I repeat for you in her name.[176]

This quote is worth keeping and reading every day. Why not read it again now? Let it sink in that Mary loves *you* very much and at every moment with no exception, no matter what. She truly is our loving Mother of Mercy, and I'll be forever grateful to St. Maximilian Kolbe for finally convincing me of it.

John Paul Finishes the Job. The other breakthrough in my devotion to Mary happened as I was writing and researching the section of *33 Days to Morning Glory* that covers the teaching on Pope John Paul II. The key insight comes from something we read in Chapter 8, namely, the Pope's amazing homily in Fatima on May 13, 1982. In that homily, John Paul made explicit the connection between Marian consecration and Divine Mercy. He said that the whole meaning of the consecration is to allow Mary to bring us to the pierced side of Jesus, the "Fountain of Mercy." In other words, her whole role is really to help us graduate from "God's school of trust," to help us come to understand, believe in, and accept God's love and mercy for us.

Now, in itself that's an amazing insight: Mary is the one who brings us to Divine Mercy. But then, when I applied it to my life, something *huge* happened. A glorious light suddenly went on in my mind, an incredible realization that totally changed my life and completely healed my relationship with Mary. Let me explain.

Recall that when I first made my Marian consecration in college, I was filled with consolation — but it only lasted a few months. Therefore, I concluded that Mary had abandoned me because she realized what a knucklehead I was. What I didn't share earlier is that during those 15 years of dryness with Mary, I fell deeply in love with the message of Divine Mercy that comes to us through St. Faustina Kowalska.

During those 15 years, through St. Faustina's testimony, I came to realize that God's ways are not our ways, that God doesn't love as we love. We tend to love people because of their gifts. We tend to love someone because he or she is attractive, funny, talented, rich, or powerful — but that's not why God loves us. He loves us because *we need his love.* He loves us because *he's good,* not because we are. He loves us because his Heart is full of merciful love, the kind of love that, like water, rushes to the lowest place.

During those 15 years, through Faustina's testimony, I came to discover the heart of the Gospel: namely, the fundamental reality of God's mercy for sinners.[177] I realized that Jesus didn't come for the righteous but for sinners, that our Good Shepherd will even leave the 99 to go out in search of the one lost sheep. I came to understand that it's our misery that attracts him, that he just wants us to let him love us, and that the more weak, broken, and sinful we are, the more his merciful Heart goes out to us. As Jesus told St. Faustina, **"The greater the sinner, the greater the right he has to My mercy."**[178]

For 15 years, I reflected on this consoling message. I gazed on the Image of Divine Mercy in my room every day and constantly prayed, "Jesus, I trust in you." Gradually, I came to believe what seemed impossible: "Jesus really does love me!" And I knew he did love me not because I'd earned it but because I was a little soul. In fact, because I was so little, I realized to my great delight, "He loves me even more!"

By the way, if you're reading this and can't relate. If you're thinking, "Well, I'm a good person, so I don't need to go crazy with this mercy stuff." I have news for you: Jesus doesn't just want "good people." He wants saints. He wants people who are *on fire* with his love. Didn't he say, "I have come to set the earth on fire, and how I wish it were already blazing!" (Lk 12:49)? When we realize how much Jesus' love demands from us, we discover that we are *all* little souls, and I mean *very little.*

Who of us is truly grateful for all that God has done for us and perpetually sings him a song of praise? Who of us prays always, as the Lord commands us to do? (See 1 Thes 5:17; Eph 6:18.) Who of us never wastes time, never procrastinates or complains, and always does what God asks? Who of us is constantly listening and looking to do the Lord's most perfect will in every situation? Who of us directs everything, every action, not to comfort, people-pleasing, and our own glory but solely to the glory of God? Who of us thinks of God day and night because we're so in love with him? In short, who of us is already a saint?

To follow the first commandment is not easy. To consciously, deliberately, and consistently put God above all else is difficult. In fact, to love God with our whole heart, mind, soul, and strength is a lifelong process, and we only truly begin when we realize that apart from him we can do nothing (see Jn 15:5). In short, we're *all* sinners. (Proverbs 24:16 says that even the just man sins seven times a day.) We're *all* in need of God's mercy, and some more than others — which brings us back to my story.

Reflecting on how, for the previous 15 years, I'd fallen so much in love with God's mercy, reflecting on how I came to believe in God's love for me and how that knowledge had grown year after year, I suddenly realized: "Oh, my gosh! Mary hasn't abandoned me for all this time. She's just been doing her job!"

Yes, at first, after I'd made my consecration, she was right there in front of me, filling me with consolation and warm fuzzies. But the Christian life isn't about warm fuzzies. So, she went from being, so to speak, right in "front" of me to going *behind me*, where I couldn't see her. I thought this meant that she'd abandoned me. On the contrary, after reading Pope John Paul's May 13, 1982, homily, I realized that she was really right there the whole time, *pushing me* from behind. Yes, for 15 beautiful years, even though I couldn't see her, she was pushing me into the rays of God's mercy, pushing me into the fountain of Divine Mercy, the pierced side of Jesus, helping me to understand how much God loves me — not because of what I've done or who I am but because of who he is and what he's done for me.

That's what Mary wants to do for each and every one of us. That's what she wants us to understand and experience. Bringing us to Divine Mercy, healing the original wound that makes us distrust God, and helping us to graduate from God's school of trust — that's Mary's mission, passion, and preoccupation as she works in the lives of all her children. And she does it best through the consecration. So let's get to know how Marian consecration is spreading today, allowing Mary to bring more and more people to the inexhaustible mercy of God.

*W*HAT THE *S*ECOND *G*REATEST *P*USH *I*S. I just shared what I believe are two miracles regarding the book *33 Days to Morning Glory:* (1) I wrote it in 10 days, and (2) it healed my devotion to Mary. But now I'd like to share another grace: the way the consecration has spread through *33 Days*, which has probably become the second greatest push for Marian consecration. Because I've been so close to this movement, because I've had the privilege of witnessing Mary's marvelous work unfold before my eyes every day, I feel the duty to share it. My hope is that, by sharing it, you'll have no doubt that Mary is on the move for something big and that she wants you to be part of it.

Mary on the Move. After *33 Days to Morning Glory* first came out, we started getting emails, letters, and phone calls from people sharing how Mary had changed their lives. Then, as time went on, the trickle turned into a torrent. My staff and I became overwhelmed by the stories that came in daily: conversions, healings, and other amazing graces. It was clear that people weren't just reading a book. They were giving themselves over to the Mother of God, and she was working miracles of mercy in their lives beyond anything we or they expected or imagined. I wish there were space enough to share those stories here, but that will have to wait for another book.

Apart from the amazing graces, people were also sharing how they were so grateful because the version of the consecration presented in *33 Days* was so easy to do. That was actually a main idea in my mind as I wrote it: I believe that our Mother of Mercy wants her consecration not just for the spiritual elites but for *all* her children. In fact, my favorite letters have been from the non-Catholics, fallen-away Catholics, and people who would write, "I went to Mass every Sunday, but I was clueless about the faith until Mary showed me who Jesus is." In fact, most of the people who have been doing the consecration are the same ones who describe themselves as previously not being very active in their faith. After the consecration, though, they often say that they're "on fire." (Perfect word choice! After all, Mary was praying in the upper room at Pentecost as her Spouse, the Holy Spirit, came down as tongues *of fire*.)

Anyway, it's through those "on fire" people that the book has really spread. Bookstore owners often tell us something like this: "In my 20 years of running my store, I've never seen a book fly off the shelves as much as this one. Somebody buys it, makes the consecration, and then they come back and buy a dozen more to give to their family and friends. We can't keep it in stock!" And this is also reflected in the Internet sales as well, because *33 Days* has consistently been among the top 10 Catholic books for online sales in the last several years.

The book has also spread because we put together a small-group program, called Hearts Afire: Parish-based Programs from the Marian Fathers of the Immaculate Conception (HAPP®), where people can go through the consecration together using not just *33 Days* but also DVDs and a workbook. That's been one of the most effective ways that whole parishes have been transformed by Our Lady. People finish the small group retreat and then invite others to do it until the whole parish is "on fire." In fact, dozens of pastors have told us that, through the consecration, Mary has transformed their parishes. But it doesn't end with the parishes. Several bishops have led their whole dioceses through the consecration with great fruit. For instance, in the Diocese of Fort Wayne-South Bend, Indiana, the bishop there led the entire diocese to do the consecration, and more than 12,000 people consecrated on the same day. Another bishop told us that the consecration is transforming his diocese, and a third orders the small-group programs himself and gives them to priests in his diocese, telling them, "This will renew your parish."

Our Lady has also been going into prisons through this ministry, where group after group of inmates — most of whom are not even Catholic — make the consecration and are so transformed that, in at least one case, the warden himself expressed his amazement at what Mary has been doing. Also, there have been several Catholic universities that have done campus-wide consecrations such that the president of one of them wrote an enthusiastic letter saying that it has deeply blessed the whole campus. Almost the entire student body of several thousand students made the consecration.

The stories go on and on. Mary truly is on the move, bringing people to God's mercy and setting them on fire with love for Jesus.

A Gift for Maria. In gratitude to Mary for all that she has been doing through the consecration, my staff and I wanted to do something special for her. So, knowing that Spanish-speakers have some of the greatest pastoral needs in the Church in the United States, we said, "What if we printed *one million* copies of *33 Days* in Spanish and gave them away for free?" The only problem was that we didn't have the money. (The book sales have gone to support the Marian Fathers' ministries and growing number of seminarians.) We prayed about it, and a benefactor stepped forward four days later and covered the whole printing!

Actually, the money wasn't the only problem. After we gave the printer the go-ahead, we found out that the books would fill *six full tractor-trailer trucks*. That's when I started to worry: "It's going to take us years to move those books! And where are we going to put them all?" That night, I left the office feeling pretty discouraged as I kept wondering if we'd made a mistake. When I got home, though, I found the following prayercard on my door, left by a fellow Marian priest who knew nothing about this situation:

Listen. Put it into your heart, my smallest
child, that the thing that frightened you,
the thing that afflicted you is nothing:
Do not let it disturb you…
Am I not here, I who am your mother?
Are you not under my shadow and protection?
Am I not the source of your joy?
Are you not in the hollow of my mantle,
In the crossing of my arms?
Do you need something more?

— Our Lady of Guadalupe, 1531

© In the Arms of Mary Foundation

And so, with that, I stopped doubting and trusted in
Mary. The next day, we sent emails to all the diocesan offices
for Hispanic ministry throughout the country and hoped for
the best. Well, within just one week, *all one million copies of the
Spanish consecration books were spoken for*. Not only that, but we
also got dozens of phone calls and emails from people telling
us, "Thank you for doing this!" One priest even wept, saying,
"I can't believe you're doing this for our people."

Counting the Spanish and English books, in just three years, with the help of our friends at Lighthouse Catholic Media, we've been able to distribute more than 2 million copies of *33 Days* in the United States and Canada alone. Also, the distribution continues to grow rapidly as the consecration reaches more and more parishes and dioceses. Thus, here in North America, it looks like we're in the midst of the second largest push for Marian consecration.

WHY THE SECOND GREATEST PUSH IS SO IMPORTANT. About a week after we sent out the emails to the offices for Hispanic ministry, I got a phone call from a man in Los Angeles who runs a thriving, Spanish-language Catholic media apostolate that reaches the United States and most of Latin America. He informed me that he had just received a special invitation from the Basilica of Our Lady of Guadalupe in Mexico City to see the tilma of Our Lady up close and "behind the vault" (the vault is a securely locked room in which the tilma is housed and from which it is displayed). He also explained that such a special viewing hadn't happened in four years and was usually just reserved for presidents, popes, and prelates. Finally, he said, "I'm allowed to take only a small group of my staff, but after hearing about the Spanish consecration book give-away, your name keeps popping into my mind. So, I think Our Lady wants you to go. Would you like to come?"

Of course, I accepted the invitation, and two days later, I was there in Mexico City, resting my head on the glass encasement of the tilma, right on the pregnant belly of Our Lady of Guadalupe. I felt she gave this beautiful gift in thanksgiving for the million books we'd given to her children who are most in need. I also believe she brought me there so I could hear an important message about the consecration, which came that same day through someone else.

A Matter of Life and Death in Mexico. The Missionaries of Charity Fathers, founded by Blessed Mother Teresa of Calcutta, live right next door to the Guadalupe Basilica.

Knowing this, I went to visit them on the same day I saw the image of Our Lady. During the visit, I offered some of the Spanish consecration books we'd just printed, so they could distribute them to the poor. The priest I spoke with, Fr. Felix, responded by saying, "I can't believe this. This is perfect timing." Then, he went on to explain a matter of life and death, which went something like this:

In the 16th century, Our Lady of Guadalupe came here to Mexico, put an end to the human sacrifice of the Aztecs, and became Queen and Mother of this land. But now the people are turning their backs on Her and going instead to "Santa Muerte" (Saint Death), who is a mockery of Our Lady of Guadalupe, the Mother of Life. In fact, the images of Santa Muerte always have the body of Our Lady but the face of a *skull* — yet the people love her! They say, "I turned to Jesus and Mary, but they didn't give me money or power, yet Santa Muerte did!"

Santa Muerte is a demon, and demons have power, which they give to people who show them devotion. (At the cost of their souls!) This is especially true in the case of the narcos [drug cartels]. They love Santa Muerte, have her tattooed all over their bodies, and use her as a recruiting tool. And then, all those brutal murders and gruesome killings you hear about on the news? That's because the Narcos show their devotion to Santa Muerte by killing. The more violent and gory the means — decapitation, dismemberment, torture — the more power Santa Muerte will give. She's giving them a lot of power because they are giving her a lot of blood.

There's power in blood, and the forces of evil are growing through it. The demons of the Aztecs knew this, and that's why human sacrifice was such an important part of the culture.[179] Well, those old demons are coming back, because the blood is beginning to flow again. While the Narcos are surely making it flow, so is abortion, which was just legalized in Mexico City a few years ago. This growing stream of blood is rousing the old demons and making their power increase in Mexico once again.

That's why this consecration is coming at the perfect time! Just as people are giving themselves to Santa Muerte more than ever, becoming her instruments of death, so Our Lady of Guadalupe wants her children to give themselves to her more than ever, so they can be her instruments of life. She wants her children to come back to her, and this is the way to do it. It's perfect timing, and if we consecrate ourselves to her, she'll conquer the evil again.

After this conversation, I decided to offer the Basilica of Our Lady of Guadalupe our 100,000 reserve Spanish copies of *33 Days* (which we'd held back to make sure every U.S. diocese who wanted them could get them). The Basilica accepted them, and one of the priests there used the books (which they've since run out of) to lead groups of people through the consecration every month throughout the year. I was later told this created quite a buzz in the city.

In the meantime, my friend who helped organize getting the books to the Basilica excitedly shared with me that at the end of that year, the Cardinal Archbishop of Mexico City (who was well aware of the consecrations taking place in the Basilica) and all the other bishops of Mexico had made a surprising announcement. With the blessing of Pope Francis, they decided to consecrate the entire country to Our Lady on her feast day, December 12, 2014. In the announcement, they expressed their belief that only the consecration of Mexico could stop the cult of Santa Muerte, abortion, and the widespread violence caused by the Narcos.[180]

Of course, the Mexican bishops were right. After all, the battle they're facing is a spiritual one, and Mary is the key to peace and the triumph of her Son over the forces of evil, as we learned through the message of Fatima (and Fr. Felix).

Hope for America. I just said the battle *they're* facing is a spiritual one. I should also say the battle *we're* facing. For if Mexico has it bad with Santa Muerte and the Narcos, the United States is in some ways a million times worse. Take, for example, the case of abortion. At present, abortion is only legal in Mexico City, but in the United States, it's legal throughout the country.

Each year, more than a million abortions are performed in the U.S. Not only that, but one could argue that the United States, more than any other country in the world, has contributed to the international spread of abortion. In view of the staggering statistic of more than *a billion* abortions worldwide over the last 30 years, that's quite an indictment. The reason this is important to mention here is because, as murder, abortion is a sin that cries out to God for punishment (see Gen 4:10). Making matters worse, it involves the murder of a completely innocent and helpless child by the will of its own parents.

It's a wonder, then, that the United States (not to mention so many other countries where the culture of death has gained the upper hand) still exists! I suggest that the only reason we haven't been wiped off the face of the earth is because, again, *now is the time of mercy.* Truly, God is showing unbelievable restraint and mercy. He's giving us time to repent and to cry out for mercy. But, eventually, something has to give. Something *is* coming. There's a reason Mary is on the move, leading the second greatest push for her consecration here in America. Is it to prepare us for the coming fire of God's justice? Or is it to bring us to a time of conversion and renewal? I believe it largely depends on us, and I have a lot of hope because people seem to realize we've come to a crucial moment, even without hearing the testimony of the second greatest story ever told. They feel the urgency, and they're ready to respond. So, let's see what we can do.

*B*EING PART OF THE STORY: THREE THINGS WE CAN DO. I'm going to keep this simple by recommending just three things we can do in response to the "time of mercy" that God is so graciously giving us: (1) Marian consecration; (2) Divine Mercy; (3) The Marian Missionaries of Divine Mercy.

(1) Marian Consecration: Make It, Renew It, Live It, Share It. If you haven't made the consecration, make it! If you've already made it, renew it! But don't just renew it every year. Renew it every day. And, above all, don't let your consecration be words alone. Live it and share it.

How do we live the consecration? By drawing close to Our Blessed Mother through turning to her in our daily lives with our needs and problems and by sharing with her our joys and sorrows. This can be done by a simple movement of the heart, through praying the Rosary, or during set times of quiet prayer with her. Remember, Mary is a real, living person. She truly is our mother, and she wants to hear from us and help us in our needs.

When we do turn to Mary, it consoles her Heart. When we forget about her, it wounds it. But her great agony is when her children go to hell. This makes her weep bitterly. So, let's be good children to her and, like St. Maximilian Kolbe, console her by offering ourselves to her, so she may use us as instruments of God's mercy. Let's allow her to use us to save souls. This gives Mary the greatest consolation, and it's the best and fullest way to live out the consecration.

But let's go even deeper by asking, "How, concretely, did Kolbe let himself be used by Mary?" *He spread her consecration.* Well, let's do the same. After all, it's the quickest, easiest, surest way to holiness. Let's tell everyone! Through the consecration, we can win the whole world for God as quickly as possible.

To obtain resources for making, renewing, living, and sharing the consecration, see the Resource Pages at the end of this book that are devoted to "Mary" and "Hearts Afire." Also, realize that part of living the consecration means heeding the request of Our Lady of Fatima, which calls for praying the Rosary daily, offering up sacrifices for unrepentant sinners, and making the Five First Saturdays of Reparation.[181]

(2) Divine Mercy: Know It, Live It, Plead for It. We've all heard of Divine Mercy, that God loves us and is merciful. However, we not only need to know it but experience and realize it in our hearts. This is not easy. The furthest distance is the road from the head to the heart! This is because of the wound of original sin, which presents us with a distorted image of God and makes us tend to fear him and hide from his love. So, even if we *know* that God is merciful, our wounded hearts often feel otherwise.

The Lord understands that we need help overcoming this wound in our hearts, especially in our day and age, where sin is so close at hand and so many hearts have become hardened. This is why he gives us our Mother Mary, who, as we learned earlier, teaches us to understand, accept, and believe in Divine Mercy, especially through the consecration. But he also gives us another help in the present time of mercy: the Divine Mercy message and devotion.

The Divine Mercy message and devotion is not some new Gospel, but rather, it reminds us of the heart of the Gospel: God's mercy for sinners. It also gives us concrete ways of discovering and experiencing Divine Mercy in our hearts: the Feast of Divine Mercy (which John Paul II established), the Image of Divine Mercy, a Novena and Chaplet of Divine Mercy, the Hour of Mercy, and the testimony of St. Faustina through her *Diary.*

Along with these devotional aspects and the reminder of God's love, the message of Divine Mercy also encourages us to *live* mercy by asking for it, being merciful to others, and completely trusting in Jesus. For we cannot expect to receive mercy if we do not show it as well (see Lk 6:38). Also, the more we trust in the Lord, the more mercy he can give us, as Jesus told St. Faustina, **"The graces of My mercy are drawn by means of one vessel only, and that is — trust. The more a soul trusts, the more it will receive."**[182]

There's no space here to explain the Divine Mercy message and devotion in detail. This book was just the appetizer.

Read the menu options for the main course in the Resource Pages devoted to "Divine Mercy."

Before moving on, I have to say something more about one aspect of the Divine Mercy devotion: the Chaplet of Divine Mercy. Please pray it! If you don't know how, see this footnote.[183] The chaplet is a perfect way to respond to John Paul's call to the whole Church to cry out for mercy in our day. It's a great way to *live* mercy.

Also, we can be encouraged to pray the Chaplet of Divine Mercy by remembering Abraham's question regarding Sodom and Gomorrah. He asked the Lord whether he would spare that sinful city if he found 10 righteous people in it. The Lord answered yes! (See Gen 18:32.) That's a reminder to us that our situation is not hopeless. Even if it seems that our society is worse than Sodom and Gomorrah and deserves a flood as in the day of Noah, victory is within reach! Indeed, just *one* person can make a huge difference. For instance, Jesus told St. Faustina, **"For your sake I withhold the hand which punishes; for your sake I bless the earth."**[184]

(3) The Marian Missionaries of Divine Mercy: Join Us. The Marian Missionaries of Divine Mercy is for all those who want to be more fully and formally involved in living and spreading Marian consecration and Divine Mercy. In fact, it's probably what St. Maximilian Kolbe's Militia Immaculata (MI) would look like if it had been founded by St. John Paul II. I say that because it combines Kolbe's Marian ideals with the Divine Mercy movement, all in the spirit of St. John Paul II. Here's the mission statement:

> *In the present "time of mercy," the Marian Missionaries of Divine Mercy, inspired by St. John Paul II, consciously and deliberately aim to win the whole world for God (prepare the world for the Lord's final coming) as quickly as possible especially through the two powerful spiritual weapons of Marian Consecration and Divine Mercy.*

Now don't be afraid of the "Lord's final coming" language. As we saw earlier, this does not mean we know the day or the hour of the Lord's coming, because we don't. (See Appendix One for what it does mean.) Nevertheless, there is a kind of urgency to the times we're living in. Moreover, according to St. John Paul II, with Mary, we *are* being called to prepare the world for the Lord's final coming, whenever it may be, by crying out for, receiving, and sharing God's mercy. The Marian Missionaries of Divine Mercy is an organization that takes this call very seriously and has three levels of participation.

Level One consists of a brotherhood of men who give a yearlong commitment to God by living an ordered life of community, prayer, formation, and service. Their main house is located three minutes down the road from the National Shrine of The Divine Mercy in Stockbridge, Massachusetts. At present, they do the works of mercy where the need is greatest (as instruments of Divine Mercy in the hands of Mary Immaculate) in the dioceses of Springfield, Massachusetts; Albany, New York; and the archdioceses of New York and Boston. If you or a young man you know may be interested in giving such a year of service to God, which is especially helpful to those who may be discerning a vocation the priesthood, religious life, or marriage, see the information pages at the end of this book.

Level Two consists of all those who, embracing the Marian Missionaries spirituality and moved by the vision of the mission, seek to aid it through either spiritual or material support or both.

Level Three consists of all those who embrace Marian Missionary spirituality and intentionally give themselves to the mission through various apostolic works, service, special projects, or administrative support. Let me introduce you to a great example of a Level-Three Marian Missionary: my friend, Brian.

Brian was the CEO of a very successful international company, a prominent figure in politics, a husband, and a father of six. He made the consecration at the invitation of a friend, and Mary changed his life. With the support of his family, he decided to sell his business, give up politics, and dedicate himself to helping spread Marian consecration and Divine Mercy throughout the country and the world. He now heads up special projects for the Marian Missionaries such as getting *33 Days to Morning Glory* translated into various languages and distributing it in many countries.

Of course, most people won't be called to give up their businesses, like Brian did, but if you feel called to do something more hands-on to spread Marian consecration and Divine Mercy but can't give a year as a Level-One Marian Missionary, there's still a place for you in Mary's army. If this describes you, then contact the Marian Missionaries Support Team today, tell them what's on your heart, and together we can explore the possibilities.

To learn more about the Marian Missionaries of Divine Mercy, you can visit the website (MarianMissionaries.org) or read about them in Appendix Two. To contact our Support Team, see the Resource Pages devoted to "Marian Missionaries."

Review. Before moving on to the conclusion, let's do a quick review of how we can respond to the time of mercy: (1) Marian consecration: Make it, renew it, live it, and share it; (2) Divine Mercy: Get to know the message and devotion, live it, and cry out to God that he may have mercy on us and on the whole world; (3) Join one of the three levels of the Marian Missionaries of Divine Mercy, which you can read more about in Appendix Two.

CONCLUSION

This book makes a bold claim. The greatest story in the history of the Church (the second greatest story after the Bible) is that surrounding the life and witness of St. John Paul II. Well, now that you have all the data, do you agree? Let's look back and see why it's so great.

First, the setting is amazing. The story begins in the 20th century, the time of greatest evil and suffering in the history of the world, right in the place that bore the worst of it: Poland. Now, such a context of unprecedented suffering makes perfect sense for the second greatest story. We know this from the central event of the first greatest story. That event — the Paschal Mystery of Christ, his suffering, death, and Resurrection — teaches us that *from the greatest suffering comes the greatest glory.* Okay, so the second greatest story has the greatest suffering part covered. Now to the glory.

Through the uniquely painful twists and turns of Polish history; through centuries of saints' scattered voices whispering words of mercy; through the blood of more martyrs than was shed at any other time; through the accumulated prayers and sacrifices inspired by the message of Fatima; through the preparatory labors, sufferings, and deaths of two of the Church's greatest saints (Faustina and Kolbe), God raised up a man to the highest office in the Church not only to free the world from the worst totalitarian regime in history but, more importantly, to give an urgent message of hope for our particularly trying times. Pope John Paul II not only confirmed the long, prophetic witness to mercy of Saints Margaret Mary, Thérèse, and Faustina but he became *the culmination of that witness.*

And what, precisely, is his witness? Again, it's that *now is the time of mercy.* It's that now is a time of unprecedented and glorious grace. It's that the spark of Divine Mercy has ignited a fire, and now this fire is preparing the world for the Lord's final coming. As the Great Mercy Pope said right before his solemn act of entrustment of the world to Divine Mercy at the Shrine in Łagiewniki, "This spark needs to be lighted by the grace of

God. This fire of mercy needs to be passed on to the world." And so it has, thanks in no small measure to St. John Paul II.

But isn't this all a bit much? Admittedly, the message of John Paul's witness is a lot to swallow. Preparation for the end of the world? Come on. A time of unprecedented grace and mercy? Really? But if it *is* true, it's a game-changer. If it is true that we are in the end times and that God is giving the world a last chance of abundant mercy before the terrible "Day of Justice" arrives, then this makes us wake up and pay attention.

But these kinds of messages or devotions are a dime-a-dozen, aren't they? I mean, there's always at least one over-zealous person at church who, as the solution to all the world's problems, says you just have to listen to this CD or read that special book, pray this no-fail novena, or go to that wonder saint, use this miraculous oil, or wear that soul-saving medal. Isn't this Divine Mercy and Marian consecration stuff the same sort of thing? Isn't it just the latest Catholic fad, another message clamoring for our attention, another unnecessary devotion?

Well, let me put it this way. Throughout this book, we haven't been dealing with obscure messages from unknown mystics or fire-and-brimstone warnings from the latest apparition. Rather, we've focused on a historic, well-vetted, Marian apparition recognized as such by pope after pope (Fatima) and widely acclaimed spiritual giants (Thérèse, Faustina, Kolbe, John Paul) whose stature in the Church leaves little room for doubt. Moreover, Divine Mercy itself, as Pope Benedict XVI pointed out, is not some "secondary devotion" but rather "an integral dimension of a Christian's faith and prayer."[185] In fact, as the central mystery of the love of the Heart of Jesus, Divine Mercy is actually *the* primary and essential "devotion" of Christians.

Still, even with these kinds of top credentials, our hearts may still remain unmoved and unimpressed. After all, it seems that every apostolate, movement, devotion, and mission has some Pope or Saint endorsing it: "Pope so-and-so says the X movement will save the world; Saint such-and-such says the X work is the most needed in the Church!"

But this message really is different. It stands out from the rest. It calls us to attention. Why? *Because of the story itself.* We're not dealing here with a one-time, isolated word or soundbite. Rather, we have a narrative, a whole web of events and meanings that converge into a clear message that speaks for itself — that speaks for God. It's a divine narrative that speaks to us. It's the Lord speaking to you and to me.

Put yourself in God's shoes. If you wanted to give a last message to humanity to prepare it for your final coming through an almost too-good-to-be-true gift of mercy, you'd wrap it up in a dazzling package. You'd save your best for last. You'd put your message right at the center of the greatest story in the history of the Church.

Of course, this story would have to involve centuries of buildup, undeniable miracles, clear fulfillment of prophecies, bold action against menacing evil, stunning victories, a most beautiful Lady, and one of the greatest men who ever lived, whose very life would be the culmination of the drama that preceded it. Then, most important of all, would be the end of that hero's life. That's where you yourself would reveal your divine hand by confirming the whole story with a glorious death that only you could arrange.

Of course, all this and more happened in the prophetic story of St. John Paul II. Yet it wasn't meant to entertain but to enlighten. It was meant to reveal a serious and urgent message: *now is the time of mercy.* It was meant to get us moving, together with a Mother who is on the move right here, right now. It was meant to bring us into the story itself and inspire us to make it our own.

Has it?

Appendix One

Regarding the Lord's Final Coming

The second greatest story ever told has to do with the "end times" and the Lord's final coming. Pope John Paul II himself underscored this point in 2002, when he dedicated the Shrine of Divine Mercy in Krakow, Poland, and entrusted the world to Divine Mercy. On that occasion, in a surprising move, he not only cited an apocalyptic passage from the *Diary of St. Faustina* but strengthened it by calling it a "binding promise":

> May this message radiate from this place to our beloved homeland and throughout the world. May the binding promise of the Lord Jesus be fulfilled: from here there must go forth "the spark which will prepare the world for [the Lord's] final coming."

The *Diary* paragraph that John Paul references (1732) isn't the only one that deals with the Lord's final coming. We also read the following words of Jesus to St. Faustina:

> **Speak to the world about My mercy. ... It is a sign for the end times. After it will come the Day of Justice. While there is still time, let them have recourse to the fount of My mercy.**[186]

> **Tell souls about this great mercy of Mine, because the awful day, the day of My justice, is near.**[187]

> **I am prolonging the time of mercy for the sake of sinners. But woe to them if they do not recognize this time of My visitation.**[188]

> **Before the Day of Justice, I am sending the Day of Mercy.**[189]

> **He who refuses to pass through the door of My Mercy must pass through the door of My Justice.**[190]

In addition to these words of our Lord, we have those of the Blessed Mother, who spoke to St. Faustina in a similar way:

> *[Y]ou have to speak to the world about His great mercy and prepare the world for the Second Coming of*

Him who will come, not as a merciful Savior, but as a just Judge. Oh how terrible is that day! Determined is the day of justice, the day of divine wrath. The angels tremble before it. Speak to souls about this great mercy while it is still the time for granting mercy.[191]

So, what are we to make of all this? And what does the Lord's final coming actually mean? I'm going to address these two questions in what follows.

WHAT ARE WE TO MAKE OF ALL THIS? Let's begin with three important points: (1) We do not know the day or the hour of the Lord's final coming; (2) There is a particular urgency to the time we're living in; (3) The apocalyptic message of the *Diary* is relatively optimistic.

First, we simply do not know when the Lord is coming. Scripture is clear about this (see Mt 24:36).

Second, while we don't know the day or hour of the Lord's coming, the *Diary* passages just cited certainly give the impression that time is running out, that the Lord is coming *soon*. When? Again, we don't know, but when the Lord says the day is "near," we're clearly dealing with an urgent message. It's telling us that the time we have now is particularly precious, and it would be foolish not to make the best use of it. As Jesus said to St. Faustina, **"He who refuses to pass through the door of My Mercy must pass through the door of My Justice."**

Third, the tone of these apocalyptic messages is relatively optimistic. While the end of the world, the "Day of Justice," is coming and won't be pretty, the good news is that God is giving us the present time of mercy (and has even extended it). So, we prepare for the Lord's coming not by being consumed with fear but by following the message of Divine Mercy. Of course, this is not some new Gospel. Rather, it brings us to the heart of the Gospel, which tells us to repent of our sins and then ask for, trust in, and receive God's mercy. The main refrain, as we see in the image of Divine Mercy, is not fear but *trust* — "Jesus, I trust in you."

By the way, if you're reading this appendix without having read the whole book, some of this may sound a bit far-fetched. If it does, I suggest going back and reading the story first.

*W*HAT DOES THE LORD'S FINAL COMING ACTUALLY MEAN? To answer this question, I'm going to adapt something I wrote in another book.[192] As we go, do keep in mind that we're dealing here with a mystery and that what follows can only amount to speculation. Nevertheless, as we'll see, this speculation is based on Sacred Scripture, papal teaching, and sound theology.

Let's begin with a reporter's question to Pope Benedict XVI about the apocalyptic dimension of St. Faustina's mission:

> About 80 years ago, Faustina Kowalska, the Polish nun canonized by John Paul II, heard Jesus say in a vision, "You will prepare the world for my final coming." Are we obliged to believe that?[193]

Here's the Pope's response:

> If one took [Jesus' words to Faustina] in a chrono-logical sense, as an injunction to get ready, as it were, immediately for the Second Coming, it would be false. But it is correct if one understands it in the spiritual sense ... as meaning that the Lord is always the One who comes and that we are always also preparing ourselves for his definitive coming, precisely when we go out to meet his mercy and allow ourselves to be formed by him. By letting ourselves be formed by God's gift of mercy as a force to counteract the mercilessness of the world, then we prepare, as it were, for his own coming in person and for his mercy.[194]

I think the key lines in the Pope's answer are "allow ourselves to be formed by him" and "letting ourselves be formed by God's gift of mercy." But what does it mean to "allow" someone to form us? More concretely, what does it mean to "allow" Jesus to form us by his "gift of mercy"? It means that we're to trust him, to have faith in him. So, when we trust in Jesus, when we say, "Jesus, I trust in you," when we are not afraid to let Jesus form us, then what does he do? How does he form us? More specifically, how does he *transform* us?

The Christian life is really about transformation. Specifically, Jesus transforms us, through the power of the Spirit, *into himself*, making us into members of his very Body. This transformation is an "already-but-not-yet process" that begins in Baptism, is nourished by the other Sacraments — especially the Eucharist — and is deepened through living a life of faith. Of course, this life of faith itself is nourished by personal prayer and devotion, is enriched by entrusting ourselves to the care of the Mother of God, and blossoms into love of God and neighbor.

So, in short, we prepare for the coming of the Lord by trusting in Jesus, by allowing him to transform us into himself, and by living a sacramental life of faith. Alright, but now here's an amazing thought: In a sense, *our transformation in Christ IS the coming of the Lord*. In the remainder of what follows, let's reflect on what this means, beginning by turning our attention to our final end.

The final end of the Christian life, our goal, the destination of our journey is communion with the Trinity.[195] We get there by going with Christ, to the Father, in the Spirit by being *transformed into Christ*. In other words, we enter into the Trinity by *becoming* one of its three members: the Son, the Word who became incarnate in Jesus Christ. Of course, there's a nuance to all this: We become Christ *as members of his Mystical Body*; we do not become the divine head of the Body, who is Jesus Christ himself.

Alright, so, in a sense, this is how the Lord comes again: *when his Body goes to him*, when we "form that perfect man who is Christ come to full stature" (Eph 4:13), when God will bring "all things in the heavens and on earth into one under Christ's headship" (Eph 1:10), when God becomes "all in all" (1 Cor 15:28).

To help us understand this coming of the Lord as including *our going to him*, let's read a passage from the beginning of the Acts of the Apostles, right after Jesus ascended into heaven:

> [Jesus] was lifted up, and a cloud took him out of their sight. And while they were gazing into heaven as he went, behold, two men stood by them in white robes, and said, "Men of Galilee, why do you stand looking into heaven? This Jesus, who was taken up from you into heaven, will come in the same way as you saw him go into heaven" (1:9-11).

That last line is most telling. Jesus "will come in the same way as you saw him go into heaven." On its surface, that's kind of a strange thought. Jesus will *come* again in the same way they saw him *go* to heaven. I think what this is saying is that part of how Jesus *comes* again is when his Body *goes* to him. Specifically, it's when his Body goes to him in the same way that he went, namely, by being "lifted up." I suggest that our being "lifted up" is not only the resurrection of our bodies at the end of time but also our ongoing transformation in Christ and that all this is included in the mystery of how the Lord will come. At least one theologian expresses a similar idea

> Instead of imagining [the Lord's] coming in glory as a kind of space travel, the reversal of what happened at the Ascension, we rather understand it as our transformation. The change will take place in us, not in him. The disproportion between our state and his will disappear, when the Spirit transforms this lowly body of ours into the likeness of his glorified body (Phil 3:21). Then we will become his members in the full sense of the word, the extension of his glorified personal body. As a result, we will then see Christ as he is in his glory, dwelling in him and he in us; and through Christ, with Christ, and in Christ, we will see the Father face to face and will recognize him as our Father.[196]

Like so much of our Christian life, we're dealing here with an "already-but-not-yet" reality. We will be "lifted up" at the resurrection of our bodies. But, again, in a sense, we are *already being lifted up* as we're transformed into Christ in this life. Thus, we could say that the more we trust in Jesus and allow him to transform us, the more we already are being lifted up, which hastens and even helps bring about the "coming of Christ," which seems to include *our going to him.*[197]

*T*HE *F*INAL *C*OMING *I*S *ABOUT* *B*ECOMING *S*AINTS. This brings us back to the relatively optimistic apocalyptic messages contained in St. Faustina's *Diary*. In the end, it's not about fear but *trust*. It's about trusting Jesus to transform us into himself. It's as if Jesus were saying to us, "Today I want to work great miracles of mercy. I want to transform you into myself quickly and relatively easily. You just have to let me do it." When, as Pope Benedict put it, "We allow ourselves to be formed" and start "letting ourselves be formed" by Jesus in this time of mercy, he does so. We just need to get out of his way. On this point, consider the following passage of St. Faustina:

> O God, one in the Holy Trinity, I want to love You as no human soul has ever loved You before; and although I am utterly miserable and small, I have, nevertheless, cast the anchor of my trust deep down into the abyss of Your mercy. ... In spite of my great misery I fear nothing, but hope to sing You a hymn of glory forever. Let no soul, even the most miserable, fall prey to doubt; for, as long as one is alive, each one can become a great saint, so great is the power of God's grace. It remains only for us not to oppose God's action.[198]

This idea of "becoming a saint" is really what our transformation into Christ is all about. And to get there, we just need to allow him to do it. Like Faustina, we need to tell the Lord, "I have ... cast the anchor of my trust deep down into the abyss of

Your mercy." We need to say, "In spite of my great misery I fear nothing." We need to get out of the way and let him do it, for "it remains only for us not to oppose God's action."

So, preparing the world for the Lord's final coming is really about becoming saints ourselves and helping others to become saints, too. And in this time of mercy, it's easier than ever before to become a saint! For, in these end times, God has saved his best miracles for last. He wants to take the weakest of souls and form them into the greatest of saints. But what does Jesus need to work miracles? He needs our faith. He needs our trust. That is why this end-times message is optimistic. It's not about fear but about trust, a trust that allows God's superabundant mercy in this time of mercy to transform us more deeply into Christ, which hastens the process of *his coming* as *we go to him* in holiness.

And while I haven't mentioned her yet in this appendix, we can't close without considering Mary's role in all this.

Mary is leading the way in this end time of mercy. As we learned in this book, it's her role to bring souls to trust in God's mercy. And she does this best when we consecrate ourselves to Jesus through her, which happens to be the "surest, easiest, shortest, and the most perfect means" to becoming a saint.[199] As St. Maximilian Kolbe taught, she is the instrument of mercy in God's hands, and she wants us to then be instruments of mercy in her immaculate hands.[200] This is the way, Kolbe was convinced, of winning the whole world for God as quickly as possible. And what does it mean to win the whole world for God but to bring it back to him by converting the world? In this time of mercy, within the context of the sacramental life of the Church, Mary and Mercy give us the quickest, easiest, and surest way. These powerful spiritual weapons help us prepare not only ourselves but the whole world for the Lord's *final coming* by helping the world to *go to him* in holiness.

[See the next appendix to learn how to help prepare the world for the Lord's final coming through Marian consecration and Divine Mercy.]

APPENDIX TWO

The Marian Missionaries of Divine Mercy

Identity, Spirituality, Mission

Outline

SECTION 1:
Identity

FIRST MOVEMENT: MARIAN CONSECRATION
SECOND MOVEMENT: DIVINE MERCY
MARIAN MISSIONARIES AS A UNIFYING PARTICIPATION
MEMBERSHIP AND LEVELS OF PARTICIPATION
SPIRITUALITY OF THE MARIAN MISSIONARIES

SECTION 2:
Level One Participation (MM-1)

COMMUNITY
PRAYER
FORMATION
SERVICE

SECTION 3:
Level Two Participation (MM-2)

SPIRITUAL SUPPORT
MATERIAL SUPPORT

SECTION 4:
Level Three Participation (MM-3)

APOSTOLATES
PARTNERS
SUPPORT TEAM

Identity

The Marian Missionaries of Divine Mercy (MMDM) is a unifying participation in two broad apostolic movements that aim to bring the whole world to God and prepare it for the Lord's final coming. [See previous appendix to learn more about this aim.]

*F*IRST *MOVEMENT: MARIAN CONSECRATION.* The first movement, Marian consecration, was pioneered by St. Louis de Montfort. De Montfort believed this movement would play a critical role in the "latter times," saying, "It was through Mary that the salvation of the world was begun, and it is through Mary that it must be consummated."[201] He stated that Mary will form the "apostles of the latter times," those who take the "surest, easiest, shortest, and most perfect" path to Christ,[202] which is Marian consecration.

Saint Maximilian Kolbe intensified the Marian apostolic thrust of de Montfort, organizing the consecration movement into a worldwide army for Mary Immaculate. The goal of his "Militia Immaculata," as he called it, is none other than to win the whole world for God under the generalship of Mary Immaculate (through the consecration) as quickly as possible. Kolbe's bold vision came from his twofold conviction that (1) the conversion of the world will come through the formation of great saints and that (2) through Marian consecration, "We can become great saints, and what is more, in an easy way."[203]

*S*ECOND *MOVEMENT: DIVINE MERCY.* Called "the largest grassroots movement in the history of the Catholic Church,"[204] the worldwide apostolic movement of Divine Mercy began with St. Faustina Kowalska and received powerful impetus from St. John Paul II and subsequent popes. At its heart, this movement, like the Marian consecration movement, has to do with the "end times." For example, the Lord told Faustina that "the spark that will prepare the world for My final coming" will come from Poland.[205] John Paul later described this as a "binding promise" from the Lord and identified the spark and subsequent fire as Divine Mercy.[206] To spread this fire,

St. Faustina envisioned a vast apostolic movement, a "work," that would be open to everyone.

At first, St. Faustina simply envisioned this work as the founding of a new religious congregation — specifically, a convent of sisters. With time, however, through subsequent revelations from Jesus, Faustina came to understand this "congregation" in a broader sense. Sister Maria Elzbieta Siepak, a member of St. Faustina's own religious community, the Sisters of Our Lady of Mercy, describes it as follows:

> The Apostolic Movement of the Divine Mercy as defined by the Lord Jesus, is as it were a newly summoned congregation, a new "calling" of the people of God who at this phase in history are to fulfill a goal set up by God as well as acquit themselves of certain precisely defined tasks, consisting in the revival of religious life, the proclamation of the mystery of the mercy of God, and entreating it for the whole world.[207]

So, this new work, what Sr. Siepak refers to as the "Apostolic Movement of Divine Mercy," is a calling by Jesus to all the people of God. In other words, he's inviting not just religious sisters and brothers, not just priests, but all the faithful, including laypeople, to invoke God's mercy, put mercy into action, and thereby prepare the world for his final coming.[208]

It is interesting to note that immediately following the above explanation of the "congregation" in her *Diary*, Faustina asks the Lord how he can tolerate so many sins and crimes in our world without punishing it. The Lord responds that he is giving us a "time of mercy" but says "woe" to us if we do not recognize our time of visitation.[209]

This concept of the "time of mercy," which is followed by the terrible day of justice, helps explain the urgent tone that accompanies the Apostolic Movement of Divine Mercy. As St. Faustina herself put it, "God's floodgates have been opened for us. Let us want to take advantage of them before the day of God's justice arrives. And that will be a dreadful day!"[210]

The idea that *now* is a special "time of mercy" comes not only from the mystic, St. Faustina. It's also something emphasized and endorsed by modern popes. For instance, St. John Paul II and Pope Francis, following the principle of Sacred Scripture that "where sin abounded, grace abounded all the more" (Rom 5:20) and reading the signs of our unprecedentedly perilous times, have determined that God's grace is truly abounding all the more *today*. In other words, they proclaim to the whole Church that *now* is the time of mercy.[211]

MARIAN MISSIONARIES AS A UNIFYING PARTICIPATION. The Marian Missionaries of Divine Mercy is a unifying participation in the two apostolic movements just presented: Marian consecration and Divine Mercy. Inspired by the teaching and example of St. John Paul II, the Marian Missionaries believe that in this "time of mercy," the message of Divine Mercy and Marian consecration are the two most effective God-given "force multipliers" to bring about the greatest possible apostolic fruitfulness and best prepare the world for the Lord's final coming. (Of course, these two force multipliers are not a substitute for or in competition with the sacramental and liturgical life of the Church. Rather, they derive from it and direct people to it. Also, of course, we do not know the day or the hour of the Lord's final coming.)

Until the Marian Missionaries of Divine Mercy, it seems there has been no other organization that so exclusively and explicitly unifies these two great apostolic movements by incorporating them into a single mission.[212] For example, some groups, such as the Militia Immaculata, primarily focus on Marian consecration (and not on Divine Mercy). Other groups, such as the Eucharistic Apostles of The Divine Mercy, primarily focus on Divine Mercy (and not on Marian consecration). Yet, Marian consecration and Divine Mercy can both become a primary focus and be unified into a single mission.

Such unification of the two movements is possible for two main reasons: (1) it is Mary who, through the consecration, best forms us into saints by bringing us to trust in and accept

Divine Mercy, as St. John Paul II taught;[213] and (2) because both missions focus on the "end times" with the goal of preparing the world for the Lord's final coming through winning the whole world for God.[214]

In view of the organic connection between Marian consecration and Divine Mercy and in light of the present time of mercy, the Marian Missionaries of Divine Mercy have adopted the following mission statement:

> *In the present "time of mercy," the Marian Missionaries of Divine Mercy, inspired by St. John Paul II, consciously and deliberately aim to win the whole world for God (prepare the world for the Lord's final coming) as quickly as possible, especially through the two powerful spiritual weapons of Marian consecration and Divine Mercy.*

*M*EMBERSHIP AND LEVELS OF PARTICIPATION. The door of membership into the Marian Missionaries is open to all: Bishops, priests, religious, and laity. Indeed, anyone who embraces the Marian Missionary spirituality (see next section) and mission (see mission statement above) can be an official Marian Missionary of Divine Mercy. Having said that, each member falls under one or two of the following three categories or levels of participation, each level containing its own contribution to the mission.

- *Level 1* – Missionaries in an intensive, yearlong commitment to the spirituality and mission.

- *Level 2* – Missionaries who give spiritual and/or material support to the mission.

- *Level 3* – Missionaries who intentionally give themselves to the mission through service, special projects, various apostolic works, and administrative support.

[For a fuller description of these three levels, see the sections that follow.]

SPIRITUALITY OF THE MARIAN MISSIONARIES. The heart of Marian Missionary spirituality is the encounter with Jesus Christ, the Divine Mercy, an encounter that brings the "joy of the Gospel"[215] into the lives of the Marian Missionaries and those they serve.

To foster this encounter with Divine Mercy, each Marian Missionary seeks to overcome his lack of trust in God's goodness and the "distorted image" of God that are results of original sin.[216] He does this especially in two ways: (1) by fostering a deep, filial Marian devotion,[217] knowing that Mary effectively obtains for us the grace to understand, accept, and trust in God's mercy; (2) by studying and living the Divine Mercy message and devotion, especially by keeping before his eyes the Image of Divine Mercy, which serves as a powerful reminder of the true face of our infinitely merciful God.

By striving to turn away from sin while coming to know, accept, and trust in God's tender mercy, Marian Missionaries become filled with the joy of the Gospel, which they generously share with others as they give testimony to the goodness, love, and mercy of God.

The following prayer expresses the spirituality at the heart of the Marian Missionaries, a prayer that all Marian Missionaries are encouraged to recite daily:

MMDM Daily Prayer

Good and gracious Father in heaven, in this time of great mercy, please grant to us Marian Missionaries of Divine Mercy the grace to understand, accept, and trust in the love and mercy pouring forth from the Heart of your Son, Jesus.

Dear Mary, our Mother, please keep us under this torrent of Grace that it may make us overflow with the joy of the Gospel. Then, with haste, bring us to those who are lonely, sad, and suffering that they may share in our joy and meet the loving gaze of God.

Through this work, may we build up the Body of Christ and thus prepare the world for the coming of him who lives and reigns forever and ever. Amen.

St. John Paul II, pray for us.

Level-One Participation
(MM-1)

The Marian Missionaries Level One (MM-1) consists of a brotherhood of single men who give at least a yearlong commitment to God through the mission, living an ordered life of **community, prayer, formation**, and **service**. Their specific contribution to the mission is as follows.

*C*OMMUNITY. As a mission with a single goal, the MMDM is by its nature communal. The more intense communal life of the MM-1 serves as a powerful sign and witness to the larger MMDM community of its unity in mission. Moreover, this more intense communal life serves as a concrete, daily challenge to practice the works of mercy where it is often most difficult: at home with the people one lives with daily. Finally, MM-1 community life can be a deep source of the joy of the Gospel, because a daily encounter with Christ in his love and mercy comes not only through encounters with Jesus Christ, the Head of the Body, but also through the members of his Body. In other words, it's through their daily encounter with Divine Mercy in one another that they also experience the joy of the Gospel.

Mary Immaculate is the special mother of each Level-One Missionary, and she preserves the bond of unity among them, brings them closer to the love and mercy of her Son, and thereby, is a cause of their joy.

*P*RAYER. To meet its goal, the mission requires prayer. Level-One Missionaries commit themselves to prayer in a manner appropriate to those taking part in active ministry.[218] Daily Mass constitutes the center of the Missionaries' prayer life, and their norms of piety include daily meditation/adoration, morning and evening prayer, and spiritual reading. Their manner of prayer includes the following emphases:

- Daily, deliberate encounters with the love and mercy of the Heart of Jesus, through Mary, that fosters the joy of the Gospel.

- Intercessory prayer in accordance with the goal of the mission, namely, that under the generalship of Mary Immaculate, the whole world will come to know and experience the love and mercy of God and that God would "have mercy on us and on the whole world." This intercessory prayer includes prayer for fellow Marian Missionaries, benefactors, specific projects, and special intentions of the mission.[219]

- Discernment of one's state in life and/or personal vocation, because each MM-1 should be open to doing God's most perfect will in his life.

FORMATION. Generally, the MMDM mission requires people of prayer and holiness who have profoundly encountered the love and mercy of Christ through Mary and who are committed to bringing the joy of the Gospel to the world (as instruments of Divine Mercy in the hands of Mary Immaculate). Level-One Missionaries become such men through the process of their formation. Moreover, because the mission requires well-formed people to be Level-Three Missionaries (see below), Level-One Missionaries are automatically considered as candidates for Level Three upon completion of their year of service.

SERVICE. The MMDM mission requires not just words and prayer but action, specifically the works of mercy. Level-One Missionaries commit themselves to the works of mercy, especially where the need is greatest and most good can be done. Their more intense commitment to the works of mercy, thereby serves as a sign to the whole movement of the importance of putting mercy into action, especially to those in greatest need. Also, as instruments of Divine Mercy in the hands of Mary Immaculate and inspired by the words of Pope Francis in *Evangelii Gaudium*, they strive to bring the joy of the Gospel to everyone, that all might encounter the love and mercy of Christ.

Level-Two Participation

(MM-2)

The Marian Missionaries Level Two (MM-2) consists of all those who, embracing the MMDM spirituality and moved by the vision of the mission, seek to aid it through either spiritual or material support or both.

SPIRITUAL SUPPORT. Regarding spiritual support, such benefactors are encouraged to make a formal prayer commitment (not binding under pain of sin) according to the following three degrees:

- *First Degree*: Those who commit to praying the MMDM Daily Prayer. (See pages 213-214.)

- *Second Degree*: Those who, in addition to praying the Daily Prayer, commit to praying regularly (for example, daily or weekly) the Chaplet of Divine Mercy, Rosary, or other such prayer for the mission.

- *Third Degree*: Those who bear extraordinary suffering and who desire to offer it for the MMDM. Such Missionaries bear the honorary title "Friends from the Cross" and make the following offering:

Friends from the Cross Daily Offering

My Father, if it be possible, let this chalice of suffering pass from me; nevertheless, not as I will, but as you will. If you do not will it to pass, then I accept to drink of it with love, obedient to your will, and uniting it to the redemptive sufferings of your Son, Jesus.

Mary, please help me in this my suffering. Intercede with your Spouse, the Consoler, that he may be close to me, giving me strength to bear my cross with love.

Merciful Mother, I offer you all the merits of my suffering. I give you permission to use them in whatever way you will. May they be for God's greatest possible glory and the salvation of souls. Also, I ask you to remember my family and friends and the intentions I hold in the silence of my heart. [Pause to recall your intentions.]

Finally, dear mother, please remember the Marian Missionaries of Divine Mercy. Through your prayers, their efforts, and this suffering I offer you, may our work of Divine Mercy win the whole world for God as quickly as possible and thus prepare it for the final coming of your divine Son, Jesus. Amen.

MATERIAL SUPPORT. Regarding material support, such benefactors can make a one-time, occasional, or monthly donation. Extraordinary benefactors, material and/or spiritual, may also be invited for special MMDM events, such as formation retreats.

Level-Three Participation

(MM-3)

The Marian Missionaries Level Three (MM-3) consists of all those who embrace MMDM spirituality and intentionally give themselves to the mission through service, special projects, various apostolic works, or administrative support.

There are three concrete ways of participating in the mission as a Level- Three Missionary: (1) Apostolates, (2) Partners, and the (3) Support Team.

*A*POSTOLATES. The MMDM Apostolates are individuals or groups (excepting Level One) who embrace MMDM spirituality, are administered and supported by the MMDM Support Team, and intentionally give themselves to the mission through service, special projects, or various apostolic works.

*P*ARTNERS. The MMDM Partners are individuals or groups who work directly with the MMDM Support Team to spread Divine Mercy and/or Marian consecration. Those who do so formally while embracing the spirituality and mission are official Partners, while those who do not formally do so are unofficial Partners. (The vast majority of people who partici-pate as Level-Three Missionaries do so as Partners.)

*S*UPPORT TEAM. The MMDM Support Team is all those who administratively support and direct the MMDM organiza-tion and its mission.

If you feel called to something more hands-on to spread Marian consecration and Divine Mercy but can't give a year as a Level-One Missionary, there's still a place for you in Mary's army of Marian Missionaries. Contact the Marian Missionaries Support Team, tell them what's on your heart, and together we can explore the possibilities. (Call 844-221-8422, email info@ MarianMissionaries.org, or visit MarianMissionaries.org. Also, see the information pages at the end of this book.)

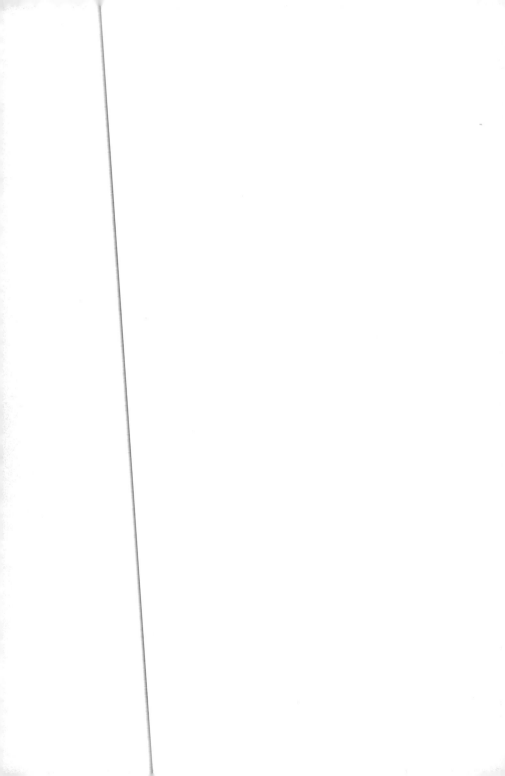

ENDNOTES

Endnotes

Introduction

[1] John Paul II, address at the Shrine of Merciful Love in Collevalenza, Italy, November 22, 1981.

[2] John Paul II, address to the Sisters of Our Lady of Mercy at the Shrine of the Divine Mercy in Krakow-Łagiewniki, Poland, June 7, 1997, 1.

[3] Benedict XVI, *Regina Caeli* address for Divine Mercy Sunday, April 23, 2006.

[4] Ibid.

[5] Francis, address to the priests of the Diocese of Rome, March 6, 2014.

Chapter 1: Regarding the First Greatest Story

[6] English translation of the *Catechism of the Catholic Church: Modifications from the Editio Typica* (Washington, D.C./Vatican: United States Catholic Conference, Inc./Libreria Editrice Vaticana, 1997), 397. Emphasis added.

[7] What exactly does personal trust in the Lord involve? Pope Benedict XVI gave us a clue when he addressed the sick at the Shrine of Divine Mercy in Krakow-Łagiewniki, Poland, on May 27, 2006. He told them:

> You who say in the silence: "Jesus, I trust in you" teach us that there is no faith more profound, no hope more alive, and no love more ardent than the faith, hope, and love of a person who in the midst of suffering places himself securely in God's hands.

Pope Benedict is stressing that when we personally trust in Jesus in a difficult situation such as suffering from a sickness, our trust is not passive. Rather, it is a concrete action that involves our exercise of all three of the theological virtues — faith, hope, and love. Our faith becomes "more profound." Our hope becomes "more alive." Our love becomes "more ardent." Through this spiritual action — in faith, hope, and love — we place ourselves "securely in God's hands." We trust in him. (This endnote was drawn from *Pope Benedict's Divine Mercy Mandate* by David Came [Stockbridge: Marian Press, 2009], pp. 68-69.)

[8] *Catechism*, 399. Emphasis added.

[9] John Paul II, encyclical letter *Dives in Misericordia*, November 13, 1980, 4. The cited text then continues, offering specific examples of when Israel appealed to the God of mercy:

> Among the events and texts of greater importance, one may recall: the beginning of the history of the Judges (Jgs 3:7-9), the prayer of Solomon at the inauguration of the Temple (1 Kgs 8:22-53), part of the prophetic work of Micah (Mi 7:18-20), the consoling assurances given by Isaiah (Is 1:18; 51:4-16), the cry of the Jews in exile (Bar 2:11-3 8), and the renewal of the covenant after the return from exile (Neh 9).

[10] See Nm 14:18; 2 Chr 30:9; Neh 9:17; Ps 85; Wis 15:1; Sir 2:11; Jl 2:13.

[11] John Paul II, encyclical letter, *Dives in Misericordia*, 4.

[12] Translation of "benefits" as his "forgivings." See Bonaventura Rinaldi, CP, *Maria di Nazareth Madre Della Chiesa: L'amore e la tenerezza essenza di Dio e di Maria* (Milan: Massimo Press, 1967), p. 91.

[13] Of course, the First Greatest Story, Biblical Salvation History, includes some first century Church history. The Second Greatest Story is certainly not greater than that! But because that relatively short part of Church history is also part of the First Greatest Story, I'm not including it in my assessment of what I'm calling "the greatest story in Church history."

Chapter 2: God's School of Trust in Church History

[14] Jesus' words to St. Margaret Mary, cited in Timothy O'Donnell, STD, *Heart of the Redeemer: An Apologia for the Contemporary and Perennial Value of the Devotion to the Sacred Heart of Jesus* (San Francisco: Ignatius Press, 1989), p. 135.

[15] Ibid., p. 131.

[16] See Procé de l'Ordinaire, 1910-11 (The Bishop's Process, 1910-11), p. 1513 and *St. Thérèse of Lisieux: By Those Who Knew Her*, ed. and trans. Christopher O'Mahony (Dublin: Veritas Publications, 1995), p. 42.

[17] See *With Empty Hands: The Message of St. Thérèse of Lisieux*, Conrad de Meester, trans. Mary Saymour (Washington, D.C.: ICS Publications, 2002), pp. 45-47.

[18] *Story of a Soul: The Autobiography of St. Thérèse of Lisieux*. 3rd edition. trans. John Clarke, OCD (Washington, D.C.: ICS Publications, 1996), p. 174.

[19] Cardinal Shönborn's words to Fr. Stefan Reuffurth, OMV, related to author in the Spring of 1999.

[20] Pius XII, Message on the occasion of the consecration of the Basilica of Lisieux on July 11, 1954. (*Acta Apostolicae Sedis*, 46 [1954], pp. 404-408.)

[21] See Warren H. Carroll, *The Building of Christendom: A History of Christendom*, vol. 2 (Front Royal: Christendom College Press, 1987), pp. 425-426.

[22] Tertullian, *Apologeticus*, ch. 50.

Chapter 3: Amazing Moments in Polish History

[23] Cited in Norman Davies, *God's Playground: A History of Poland*, revised edition, Vol. II (New York: Columbia University Press, 2005), p. 7.

[24] Juliusz Slowacki, "Into the midst of riotous squabblers," trans. Sandra Celt, *Info Poland University at Buffalo*, accessed December 15, 2014, http://info-poland.buffalo.edu/web/arts_culture/literature/poetry/slowacki/poems/midst.shtml.

[25] Fr. Seraphim Michalenko, MIC, a priest in my community, shared that he was in Wawel Cathedral in Krakow for John Paul II's first visit

to Poland. As the Pope entered the Cathedral, the choir was singing Słowacki's poem. Then, when he arrived at the throne or cathedra, which was a few yards from Słowacki's tomb, the choir sang the verse "and the angels will prepare his throne."

26 See Christopher Hitchens, "Why the suicide killers chose September 11," *The Guardian*, October 3, 2001, accessed December 15, 2014, http://www.theguardian.com/world/2001/oct/03/september11.usa2. While he gets the date wrong for the Christian victory at the Battle of Vienna — he erroneously writes that it occurred on September 11 — he makes the point: "[I]n the Islamic world, and especially among extremists, [the date of Christian victory] is remembered as a humiliation in itself and a prelude to later ones."

27 Cited in Norman Davies, *God's Playground: A History of Poland*, Revised Edition, Vol. I (New York: Columbia University Press, 2005), p. 366.

28 "Letter from King Sobieski to his Wife." University of Gdansk, Department of Cultural Studies. Faculty of Philology. Retrieved August 4, 2011.

29 Cited in Davies, Vol. I, p. 386.

30 Cited in Davies, Vol. II, p. 290.

31 Adrian Hyde-Price, *Germany and European Order* (Manchester: Manchester University Press, 2001), p. 75.

32 Cited in Davies, Vol. II, p, 294.

33 Ibid., p. 297.

34 In acknowledgment of Pope John Paul II's support for Solidarity, Lech Wałesa signed the 1980 Gdansk Agreement between the Solidarity labor movement and Poland's Communist government using a huge, souvenir-type pen that bore a large image of the Pope.

Chapter 4: The Story Begins

35 *Diary of St. Maria Faustina Kowalska: Divine Mercy In My Soul* (Stockbridge: Marian Press, 1987), 1588.

36 Pope Benedict XVI as Joseph Cardinal Ratzinger describes a prophet:

What is a prophet? A prophet is not a soothsayer; the essential element of the prophet is not the prediction of future events. The prophet is someone who tells the truth on the strength of his contact with God — the truth for today, which also, naturally, sheds light on the future. It is not a question of foretelling the future in detail, but of rendering the truth of God present at this moment in time and of pointing us in the right direction (Niels Christian Hvidt, *Christian Prophesy: The Post Bibical Tradition* [Oxford: Oxford University Press, 2007], pp. vii).

Clearly, this description fits the saints that follow in the text.

[37] *Diary,* 150. Emphasis added. While one could say that St. Thérèse's appearance to St. Faustina was "only a dream," Faustina herself added that three days later, all her difficulties got worked out, as Thérèse said they would.

[38] Ibid., 281.

[39] Ibid., 429.

[40] See page 197.

[41] *Diary,* 1732.

[42] Regarding St. Faustina's prediction of World War II, her spiritual director, Blessed Fr. Michael Sopocko, offered the following sworn testimony during her beatification process:

> [Sister Faustina] also foretold the destruction that would afflict the Fatherland (Poland), that there would come most sorrowful times. She saw her fellow citizens expelled to the East and to the West.
>
> She wrote in her *Diary* that Jesus himself said he was about to destroy one of the most beautiful cities of our country like Sodom on account of the crimes committed there.
>
> Having read these things in her *Diary,* I asked her what this prophecy meant. She answered confirming the things she wrote, and, responding to a further question of mine: On account of what sins God would inflict these punishments, she replied, "especially on account of the slaughter of infants not yet born, as the most grievous crime of all" (*Beatificationis et canonizationis servae dei Faustinae Kowalska Instituti Sororum B.M.V. a Misericordia [1905-1938]: Summarium,* p. 95, 25.1).

[43] *Diary,* 1379.

[44] *The Letters of St. Faustina,* trans. Piotr Mizia (Krakow: "Misericordia" Publications, 2006), pp. 107-108.

[45] The information that follows regarding Fr. Joseph Jarzebowski, MIC, and Divine Mercy was related to the author by Fr. Kazimierz Chwalek, MIC, who provided oral history, and Fr. Seraphim Michalenko, MIC, who knew Fr. Jarzebowski personally and shared several documents and letters describing the events that follow.

[46] This whole story about St. John XXIII was related to me by Fr. Seraphim Michalenko, MIC, who heard it from Fr. Carlo Vivaldelli in Trent, who had been the seminary classmate of the secretary of St. John XXIII. The secretary had witnessed it when it happened, knew that Fr. Vivaldelli was deeply devoted to Divine Mercy, and so called Fr. Vivaldelli immediately after witnessing this event.

[47] *Acta Apostolicae Sedis,* April, 25, 1959 (Ser. III, v. I-N. 5). To learn other ways that Pope John XXIII was involved with Divine Mercy, see "Trifecta of Mercy: Three Mercy Popes will come together in the

'winner's circle of grace' this Mercy Sunday" by Fr. Joseph, MIC, in *Marian Helper* magazine (Spring 2014), pp. 14-16.

[48] The Marian Fathers, who had printed thousands of Divine Mercy holy cards, pamphlets, and images had to lock them up after the 1959 Notification. The Marians' Superior General warned that if they gave out even one holy card there would be grievous consequences. Eventually, during the ban, these prohibited materials were buried on Eden Hill in Stockbridge, Massachusetts.

[49] *Diary*, 378. Another passage from the *Diary* of St. Faustina refers to the attacks against the work of mercy:

> The glory of the Divine Mercy is resounding, even now, in spite of the efforts of its enemies and of Satan himself, who has a great hatred for God's mercy. This work will snatch a great number of souls from him, and that is why the spirit of darkness sometimes tempts good people violently, so that they may hinder the work. But I have clearly seen that the will of God is already being carried out, and that it will be accomplished to the very last detail. The enemy's greatest efforts will not thwart the smallest detail of what the Lord has decreed. No matter if there are times when the work seems to be completely destroyed; it is then that the work is being all the more consolidated (1659).

[50] Fr. Sopocko died in 1975, three years before the ban was lifted. Regarding the Lord's love for this priest who poured himself out for the message of Divine Mercy, we can read the following words of Jesus to St. Faustina:

> **He is a priest after My own Heart; his efforts are pleasing to Me. ... Through him it pleased Me to proclaim the worship of My mercy. And through this work of mercy more souls will come close to Me than otherwise would have, even if he had kept giving absolution day and night for the rest of his life, because by so doing, he would have labored only for as long as he lived; whereas, thanks to this work of mercy, he will be laboring till the end of the world (1256).**

[51] Adam Boniecki, MIC, *The Making of the Pope of the Millennium: Kalendarium of the Life of Karol Wojtyła*, trans. Thaddeus Mirecki (Stockbridge: Marian Press, 2000), p. 254.
[52] Ibid., p. 253.
[53] Related by Andrew Cardinal Deskur to Fr. Seraphim Michalenko, MIC.
[54] Cited in *Diary*, p. 666. Also, on July 12, 1979, in response to the Superior General of the Congregation of Marian Fathers of the Immaculate Conception, who, in the name of the Provincial Superior of the

American Province of St. Stanislaus Kostka of said Congregation, had asked for an authoritative explanation of the scope of the text in the "Notification" of 1978, rescinding the prohibitions to spread the devotion to The Divine Mercy proposed by Sister Faustina Kowalska, the Prefect of the Sacred Congregation for the Doctrine of the Faith replied:

> In reference to that matter (raised in the letter of Father General) I have the honor of informing you that with the new "Notification" (A.A.S., 30 June 1978, p. 350), arrived at in the light of original documentation examined also by the careful informative intervention of the then Archbishop of Cracow, Card. Karol Wojtyła, it was the intention of the Holy See to revoke the prohibition contained in the preceding "Notification" of 1959 (A.A.S., 1959, p. 271), in virtue of which it is understood that there no longer exists, on the part of this S. Congregation, any impediment to the spreading of the devotion to The Divine Mercy in the authentic forms proposed by the Religious Sister mentioned above [The Servant of God Sister Faustina Kowalska] (cited in Ibid, p. 667).

Chapter 5: Mercy Pope

55 John Paul II, remarks on arrival at Fatima, May 12, 1982, in *Insegnamenti di Giovanni Paulo II, 1982*.
56 George Weigel, *Witness to Hope: The Biography of Pope John Paul II* (New York: HarperCollins, 1999), p. 388.
57 Ibid., p. 387.
58 *Dives in Misericordia*, 15.
59 Ibid.
60 Ibid., 7.
61 Ibid.
62 There is some interesting background to this remarkable statement: After the assassination attempt, as Pope John Paul II recovered in the summer and fall of 1981, he asked to have read to him *both the Fatima message and Faustina's Diary*. He then made his first public visit outside of Rome following his lengthy recuperation on November 22, 1981, the feast of Christ the King, to the Shrine of Merciful Love in Collevalenza near Todi, Italy. He choose to go there because an international congress was being held on his encyclical *Dives in Misericordia* (*Rich in Mercy*) one year after its publication. Significantly, he said on that occasion:

> A year ago I published the encyclical *Dives in Misericordia*. This circumstance made me come to the Shrine of Merciful Love today. By my presence I wish to reconfirm, in a way, the message of that encyclical. I wish to read it again and deliver it again.

It's fascinating to think that John Paul seems never again to have publicly read or delivered any of his other encyclicals.

[63] For a fuller treatment of the Great Jubilee 2000, see chapters 5-6 in George Weigel, *The End and the Beginning: Pope John Paul II — The Victory of Freedom, the Last Years, the Legacy* (New York: Image Books, 2010).

[64] "Testament of the Holy Father John Paul II," *Libreria Editrice Vaticana*, accessed December 15, 2014, http://www.vatican.va/gpII/documents/testamento-jp-ii_20050407_en.html. It is interesting to note that in this testament, Pope John Paul II highlights Mary's role during Poland's millennial time of grace while describing Cardinal Wyszynski's role in preparing Poland for it:

> I witnessed [Wyszynski's] mission, his total confidence, his struggles and his triumph. "When victory is won, it will be a victory through Mary": The Primate of the Millennium was fond of repeating these words of his Predecessor, Cardinal August Hlond.

Surely John Paul II had great confidence in Mary's powerful intercession as he would lead the Church to the triumph of her Immaculate Heart, which, as we'll see, is also the triumph of Divine Mercy.

[65] John Paul II, apostolic letter *Tertio Millennio Adveniente*, November 10, 1994, 18. See also Pope John Paul II's Bull of Indiction of the Great Jubilee of the Year 2000, *Incarnationis Mysterium*, November 29, 1998, 2.

[66] See Ibid., 11-14

[67] During the Great Jubilee Year, the Church offered a superabundance of opportunities to receive indulgences (see the Bull of Indiction, *Incarnationis Mysterium*), and the response was overwhelming. For instance, millions of pilgrims came to Rome during the Jubilee Year to pass through the Holy Door — which was symbolically wider than those of previous Jubilees — and receive the Jubilee indulgence. Also, the number of confessions, conversions, and vocations exploded. Finally, the Church herself, on March 12, 2000, the First Sunday of Lent, held a "Day of Pardon," which involved a profound examination of conscience of past sins and the petition of the Lord's merciful forgiveness. In this way, the Church specially prepared herself for Easter and the great blessing of Divine Mercy Sunday, 2000.

[68] John Paul II, homily for the canonization of Sr. Maria Faustina Kowalska, April 30, 2000, 7.

[69] Ibid., 8.

[70] *Diary*, 1044-1049.

[71] Ibid., 341.

[72] These words of Pope John Paul II were related by Dr. Fuster to Fr. Seraphim Michalenko, MIC.

[73] John Paul II, homily at the dedication of the Shrine of Divine Mercy in Krakow-Lagiewniki, Poland, August 17, 2002.

[74] *Diary*, 1689.

[75] In the summer of 2005, as a seminarian, I attended an international retreat for priests and their pastoral teams led by Cardinal Shönborn at the Shrine of Divine Mercy in Krakow-Lagiewniki, Poland. It was during that retreat that the Cardinal shared about the impact Pope John Paul II's words made on him during the 2002 homily of dedication of the Shrine. It was from that retreat that the inspiration and resolution came to begin the World Apostolic Congresses on Mercy, which were enthusiastically endorsed by Pope Benedict XVI and attended by Cardinal Jorge Bergolio, the future Pope Francis.

[76] Benedict XVI, *Regina Caeli* address for Divine Mercy Sunday, April 23, 2006.

[77] John Paul II, homily at the dedication of the Shrine of Divine Mercy in Krakow-Lagiewniki, Poland, August 17, 2002, 5.

[78] *Diary*, 1732.

[79] John Paul II, homily at the beatification of four Servants of God of the Polish nation in Krakow, Poland, August 18, 2002, 3.

[80] See Cardinal Stanislaw Dziwisz, *A Life with Karol: My Forty-Year friendship with the Man Who Became Pope*, trans. Adrian Walker (New York: Doubleday, 2007), p. 258.

[81] Here is a more complete citation: "The Servant of God Pope John Paul II ... wanted the Sunday after Easter to be dedicated in a special way to Divine Mercy, and providence disposed that he should die precisely on the vigil of that day in the arms of Divine Mercy" (Benedict XVI, *Regina Caeli* address for Divine Mercy Sunday, April 23, 2006).

[82] Regarding Divine Mercy Sunday, not only did John Paul II die on the vigil of that feast, but he was beatified (in 2011) and then canonized (in 2014) on the feast itself. In fact, it's almost as if Divine Providence adds an exclamation point to his legacy of mercy when we learn that the miracle recognized for his canonization occurred on the very day of his beatification, which was, of course, Divine Mercy Sunday!

[83] This information was given by a Polish priest, Msgr. Jarek Cielecki, director of Rome's Vatican News Service and close friend of Pope John Paul II.

[84] *Regina Caeli* message for Divine Mercy Sunday, prepared by Pope John Paul II, but delivered as the homily for the Mass for the repose of his soul on April 3, 2005.

[85] Compiled from various papal addresses of John Paul II: (1) address at the Shrine of Divine Mercy, Krakow, Poland, June 7, 1997, 1; (2) *Regina Caeli* address, Rome, April 10, 1994, 2 ; (3) homily at the dedication of the Shrine of Divine Mercy in Krakow-Lagiewniki, Poland, August 17, 2002, 1; (4) Ibid., 5.

Chapter 6: Fatima

[86] Benedict XV, letter to Cardinal Pietro Gasparri, his Secretary of State, May 5, 1917. See next note for further citation information.

[87] Cited in Warren Carroll, *1917: Red Banners, White Mantle* (Front Royal, VA: Christendom Press, 1981), p. 71.

[88] Ibid., p. 72.

[89] Like the later D-day invasion of Europe by the Allied Forces, perhaps Mary wanted to establish a beachhead of peace that would eventually conquer the continent.

[90] Sr. Mary Lucia dos Santos of the Immaculate Heart, *Fatima in Lucia's Own Words*, ed. Louis Kondor, SVD, trans. Dominican Nuns of Perpetual Rosary (Fatima: Postulation Centre, 1989), p. 104.

[91] St. Thérèse of Lisieux *General Correspondence Vol. I,* trans. John Clarke, OCD (Washington, D.C.: ICS Publications, 1982), p. 578.

[92] *Fatima in Lucia's Own Words*, pp. 104-105.

[93] Regarding the Five First Saturdays devotion, Jesus and Mary asked that on the first Saturdays of five consecutive months, we go to confession, receive Holy Communion, say a Rosary, and then meditate for fifteen minutes on the mysteries of the Rosary. This should all be done with the intention of making reparation to the Immaculate Heart of Mary for the countless sins and blasphemies that daily offend her. Our Lady promised that to those who would keep this devotion, she would assist them at the hour of their deaths with all the graces necessary for salvation. Jesus emphasized that this devotion should not just be made only once but again and again.

[94] Cited in Fr. Andrew Apostoli, CFR, *Fatima for Today: The Urgent Marian Message of Hope* (San Francisco: Ignatius Press, 2010). p. 170.

[95] "The Message of Fatima," Congregation for the Doctrine of the Faith, June 26, 2000, accessed December 27, 2014, http://www.vatican.va/roman_curia/congregations/cfaith/documents/rc_con_cfaith_doc_20000626_message-fatima_en.html.

[96] Ibid.

[97] *Fatima in Lucia's Own Words*, p. 161.

[98] Ibid., p. 168.

[99] Cited in Apostoli, pp. 129-130.

[100] Cited in Ibid., pp. 131-132.

[101] Cited in Ibid., pp. 133-134.

[102] Cited in Ibid., pp. 132-133.

[103] The remarkable video footage of Our Lady of Zeitoun, Egypt is readily available on the Internet. Simply search for "Our Lady of Zeitoun."

Chapter 7: Fatima and the Mercy Secret

[104] "The Message of Fatima," Congregation for the Doctrine of the Faith, June 26, 2000, accessed December 27, 2014, http://www.vatican.va/roman_curia/congregations/cfaith/documents/rc_con_cfaith_doc_20000626_message-fatima_en.html.

[105] Regarding psychics, palm readers, and the like, the *Catechism of the Catholic Church* warns:

> All forms of *divination* are to be rejected: recourse to Satan or demons, conjuring up the dead or other practices falsely supposed to "unveil" the future. Consulting horoscopes, astrology, palm reading, interpretation of omens and lots, the phenomena of clairvoyance, and recourse to mediums all conceal a desire for power over time, history, and, in the last analysis, other human beings, as well as a wish to conciliate hidden powers. They contradict the honor, respect, and loving fear that we owe to God alone (2116).

[106] See Apostoli for several examples, pp. 83-86.

[107] "The Message of Fatima," Congregation for the Doctrine of the Faith, June 26, 2000, accessed December 27, 2014, http://www.vatican.va/roman_curia/congregations/cfaith/documents/rc_con_cfaith_doc_20000626_message-fatima_en.html.

[108] Weigel, p. 413.

[109] Ibid., p. 412.

[110] This fact about the reading of the *Diary* was related to me by Fr. Seraphim Michalenko, MIC, who had heard it from Archbishop Deskur himself. The background as to how the Archbishop obtained the *Diary* (and the Pope's reaction) is interesting.

From the end of March to the beginning of April, 1981, Fr. Michalenko had gone on a pilgrimage to Poland and Rome with Bob and Maureen Digan and their son, Bobby. During the pilgrimage, Maureen experienced a miracle that would lead to the beatification of Sr. Faustina Kowalska. While in Rome, after the miracle had taken place, the first *Diary of St. Faustina* was published through the efforts of Fr. Michalenko. On the last day of the pilgrimage, Fr. Michalenko delivered the first copy to Archbishop Deskur, who playfully showed it to the Pope, saying, "I've got a copy of the *Diary of St. Faustina!*" The Pope then asked his longtime friend, "Where's my copy?" The Archbishop explained that the papal copy was being specially bound in white. The Pope responded that he wasn't worried about the cover. He just wanted his copy! About a month later, John Paul II was shot. By then, he still didn't have his copy of the *Diary*, so he asked Archbishop Deskur to come to the hospital and read his copy to him, which the Archbishop did.

[111] Dziwisz, p. 136.

[112] Ibid., p. 137.

[113] C.S. Lewis, *The Lion, the Witch and the Wardrobe* — Book Two in the Chronicles of Narnia (New York: HarperCollins, 1950), p. 156.

[114] Ibid., p. 142.

[115] Ibid., p. 163.

[116] Saint Thomas Aquinas, *Summa Theologiae*, III, q. 46, a. 3.

[117] I am grateful to my friend, Marian Press Editor, David Came, for the remarkable insights of the next four paragraphs, which come entirely from him and were composed by him. These insights are particularly meaningful because David Came, who is deeply devoted to St. John Paul II, suffers from the same disease as the Pope. Following the Holy Father's example, David has been soldiering on for the last several years, despite the debilitating effects of his Parkinson's. This is one of his last books as a full-time employee for Marian Press, and I'm grateful to him not only for these insights and his example but for his mentorship and the invaluable help he has given me with every one of my books thus far.

[118] See George Weigel, *The End and the Beginning: Pope John Paul II — The Victory of Freedom, the Last Years, the Legacy* (New York: Image Books, 2010), p. 369ff.

[119] *Fatima in Lucia's Own Words*, p. 62. Emphasis added.

[120] Cited in Apostoli, p. 161.

[121] Cited in Ibid., pp. 168-169.

[122] Cited in Ibid., p. 173.

[123] Ibid., p. 123.

[124] See endnote 110.

Chapter 8: World Consecration and the Triumph

[125] Address to the de Montfort Fathers, cited in St. Louis de Montfort, *True Devotion to Mary*, trans. Frederick W. Faber (Rockford, IL: TAN Books, 1985), p. vi.

[126] Ibid., 266.

[127] John Paul II, Act of Entrustment, May 13, 1982, 9.

[128] John Paul II, homily in Fatima, Portugal, May 13, 1982, 8.

[129] This phrase comes from John Paul's greeting to the English-speaking pilgrims at his first general audience in Rome after his return from Fatima (May, 1982), cited by Arthur Calkins in *Totus Tuus: John Paul II's Program of Marian Consecration and Entrustment* (Libertyville, IL: Academy of the Immaculate, 1992), p. 177. For the full text, see the next block citation in the book text.

[130] John Paul II, homily in Fatima, Portugal, May 13, 1982, 9.

[131] Act of Entrustment, May 13, 1982, 2.

[132] Ibid.

[133] John Paul II, general audience, greeting to the English-speaking pilgrims, May 19, 1982. Emphasis added.

[134] In May of 1982, Pope John Paul II traveled to Fatima, Portugal to give thanks to the mercy of God and Our Lady of Fatima for sparing his life the previous year. For the occasion, one of the bullets from Mehmet Ali Ağca's Browning 9-mm semiautomatic had been placed in the crown of Our Lady of Fatima's statue.

[135] Apostoli, p. 195.

[136] Cited in Ibid., p. 197.

[137] Conversation with Deacon Bob Ellis from the World Apostolate of Fatima.

[138] Cited in Apostoli, p. 104.
[139] John Laul II, Act of Entrustment, St. Peter's Square, Rome, March 25, 1984.
[140] Apostoli, p. 170.
[141] Again, see the examples provided in Apostoli, pp. 81-86.
[142] "The Remembrances of Twenty Cardinals" on the *30 Days* website, accessed December 20, 2014, http://www.30giorni.it/articoli_id_8513_l3.htm.

Chapter 9: Personal Consecration and the Triumph

[143] The "Miraculous Medal" is a sacramental that originates from an apparition of Mary to a French nun, St. Catherine of Laboré, that occurred on November 27, 1830. The front of the medal bears an image of Mary and the prayer, "O Mary, conceived without sin, pray for us who have recourse to thee." The back has an image of an "M" with a bar across it and a cross arising from the middle. Below the two columns of the "M" appear two hearts: The Sacred Heart and the Immaculate Heart. It's called the "Miraculous Medal" because countless people who have worn it with devotion have experienced great graces from God by means of Mary's powerful intercession.
[144] Roy H. Schoeman, *Salvation is from the Jews* (San Francisco: Ignatius Press, 2003), pp. 330-331. It is interesting to note the mercy theme in Ratisbonne's testimony of his life-changing mystical experience. For instance, he described Mary as "beautiful and full of mercy" and, describing himself, said "I could see into the depths of my frightful misery, from which infinite mercy had liberated me." *The Kolbe Reader: The Writings of St. Maximilian Kolbe, OFM Conv.*, ed. and commentary, Fr. Anselm W. Romb, OFM, Cap. (Libertyville, Ill.: Marytown Press, 2007), pp. 27-29.
[145] *True Devotion to Mary*, 55. See also 152-168.
[146] See *True Devotion to Mary*, 55-59, 114.
[147] *The Kolbe Reader*, p. 39.
[148] Ibid., pp. 148-149.
[149] Ibid., pp. 13-15.
[150] Ibid., pp. 93-94.
[151] Ibid., pp. 61-62.
[152] See, for example, *True Devotion to Mary*, 78-80, 85, 143. Here's one of the problematic lines: "... Our Lord, who is infinitely pure and hates infinitely the least stain of sin upon our souls, will not unite Himself to us, and will cast us out from His presence" (78).
[153] Mother Teresa's letter to the Missionaries of Charity family, 25th March 1993 © 2011 Missionaries of Charity Sisters, c/o Mother Teresa Center.
[154] Blessed Mother Teresa said, "If Our Lady had not been there with me that day, I never would have known what Jesus meant when he said, 'I thirst' ... " Recounted by Fr. Joseph Langford, MC, *Mother Teresa:*

In the Shadow of Our Lady (Huntington, Ind.: Our Sunday Visitor, 2007), p. 40.

[155] Mary's role leading us to Divine Mercy is directly related to her "co-redemptive role" at the Cross of Calvary, which we'll examine now.

Mary participated in the suffering of Christ more than anyone, and her suffering has the greatest redemptive role, after Christ. Of course, Mary is not the Redeemer, but God is pleased to include Mary (and all Christians) in the work of redemption, in which suffering united to love has a primary role. Indeed, the Lord invited Mary (and each of us) to unite her suffering with his in order to save souls: He invited her and us to be "co-redeemers," redeemers "with him," though in an entirely subordinate way to himself.

We approach the mystery of "co-redemption" when we reflect on some potentially puzzling words of St. Paul: "I rejoice in my sufferings for your sake, and in my flesh I complete what is lacking in the suffering of Christ for the sake of his body, the Church ... " (Col 1:24) How can St. Paul write that there's something "lacking" in the suffering of Christ? After all, Jesus' suffering is objectively enough to save everyone, and the graces of his suffering are available to all (objective redemption). In this sense, there's absolutely nothing lacking in his suffering. Yet there's a kind of "lack" in Christ's suffering in the sense that not everyone subjectively accepts his grace and mercy (subjective redemption). Moreover, there's also a lack in his suffering when people don't fully accept his grace and mercy, that is, when they do so halfheartedly and with reservations and conditions. It's precisely such situations where people reject or don't fully accept God's grace and mercy that our sufferings and prayers can come in to "compete what is lacking."

Now, because Mary suffered the most with Christ and in a uniquely privileged way, it is her special role to help us accept the graces and mercy of Christ more than any other. Again, she's not the Source of Mercy (which has to do with "objective redemption"), but rather, *she's the great instrument of Divine Mercy* leading people to the Source of Mercy (which has to do with "subjective redemption"). And while we're all called to lead people to God's mercy (as the text will go on to say), Mary does this in a supremely important way. For, indeed, her Heart was pierced with a sword of suffering at the foot of the Cross so many hearts would be laid bare and opened to God's mercy (see Lk 2:35). For, indeed, she is *the New Eve* who instead of leading us to a tree of death, as did the Old Eve, she leads us to the Tree of Life, the Cross. For, indeed, she is the Spouse of the Holy Spirit, whose hidden action prepares and moves hearts to receive the Savior and his Divine Mercy.

[156] Regarding this prayer of the Marian Missionaries, they also pray, "Mary, if we're not attentive enough to recognize who you want us to visit, then you bring them to us." And she does. (They have many amazing stories of her doing that as well.)

[157] Regarding God's justice and mercy, St. Thérèse of Lisieux writes:

To me [God] has granted His *infinite Mercy*, and *through it* I contemplate and adore the other divine perfections! All of these perfections appear to be resplendent *with love*; even His Justice (and perhaps this even more so than the others) seems to me clothed in *love*. What a sweet joy it is to think that God is *Just*, i.e., that He takes into account our weakness that He is perfectly aware of our fragile nature. What should I fear then? (*Story of a Soul*, p. 180).

158 *The Kolbe Reader*, commentary of the editor, p. 37.
159 Ibid., p. 159.
160 Ibid., p. 160.
161 Ibid., p. 154.
162 André Frossard, "*Forget Not Love*": *The Passion of Maximilian Kolbe*, trans. Cendrine Fontan (San Francisco: Ignatius Press), p. 50.
163 Regarding the consecration to Mary Immaculate as the source of renewal for his Order, Kolbe writes:

As for the purpose we pursue, one might indicate that among others the need for a rebirth of the Order. ... [I]t is really not helpful to make excuses ... and to say that our Order has grown old by now, and is therefore run down; for the spirit does not grow old. Only the falling away from one's ideal, on the one hand, and the lack of flexibility in adapting oneself to conditions and circumstances which constantly change, on the other hand, bring about a diminution of vitality, of life, a deterioration.

For the revival of the Order even the wisest prescriptions, sanctioned by the sternest of penalties, will not suffice. In this field supernatural grace is indispensable, the grace of sanctification for our religious. And since the Immaculate is the Mediatrix of all graces, it follows that the nearer one approaches her, the more flourishing will his spiritual life become. But without doubt the most perfect manner of approaching her is the total consecration of oneself. Hence it will be the consecration to the Immaculate not only of individual religious, friaries or even provinces, but of the Order as such which will bring about its rebirth. Today the breath of the Immaculate is beginning to vivify in a marvelous manner those members of the Order who have drawn closer to her in a very special manner (*Kolbe Reader*, p. 134).

164 Ibid.
165 Ibid. p. 53.
166 Claude R. Foster, *Mary's Knight: The Mission and Martyrdom of Saint Maksymilian Maria Kolbe* (Libertyville, Ill.: Marytown Press, 2002), p. 258. Also worthy of note is that St. Faustina's future spiritual

director, Blessed Michael Sopocko, went to visit Kolbe and his printing operation in Grodno in 1924, two years before St. Faustina entered her novitiate. Kolbe himself showed Sopocko around the printing facility. (See Grzegoz Górny, *Ufajacy: Sladami Błogosławionego Michała Sopocki*, photos Janusz Rosikon [Rosikon Press, 2012]), p. 77.

167 Patricia Treece, *A Man for Others: Maximilian Kolbe, Saint of Auschwitz* (Huntington, Ind.: Our Sunday Visitor, 1982), p. 35.

168 See *Mary's Knight*, pp. 567-568.

169 See John Paul II, *Gift and Mystery: On the Fiftieth Anniversary of My Priestly Ordination* (New York: Doubleday, 1996), pp. 34-40.

170 It is interesting to note that Mary not only brought St. Maximilian to Nagasaki but also the message of Divine Mercy. Recall that Fr. Joseph Jarzebowski, when he escaped to the United States from Europe during World War II, passed through Japan and stayed at the Franciscan's Mugenzai no Sono Monastery where he gave a Divine Mercy-themed retreat. His remarkable story surely inspired the friars to trust in Divine Mercy even more, and it's easy to imagine those Polish friars then bringing this consoling message of Divine Mercy to the people of Nagasaki both before and after the blast.

171 *Catechism*, 692.

172 Mary is the Mediatrix of all grace because we received Jesus, the source of grace, through her, at the moment of the Incarnation, when the Second Person of the Trinity assumed a human nature from her. Also, because Mary suffered with Christ on Calvary "in an altogether singular way … to restore supernatural life to souls" (*Lumen Gentium*, 61), it is fitting that she would also be involved "in an altogether singular way" in the distribution of this supernatural life to souls. In other words, it is fitting that she who was associated with Christ in obtaining grace for us would also be associated with him in distributing grace to us. But here is the key distinction: Christ is the source of grace while Mary is the channel through which the grace of her Son comes to us. Put differently, through his Paschal Mystery, Christ obtained all the graces necessary for the salvation of the human race, and Mary, as our mother in the order of grace and mediatrix of all grace, distributes those graces to humanity. Of course, for Mary to have such a role is not necessary; God did not have to honor Mary in this way. Nevertheless, he chose to do so, and again, it is fitting because of how Jesus came to us (through her) and how he won our salvation, namely, through his suffering on the Cross, which Mary uniquely participated in through her motherly compassion and tender love for her Son. It is also fitting, considering that Mary is the spouse of the Holy Spirit. Her Divine Spouse is pleased to work through her and can work through her perfectly because she is immaculate.

173 John Paul II, encyclical letter *Redemptoris Mater*, March 25, 1987, 45.

Chapter 10: The Story Continues

174 Francis, address to the priests of the Diocese of Rome, March 6, 2014. Pope Francis also said something very similar during a press conference on the return flight from his apostolic journey to Rio de Janeiro for World Youth Day, 2013:

> I believe that this is the season of mercy. ... And I believe that this is a *kairos*: this time is a *kairos* of mercy. But John Paul II had the first intuition of this, when he began with Faustina Kowalska, the Divine Mercy ... . He had something, he had intuited that this was a need in our time.

Pope Benedict XVI also recognized the powerful intuition of John Paul II that now is the time of mercy. For instance, in his September 16, 2007, *Angelus* message, he says:

> In our time, humanity needs a strong proclamation and witness to God's mercy. Beloved John Paul II, a great apostle of Divine Mercy, prophetically intuited this urgent pastoral need. He dedicated his second Encyclical to it and throughout his Pontificate made himself the missionary of God's love to all peoples.

175 Treece, p. 66.

176 *The Kolbe Reader*, p. 96.

177 Regarding Divine Mercy as the heart of the Gospel, the *Catechism* states: "The Gospel is the revelation in Jesus Christ of God's mercy to sinners" (1846). Also, Pope Benedict XVI, in a *Regina Caeli* message on Divine Mercy Sunday, March 30, 2008, called mercy "the central nucleus of the Gospel message." He went on to say "it is the very name of God, the Face with which he revealed himself in the Old Covenant and fully in Jesus Christ."

178 *Diary* 723.

179 Any culture that has as its highest religious expression the murder of innocent people is clearly influenced by demons and by he who is "a murderer from the beginning" (Jn 8:44) and not by the Lord of Life who came that we may "have life and have it abundantly" (Jn 10:10). See also G.K. Chesterton, *The Everlasting Man*, chapter 6, "The Demons and the Philosophers."

180 The most detailed report on the consecration came from a communication put out by the "Union de Voluntades" in Mexico City on November 26, 2014.

181 Regarding the Five First Saturdays devotion, Jesus and Mary asked that on the first Saturdays of five consecutive months we go to confession, receive Holy Communion, say a Rosary, and then meditate for fifteen minutes on the mysteries of the Rosary. This should all be done

with the intention of making reparation to the Immaculate Heart of Mary for the countless sins and blasphemies that daily offend her. Our Lady promised that to those who would keep this devotion, she would assist them at the hour of their deaths with all the graces necessary for salvation. Jesus emphasized that this devotion should not just be made only once but again and again.

[182] *Diary*, 1578.

[183] How to pray the Chaplet of Divine Mercy:

1. Make the Sign of the Cross

2. Optional Opening Prayers
You expired, Jesus, but the source of life gushed forth for souls, and the ocean of mercy opened up for the whole world. O Fount of Life, unfathomable Divine Mercy, envelop the whole world and empty Yourself out upon us. O Blood and Water, which gushed forth from the Heart of Jesus as a fountain of Mercy for us, I trust in You.

3. Our Father

4. Hail Mary

5. The Apostle's Creed

6. The Eternal Father
Eternal Father, I offer You the Body and Blood, Soul and Divinity of Your Dearly Beloved Son, Our Lord, Jesus Christ, in atonement for our sins and those of the whole world.

7. On the Ten Small Beads of Each Decade
For the sake of His sorrowful Passion, have mercy on us and on the whole world.

8. Repeat for the remaining four decades
Say the "Eternal Father" (6) on the "Our Father" bead and then 10 "For the sake of His sorrowful Passion" (7) on the following "Hail Mary" beads.

9. Conclude with Holy God (Repeat three times)
Holy God, Holy Mighty One, Holy Immortal One, have mercy on us and on the whole world.

10. Optional Closing Prayer
Eternal God, in whom mercy is endless and the treasury of compassion — inexhaustible, look kindly upon us and increase Your mercy in us, that in difficult moments we might not despair nor become despondent, but with great confidence submit ourselves to Your holy will, which is Love and Mercy itself. Amen.

[184] *Diary*, 431. See also the following words of the Lord to St. Faustina:

> For your sake I bless the world. ... For the sake of your love, I withhold the just chastisements, which mankind has deserved (1061, 1489).

Conclusion

[185] Benedict XVI, *Regina Caeli* address for Divine Mercy Sunday, April 23, 2006.

Appendix One: Regarding the Lord's Final Coming

[186] *Diary*, 848.
[187] Ibid., 965.
[188] Ibid., 1160.
[189] Ibid., 1588.
[190] Ibid., 1146.
[191] Ibid., 635.
[192] See *The 'One Thing' Is Three: How the Most Holy Trinity Explains Everything* (Stockbridge: Marian Press, 2012), pp. 132-135.
[193] Peter Seewald, *Light of the World: The Pope, the Church and the Signs of the Times* (San Francisco: Ignatius Press, 2010), p. 180. The original translation of this journalist's quote includes the Lord's words, "You will prepare the world for my definitive return," but this does not reflect the official English translation of the *Diary*, which presently appears in the text.
[194] Ibid., pp. 180-181.
[195] *Catechism*, 260.
[196] Roch Kereszty, O. Cist., *Jesus Christ: Fundamentals of Christology* (New York: Alba House, 1991), p. 359.
[197] This idea of the Lord's coming as including our going to him does not contradict the Church's traditional faith that Christ will, in fact, return to earth (see *Catechism*, 677). Somehow it can be true that the Lord's "coming down" from heaven includes our being "taken up" to heaven. In view of this "somehow," we can ponder the following reflection by Pope Benedict on the Liturgy of the Eucharist:

> Every Mass is ... an act of going out to meet the One who is coming. In this way, his coming is also anticipated, as it were; we go out to meet him — and he comes, anticipatively, already now. I like to compare this with the account of the wedding of Cana. The first thing the Lord says to Mary there is "My hour has not yet come." But then, in spite of that, he gives the new wine, as it were, anticipating his hour, which is yet to come. This eschatological realism becomes present in the Eucharist: we go out to meet him — as the One who comes — and he comes already now in anticipa-

tion for this hour, which one day will arrive once and for all. If we understand this as we should, we will go out to meet the Lord who has already been coming all along, we will enter into his coming — and so will allow ourselves to be fitted into a greater reality, beyond the everyday (*Light of the World*, p. 180).

[198] *Diary*, 283.

[199] *True Devotion to Mary*, 55. See also 152-168.

[200] *The Kolbe Reader*, p. 15.

Appendix Two: The Marian Missionaries of Divine Mercy

[201] *True Devotion to Mary*, 55.

[202] Ibid.

[203] *Aim Higher!: Spiritual and Marian Reflections of St. Maximilian Kolbe*, trans. Dominic Wisz, OFM Conv. (Libertyville, IL: Marytown Press, 2007), p. 15.

[204] This statement was made by Divine Mercy expert, Fr. Seraphim Michalenko, MIC, who was the vice-postulator for the cause of St. Faustina Kowalska.

[205] *Diary*, 1732. Regarding the "final coming" of Jesus, see Appendix One.

[206] John Paul II, homily at dedication of Shrine of Divine Mercy in Krakow-Łagiewniki on August 17, 2002.

[207] Sr. Maria Elzbieta Siepak, ZMBM, *The New "Congregation" of Sister Faustina: The Apostolic Movement of the Divine Mercy* (Krakow: "*Misericordia*" Publications, 2003), p. 26.

[208] See *Diary*, 1155-1158.

[209] Ibid., 1160.

[210] Ibid., 1159.

[211] See, for example, Pope Francis's address to the priests of the Diocese of Rome on March 6, 2014, which best express this emphasis of both popes and is cited on pages 165-166.

[212] After the MMDM, the Marian Fathers of the Immaculate Conception is probably the organization that comes closest to explicitly embracing this mission. While its official charism does not explicitly endorse the worldwide apostolate of Marian consecration, as it does the promotion of Divine Mercy, its emphasis on the promotion of Marian devotion gives implicit endorsement to it.

[213] See pp. 125-127.

[214] To learn what is meant by preparing the world for the Lord's coming by winning the whole world for God, see Appendix One.

[215] See Pope Francis's apostolic exhortation, *Evangelii Gaudium*, November 24, 2013, 1-8.

[216] See *Catechism*, 397, 399.

[217] This includes making a total consecration of oneself to Jesus through Mary, which is a condition for becoming a MMDM.

[218] For this reason, Ignatian spirituality serves as a foundation for MMDM spiritual formation.

[219] The Chaplet of Divine Mercy takes pride of place during such intercessory prayer in the life of each Marian Missionary.

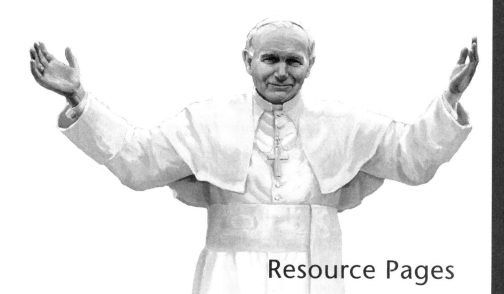

Resource Pages

Divine Mercy Resources

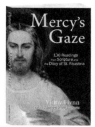

Mercy's Gaze
Inclues 100 parallel passages from Scripture and the *Diary of St. Faustina* that develop key mercy themes and encourage you to gaze on Jesus daily. Paperback. Includes pages for reflection and an appendix of prayers. (170 pages.) **GAZE**

Loved, Lost, Found:
17 Divine Mercy Conversions

Profiles 17 everyday people who discover God's extraordinary mercy. **LLF17**

Make the Consecration as a group!

The group retreat is…

- Parish-based
- Easy to implement
- Short in length
- Solidly Catholic
- Affordable
- Life-changing
- Parish-transforming

Here's How the Group Retreat Works:

1. Gather a group.
Better yet, gather several groups of six to twelve people who want to consecrate themselves to Jesus through Mary.

2. Find a place to meet.
Ideally, this would be at a parish with the permission of the pastor, but your group can also meet at someone's home.

3. Read, Ponder, Meet ("RPM")
Get revved up! and...

- *Read...*
  Read the daily meditation in the retreat book, *33 Days to Morning Glory.*

  - *Ponder...*
    Ponder the daily meditation with the help of the *Retreat Companion.*

  - *Meet...*
    Meet with your group for weekly prayer, discussion, and to watch the accompanying talks on DVD.

Here's What You'll Need:

(Details to follow.)

1. The Retreat Book

Everyone will need
one of these.

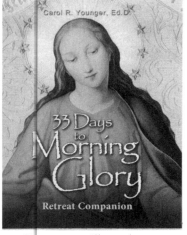

2. The *Retreat Companion*

Everyone will need one
of these, too.

3. DVD Set

Just the Retreat Coordinator will need this.

How to Get What You'll Need:

1. Choose a Retreat Coordinator

The Retreat Coordinator is the person who will organize and run the group retreat.

(The responsibilities of the Retreat Coordinator are explained in the video tutorial and free, downloadable guide available at our website, AllHeartsAfire.org.)

2. Order Your Retreat Materials

Typically, the Retreat Coordinator orders all the materials for the group retreat at the same time to save on shipping. But anyone can order their own materials. To place your order, call toll-free or visit:

1-866-767-3155
LighthouseCatholicMedia.org/HAPP

3. Have Product Codes Ready

The materials mentioned on the previous page come in packets or kits. *The Retreat Coordinators get the kits; the Retreat Participants get the packets.* There are four product codes to choose from for the retreat materials. Have them handy when you order:

PARTICIPANT PACKET (*with* retreat book) = **LH_PTPKWB**

PARTICIPANT PACKET (*without* retreat book*) = **LH_PTPK**

COORDINATOR KIT (*with* retreat book) = **LH_COKTWB**

COORDINATOR KIT (*without* retreat book*) = **LH_COKT**

---

* If you already have the retreat book, *33 Days to Morning Glory: A Do-It Yourself Retreat in Preparation for Marian Consecration*, you can order your packet or kit without it.

HEARTS AFIRE

The Participant Packet
and Coordinator Kit

PARTICIPANT PACKET INCLUDES:

- *33 Days to Morning Glory Retreat Companion*
- Prayer Card with Consecration Prayer
- *Collection of Daily Prayers,* a greeting-card-sized compilation of the daily prayers for each week.
- Rosary (colors will vary)
- Pamphlet on How to Pray the Rosary
- Miraculous Medal
- 8 ½ x 11 full-color Consecration Day Certificate

COORDINATOR KIT INCLUDES:

- 33 Days to Morning Glory Participant Packet
  - *33 Days to Morning Glory Retreat Companion*
  - Prayer Card with Consecration Prayer
  - *Collection of Daily Prayers,* a greeting-card-sized compilation of the daily prayers for each week.
  - Rosary (colors will vary)
  - Pamphlet on How to Pray the Rosary
  - Miraculous Medal
  - 8 ½ x 11 full-color Consecration Day Certificate

- *33 Days to Morning Glory: Retreat Talks by Fr. Michael Gaitley, MIC* (DVD set: six sessions, approximately 36-min each)
- *Retreat Coordinator's Guide*

*Both the Participant Packet and Coordinator Kit are available with or without the Retreat Book, *33 Days to Morning Glory.* (See product code information on oppostite page.) Photos above include the Retreat Book.

Up Next...

Continue your small-group experience with the next group retreat based on the best-selling book, *Consoling the Heart of Jesus*. This retreat is the second part of Stage One of the Hearts Afire Program.

And Then...

Proceed to Stage Two of the Hearts Afire Program: Wisdom & Works of Mercy. Features The 'One Thing' Is Three Group Study and concludes with a program for works of mercy based on the book '*You Did It to Me.*'

For more information about the Consoling the Heart of Jesus Group Retreat and other programs, please visit:
LighthouseCatholicMedia.org/HAPP

Parish-based Programs from the
Marian Fathers of the Immaculate Conception

The 33 Days to Morning Glory and Consoling the Heart of Jesus group retreats and The 'One Thing' Is Three group study are brought to you by Hearts Afire: Parish-based Programs from the Marian Fathers of the Immaculate Conception (HAPP®), and Marian Press, the Marian's publishing apostolate.

Join the Association of Marian Helpers!

**An invitation from
Director Fr. Chris Alar, MIC**

When you and your family become members
of the Association, you'll share in the
benefits of all the daily Masses, prayers,
and good works of Marian priests
and brothers all over the world.
In addition, you'll receive a
specific remembrance in the
following ways:

MARIAN HELPERS

- A daily Holy Mass celebrated for all Marian Helpers

- A Holy Mass offered for members on the First Friday and First
Saturday of each month

- A Holy Mass offered for deceased members on All Souls' Day

- A special Mass offered on each feast day of Our Savior
and His Blessed Mother, including The Presentation (Feb. 2),
The Annunciation (Mar. 25), The Assumption (Aug. 15), The Birth
of Mary (Sept. 8), and The Immaculate Conception (Dec. 8)

- The continuous Novena to The Divine Mercy at the National
Shrine of The Divine Mercy in Stockbridge, Mass.

- The daily prayers offered by workers at the National Shrine
of The Divine Mercy and the Marian Helpers Center.

**The Marian Fathers of the Immaculate Conception of the
Blessed Virgin Mary is a religious congregation of nearly
500 priests and brothers around the world.**

*With my fellow Marians, including Fr. Michael Gaitley and
Fr. Seraphim Michalenko, I'm committed to praying for you!*

A Minute with Fr. Chris:

We get a lot of questions about the Association and its dedication to praying for its members. So I've summed it up for you!

What is the Association of Marian Helpers?

The Association is a group of faithful men and women officially recognized by the Holy See, which also decreed that Association members share in the spiritual benefits of all the prayers, good works, and Masses of the Marian Fathers.

Who can join?

Men, women, moms, dads, grandparents, and entire families who desire to support the mission of the Marian Fathers in various ways can join the Association. They are people who, maybe just like you, are looking for ways to belong to something that is doing great good in the Church and around the world.

What's an enrollment?

An enrollment is a formal request to join the Association and share in the spiritual benefits. You can join the Association by enrolling yourself or a loved one (living or deceased) for one year, several years, or perpetually.

How do I use the enrollment cards and folders*?

Enrollment cards and folders are ways to enroll a loved one in the Association of Marian Helpers. Just like greeting cards you find in the store, our enrollment cards express your heartfelt support during occasions like birthdays, weddings, anniversaries, illness, ordinations, and even in times of sympathy.

But our cards and folders are *very different* than your store-bought greeting cards: Our cards and folders include the gift of prayer through an enrollment in the Association.

*Folders are essentially more formal cards, and usually offer a longer enrollment, such as for 15 years or perpetually.

How do I enroll someone?

It can be as simple as calling us or going online and enrolling yourself or a loved one. You can even request enrollment cards and send them out yourself, or have us send a card to someone on your behalf.

MARIAN HELPERS

MARIAN MISSIONARIES

WANTED:

Men and women who desire to live lives unified through Divine Mercy and Marian consecration.

Men and women who want to respond to the call for mercy in this "time of mercy."

Men and women who aim to support the work of evangelization of the MMDM.

is this you?

Be part of the mission.

MARIAN MISSIONARIES
OF DIVINE MERCY
SET ALL AFIRE

Membership and Levels of Participation in the Mission.

The door of membership into the Marian Missionaries is open to all: Bishops, priests, religious, and laity. Indeed, anyone who embraces the Marian Missionary spirituality and mission can be a Marian Missionary of Divine Mercy.

Each member falls under one or two of the following three categories or levels of participation, each level containing its own contribution to the mission.

Level 1 – Missionaries in an intensive, yearlong commitment to the spirituality and mission.

Level 2 – Missionaries who give spiritual and/or material support to the mission.

Level 3 – Missionaries who intentionally give themselves to the mission through service, special projects, various apostolic works, and administrative support.

Contact Us:
Info@MarianMissionaries.org
MarianMissionaries.org
844-221-8422

MARIAN MISSIONARIES